THE CHELSEA WHISTLE

Michelle Tea

A Memoir

SEAL PRESS

THE CHELSEA WHISTLE

A Memoir

Seal Press
A Member of the Perseus Books Group
1700 Fourth Street
Berkeley, CA 94710

9 8 7 6 5 4 3 2 1

Acknowledgment is hereby made for permission to quote song material and prose from the following publishers and copyright holders, to whom all rights are reserved: "Kids in America." Written by R. Wilde. M. Wilde. © Finchley Music Corporation. "Our Lips are Sealed." Written by Terry Hall/Jane Wiedlin. © 1981 BMG Songs, Inc. (ASCAP): Plangent Visions Music, Ltd. Lyric excerpt from "names and dates and places" by Ani DiFranco. Copyright 1993 Righteous Babe Music. All rights reserved. Used by permission.

Library of Congress Cataloging-in-Publication Data is available.

ISBN-10: 1-58005-239-8
ISBN-13: 978-1-58005-239-9

Cover and Interior Design by Domini Dragoone
Printed in the United States by Maple-Vail
Distributed by Publishers Group West

For Eileen Myles

CONTENTS

INTRODUCTION

It feels totally weird to write an introduction to a memoir. This is my third attempt; the first two got scrapped when I realized I'd gone over my word count by a million words and had only managed to detail the effect that growing up in a tough, low-income city such as Chelsea had on me, something the book hopefully does on its own. I've already talked so much about myself in these pages, the experience of sitting down to write about how I've written about myself seems I think post-modern, but I'm not sure. I didn't go to college, and have never fully grasped what post-modernism is. I'm from Chelsea.

I wrote this book with the help of a foundation, The Rona Jaffe Foundation, who blew my mind by awarding me a cash prize they give to a handful of aspiring female writers each year. I should have thanked them in the pages of this book, and didn't. I wrote a lot of the *The Chelsea Whistle* at Flann O'Brien's, an Irish bar in Roxbury, Massachusetts, when I used the Rona

Jaffe money to escape my messy San Francisco love life and do "research" in Boston. I was supposed to thank the bar, too, for all the free beers the bartenders floated me, and I forgot that as well.

Returning to Boston for research, to remember Chelsea's essence, didn't work. Like a lot of low-income places, the landscape changes rapidly, and my 80s-era Chelsea was long gone when I returned. The Chelsea I re-created in my book has occasionally been an insult to older generations, who experienced a Chelsea less depressing and depressed, a hardy working-class town with a lot of pride and options, being located so close to Boston and its culture. They've got a pure, possibly nostalgic, hometown pride, and I offended it. Of course, they tend to be guys, and their experience of the place is absolutely influenced by that massive fact. The Chelsea girls of that generation may be a bit more understanding of my perspective. But there have also been a few contemporary Chelsea residents, male and female, pissed that I've talked such shit about their home. Their defensiveness is like the protective rage one might feel about having their no-good drunken disaster of a parent called a no-good drunken disaster of a parent: yeah they may be drunk, a disaster, no good, but they're still your *parent*. Chelsea, like all of New England, is a region where townieism rules. Townieism: a low-rent nationalism. Whatever close-minded chunk of hell you wound up being born into *rules* simply because you live there. Calling out your town for being racist and violent, depressed and depressing, is not something a Townie does.

I mentioned parents. People often ask how mine feel about my writing a book that exposes not only my city's impersonal flaws, but the deep, traumatic family business that everyone, Townie or not, is supposed to keep quiet about. My sister, my biggest hero and best friend, has always been amazing. She is deeper, more complex, strong and brainy than I have the talent to wholly capture in words. Her support and belief in my writing helped free me up to be as honest and fearless in my dredging of my past as possible.

My mother hates it. When I awkwardly told her I was writing a book about Chelsea, about growing up there, about our family and what happened to it, she asked me a series of existential questions: Why? Why write? Why publish what you've written? The answers were mysterious, or they were selfish. I don't know why I need to write, or why the writing I need to do is so often about my own life. According to Alice Weaver Flaherty, in her book *The Midnight Disease: The Drive to Write, Writer's Block and the Creative Brain*, it may in fact be a neurological disorder. It definitely feels like one. But why publish? Unlike writing, publishing wasn't something I was afflicted with, it was something I pursued.

My first, most defensive response was perhaps the most true: Do You Want Me To Work At Taco Bell My Whole Life Instead? For the record, I have never worked at a Taco Bell, but in my mind — warped by brokenness and few options and Chelsea — the possibility that I could live out my days slaving at a massive fast-food chain, like so many other working poor people with my background, was real, a monster constantly snoozing under my bed. That I was given the ability and drive to write saved my life; it gave it meaning, gave me purpose, plunked me into a cool community.

But there were less utilitarian, more emotional, and political, reasons to publish a book like *The Chelsea Whistle*. When my family imploded, the message I got from the few adult family members I'd reached out to was: It's not that big of a deal. Get over it. What happened was bad, but you shouldn't have any feelings about it, and you certainly shouldn't be talking about it, or acting out around it. I knew they were wrong, and that their acceptance of lousy, disappointing behavior was no different than their acceptance of so many ills, from racism to the government to their own lot in life. Of course it was idealistic to imagine a small feminist revolution rising up from a people who were fearfully small-minded, but these fearful, small-minded people were my family, and I needed their support. I didn't get it. I wrote a book, and got it from a whole other world instead. And in getting it, I gave it; telling my story gave comfort and resolve to other girls who were struggling with their family's denial and dynamics, one of the best, most magical things a book can do.

Of course I didn't know that a faceless readership would give me a little bit of what I tried and failed to get from my family. I wasn't consciously hoping for that, and couldn't have imagined really having a readership at that point. I did know that, politically, as a feminist, it wasn't my job to protect my family from the results of their dumb actions. I wasn't about to censor my writing so that a man who'd made bad decisions fueled largely by sexism and privilege could live more comfortably while I ached. The least I could do was indulge my writing with same sense of entitlement he'd had toward my body. Yay, feminism! Without that frame through which to understand my experience, I would have been forever knocked on my ass by it. Of course, I foundered for a while in a particularly extreme strain of radical lesbian feminist separatism that was, like all fundamentalist religions, delusional and debilitating, but it got me out of Chelsea.

When I go back to Chelsea now, it is like certain recurring dreams I have, when I am navigating my way around a foreign city, intuitively knowing where I'm going in a landscape visually unfamiliar but deeply, cellularly, *known*. I like to visit in the summer, when I am most nostalgic for the place. Though I remembered the city as barren, and wrote as much in the book, it is not; there are big, old trees everywhere, and when they are full and green they give the city a quaint look. The old homes look worn, not poor. I'm thirty-six years old, and the streets are not full of boys and girls who want to kick my ass. The effects of gentrification have been hard and helpful and occasionally bizarre. Low-income renters are no doubt facing evictions as home buyers priced out of Boston realize there are places going cheaper a mere five minutes outside the city. The lower rents have been sniffed out by the famous first wave of gentrification, queers; and when I did a reading in Chelsea while on tour for this book, a few queer girls showed up to listen. That there was even a venue to *have* a literary reading in Chelsea was shocking; the city had no such culture when I lived there. But on the site of the old Sparta Spa is now an artsy café called The Chelsea City, which surely caters less to natives, who get their coffees "regular" at the Dunkin' Donuts drive-through than to the new arrivals.

The other first-wave gentrifiers, artists (overlap withstanding) have also helped the city by bringing art walks, community theater, and workshops for local kids. There has been a movement to clean up the crusty old creek, so successful that I've heard dolphins have been spotted in its waters. This reeks of urban legend, but Chelsea is such a strange place, who knows? It wouldn't be any crazier than Our Lady of Assumption School being sold to condo developers who are selling off the church, rectory, and the school as, yes, condos. My strange, occasional urge to move back to Chelsea got *way* inflamed when I learned I could possibly *live* in one of my old classrooms. That this sounds at all appealing is surely a mental condition related to Stockholm Syndrome, but the desire is there. There would be something triumphant about returning to a place of such personal struggle and seeing how the landscape has changed to accommodate you — culture and cafes and a cozy bedroom in the place where once a mean nun berated you. That feels like victory. That all the Catholic schools, which made my life miserable, have closed down feels like victory. That there is a place for creative kids to learn art or hang out feels like victory. That I got out feels like I won, and that if I want to I can come back feels like victory, but mostly, getting to tell my story and watching, amazed, as my story then creates for me a life, feels like the biggest Megabucks hit of them all.

With a much belated thank you to The Rona Jaffe Foundation, for their incredible, unexpected support. To be recognized by such a foundation truly astounded me, and changed my life by showing me that a writing career was a true possibility.

And a thank you to Flann O'Brien's, for painting the bar with portraits of great dead writers, and welcoming an aspiring live one with good vibes and free beer.

Michelle Tea
San Francisco
September 2007

Childhood is morbid. That's a word I learned from my mother. You kids are morbid, she said, spying on me and my sister, small Madeline, playing with our cousin Allen, who everyone said was going to turn out gay from all the dolls his grandmother bought him. It was the era of "William Wants a Doll," a tune that didn't quite reach Chelsea, Massachusetts, a town five minutes from Boston that might as well have been five hours, five days. People in Chelsea went to neighboring towns like Revere, Everett, East Boston—similarly connected to the big city and all its culture but, like Chelsea, sealed off, retarded by the local yokels' fears of big cities and all the different people who dwell there. Not that you'd call the sort of stunted human that occupied my town a yokel. Yokels were trailer trash living in wild rural areas deep in the jungles of America, a television myth. These low-bailers were "townies." And they were proud of it. As if being born into this grimy pocket of New England were a cosmic lottery hit. East Boston—Eastie—had a tunnel that shot you into Boston, and in Chelsea we had the big green bridge that looped the edge of town, a dead warehouse district. You had to pay a guy in a little booth fifty cents to pass into Boston. That made sense. The city was holding us hostage. What didn't make sense was having to toss the guy quarters on your way back, too. A toll to get into Chelsea? Its cracked pavement and trashy curbs, plastic playgrounds stained with spray paint and mean kids on every corner, wanting to kick your ass—that was Chelsea, and they made you give them two quarters to get into it. Like being bullied out of your lunch money. They'll nickel and dime ya to death, my parents would often lament, and I'd think of this phrase as the twin coins were tossed into the giant basket on the Tobin Bridge, tumbling into the hole that would lift the bar and allow our car entrance to Chelsea. Outside of our misanthropic city, in Boston, children were free to be you and me, and William was serenaded for his dolly desires, but it never reached us. It was like a cable station we just didn't get. We got other things.

We got to play dead. I was teaching my cousin Allen that it wasn't like sleeping—you didn't just lie there and relax, limp, tiny bird-bone rib cage fluttering up and down on kid's breath. Playing dead was hard and took practice—you kept your eyes open and you didn't blink, and your eyeballs got drier and drier until it seemed you'd go nuts if you couldn't snap them shut, and everything blurred and the ball of your eye seemed to twist in its socket. And you held your body still, no breath coming and going like kids on a hot day dashing to and from the backyard while a mother is trying to clean or pay bills or just have one damn second of peace, just to think, and she says, You're in or you're out.

That's like your breath when you're playing dead—it's in or out. And you are still, no blinks from the dry, dry eyes, no relieving gasps from the body, just lie there and suffer beneath the eyes of your marveling friends who coo and gasp at how good you are at being dead. Inside, you are close to combustion, and the seconds that tick you toward it are delicious, an accomplishment. Advanced dead children could challenge themselves by attempting a faux death in various crumpled heaps, the way people really die, all folded and snapping at odd angles. But to start you just lay there, like a princess in a book, thumb skin pricked, apple flesh sitting poisonous in your belly. Ma opened the bedroom door and observed her eldest in just such a position, my favorite because it seemed so beautiful. I could have been a model holding a difficult pose for an artist, if it weren't for the frozen grossness of my blankly staring eyeballs. Madeline and Allen gazed down at me, impressed. Don't play like that, my mother said, with a catch in her voice like her kids were a couple of Sickos. God forbid, she said, waving her hand like somebody had farted. Embarrassed, I scrambled from the floor, my eyes stinging as moist lids snapped over them, a little sprinkle of thankful tears and I hauled huge gusts of air into my lungs. It was a strange, inverted sort of athleticism. My body was cramped and proud.

If you were a kid in Chelsea, there were so many things that could kill you. Men bearing candy, cars plowing you down on the busier streets, and on the more desolate ones wild trains and packs of boys on dirt bikes. A van full of naked clowns, naked from the waist down so that at first glance you thought the circus had come to town—you'd see only their loopy costumes, the floppy collars and greasy smiles, and then they'd yank you into their van just like nothing, like a sack of potatoes, an extra-heavy book bag. Kids are light as air and once the clown had seized you with his bulbous, gloved hand, you were doomed, cause they had their wieners out and were ready to stab you with them, to kill you forever. There were Mickey Mouse candies that were really LSD, planted on the sidewalk by evil druggies. The sinister slits of electrical outlets, which I could never imagine being able to fit my finger into, but if I did would leave me charred and smoking, my hair a stiff brush like a cartoon fool. Childhood was an endless backyard obstacle course filled with everything deadly that stood between you and adulthood, at which point no one would try to kidnap you, and you could relax and be alive. Razors in apples on Halloween night, sweet harmless brownies handed out in baggies by an old lady who looked like a grandma, but you never know. They don't have horns on their heads, my mother would say. She was talking about Sickos. They looked just like everyone, you couldn't ever, ever know. The skanky man in Bellingham Square, the one who always sat around near the post office in his stained wool coat, sloshing a bottle that smelled like you were maybe supposed to clean the house with it, not drink it, whom every-one knew as Johnny Cornflakes and who talked to himself and got kicked off the bus for falling down, his pants torn and hands scuffed to scabs—you might think this guy was one of them, a Sicko. But really he just needed some help because he was crazy, not Sicko crazy but alcoholic crazy, sad crazy. Now, look over there on the other side of the street, at the older guy, cute, Italian, very dark hair set into swirls with sweet-smelling gel. He's got this real nice car, candy-apple red, red like the tin of a Coke can, and it's so clean it shines, so clean you can smell the color of the tree that dangles from the rearview mirror. It's summertime and he's lying across the front seat of his car, his head is tucked beneath the steering wheel because he's fixing something—there are tools on the sidewalk. His legs are splayed onto the sidewalk, and if you skate your gaze up his tanned calves, up his thighs, you will spot the most odious, purpley ugh, purple penis, jutting grotesquely from the edge of his nylon running shorts. This man, who looks so normal, looks even attractive in much the way a man on a soap opera does, is actually a Sicko. If you stopped and made a scene, he would leap from his car, gasp and apologize, feigning terrific embarrassment, but you'd know he was full of lies. Because (as my mother wisely said) he has no horns on his head, this awful man will be able to get away with being a Sicko for his entire life, yanking his dick out from his clothing every day and blushing red so that you feel bad for embarrassing him. And meanwhile, poor old Johnny Cornflakes gets yelled at by mean gangs of kids and kicked off buses, and mothers grab their children when he totters by, even though, I promise you, the man's dick will stay tucked there in his grody underwear and no kid will ever be forced to behold its horror. That's a little something about Sickos.

Also, you could get leukemia if you were a kid. You could be a thin bald girl on a telethon, smiling bravely from a hospital bed with teeth that take up all the space on your small, wasting face. Doctors would administer medicines and poisons, killing a bunch of your body in hopes of killing the thing killing you, and celebrities would visit you with a camera crew and take you to Disney World, and maybe you'd get better and go on to college and discover a cure so no other kid would ever have to suffer like you and you would be a hero. Maybe you would simply die and your family would be eternally puzzled by life's cruel lack of meaning. If you thought about it, there seemed to be no end to things that could kill kids. So we would play these great and sexy games about being dead. And I'm telling you, they were sexy, maybe just cause sex was a similar threat that loomed in our future, one tucked in the pockets of the Sickos. Like death, we would encounter sex first-hand, eventually, though hopefully not until we were very grown up. So we swirled both of them together and choreographed them into dramatic play scenarios involving Kiss. I mean the band Kiss, giants on stacked heels, leathery contraptions stretched across their bodies, sci-fi grease paint masking their faces. I didn't even know Kiss, not their music. I had only seen them once, on a telethon for sick and dying children, and it had confused me to see them take the stage between clips of the holy, scrawny children quickly on their way to being dead. Kiss was evil, they spit blood—that was one thing I knew about them. The head one did, the pointy guy who was the most evil. His makeup looked like slick black claws stretched menacingly across his cheeks. In our room, me and Madeline would wade through a sea of blood at a Kiss concert, imagining that guy at the top of our bunk beds, leering down at us and spitting. We would swim through the invisible red and finally drown, twisting and collapsing onto our dusty wooden floor, and envision the evil bad man, his strangely long tongue pushed from his lips, drooling a slick river of blood. It was sexy. It was gross and wrong and if Mom caught us she'd think we were Sickos, our games disturbingly morbid.

There were lots of dirty jokes that were pretty morbid. The one about the guy shaving his face while looking out the window naked. He lives upstairs from a pickle factory, and when he accidentally drops his razor, it slices off his dick, which falls neatly into a pickle jar below and is mistakenly eaten by a lady. What were dicks? Something shaped like a pickle, ladies put them in their mouths. It's called a blowjob. Some girls in the neighborhood knew the names for everything. Sixty-nine, fucking. It was hard to get your head around some of them. Fucking was easier. Guys had the pickle and we had a hole and they went together. Me and Madeline would play fucking. There was a dirty joke called Johnny Deeper and it involved a teacher fucking her student named Johnny Deeper, and I would be the teacher and I would make my sister be Johnny. I would always make Madeline be the guy, Danny to my Sandy when I stretched the collar of my shirt down over my shoulders and stole Mom's clogs with the big heels. She would be Ponch and I would be the hitchhiker in distress on the California highway. She was Bo or Luke Duke while I was Daisy, stretched out on my bed like it was the General Lee. She would lie on top of me and we would kiss. Madeline rarely wanted to do this. I would have to nag her into it the way I'd bully her into being Carrie when we played Little House on the Prairie so I could be Half-Pint, or coerce her into playing any other game that was okay to play, and not sick or morbid. It just seemed like the normal type of bullying I would engage in because sometimes you really had to push Madeline into doing something fun. Like the time at my grandmother's house, which was across the street from the cemetery and so close to the airport that planes shook the shingles as they crashed through the sky outside. It was summer and the house was so hot that vegetable cuttings and slop from dinner plates got dumped into old milk containers and shoved in the freezer so they didn't rot into a stink cloud on the back porch, where the trash was kept. The slop was called "swill," the back porch was the "piazza," the living room was the "parlor" and on hot days it was blocked off by a sheet tacked to the doorjamb, to keep the cool air-conditioned air in my grandparents' bedroom only. The AC was an old hulk that got heaved into the window each summer, humming out tinny air that tasted like hotels, that chilled us. In the cool room, me and Madeline dove under the blankets on my grandparents' bed, and it was a spaceship, and we were on Battlestar Galactica. I made Madeline be Dirk, the guy with the cigar, and we kissed. The sheet flapped open and you could feel my grandmother move into the room like a weather front. Get out from there, you'll suffocate, she said, edgy. Oh, Leave 'em alone, they're not gonna suffocate! Papa bellowed from the parlor. He sat out there in his humid chair, his sore feet up on the round footstool. Papa had the gout. I imagined it as an old gnome that lived in his toe, a swollen, oniony thing he'd soak in water doused with Epsom salt, which was not the salt you ate on your food. Papa watched black-and-white television. The Three Stooges, Abbott and Costello. Old dead guys who were shrill, not funny, back from a time when there wasn't any color. It depressed me to watch my grandparents' TV. They just wouldn't get cable because then my grandfather would watch dirty movies with boobs in them. So he watched these other boobs whacking each other with frying pans and sticking out black shoes to trip a black pant leg, smoking his filterless cigarettes that hazed up the room, the ssssvt, sssvt, sssvt sound of loose tobacco being spit from his lips. Papa said, Leave 'em alone, and Nana did, lifting the faded sheet reluctantly and walking back into the parlor to sit on the sofa and watch TV. But the Battlestar Galactica was gone, it was just a bed, wide and lumpy, no man with a sinister cigar, only me, and I was the sinister one, the Sicko, playing bad games. I pulled the sheet from our heads and breathed the cold, conditioned air.

Back at our house I lay in the dark, in my bed, and my bones were filled with how awful I was. An awfulness that sucked out all the marrow, like those sick and dying children on the telethon. Only they were good. I would go to hell. For kissing Madeline, for making her be a man. I lay with my awfulness, as still as I could, and pretended to be paralyzed. It would probably happen, God would find a way to hurt me for this. Not that God was trying to hurt paralyzed children or children kidnapped by evil clowns or any of those fates already mentioned. God was with those children in their unimaginable moments of terror, as surely as he was turning his broad back on me—a molester, a Sicko. Lying so still, I felt everything sink into my sheets and dissolve there, until all I could feel was my brain, no body. I opened my eyes and the room was black like a shut-off TV, and I was blind. I stared out into the void of my bedroom, and after a while a looping pattern like neon began to hang there in the dark, swirling and making me sick. As my eyes adjusted, I began to recognize the plastic Goofy bank on my dresser, how it sort of glowed in an awful way, its bulging eyeballs and slobbery plastic snout. I shut my eyes against it but it had burned itself into my sickened brain, twisting into the phantom neon loops, a hideous face. I just wanted to sleep, but why did I deserve to when I kissed my own sister and laughed at jokes about women eating pickled dicks? Why should I have peace when so many children, good children, had none? I thought of

Sister Maria, my first-grade nun. She was so short, Ma said, that you could eat beans off her head. A little woman with a little bowl haircut, shabby, and little bifocal glasses. She was one of the more modern nuns who had stopped wearing her habit, had traded the uniform of dour black or navy polyester for the uniform of a normal, if conservative and outdated, older female. Sister Maria had lined us all up against the walls of our classroom, sitting down, our legs jutting out on the wood floor. Girl legs with blue knee socks and fleshy knee bones, and boy legs in blue slacks. She had us close our eyes and relax each part of our body, piece by piece, chanting, My feet are relaxing my feet are relaxing my feet are relaxed. My legs are relaxing my legs are relaxing my legs are relaxed. All the way up to our head until our whole body buzzed this gentle buzz that must have been holy since Maria was a nun. It was better than phonics. I tried it then in my bed until I was a flat girl, a paper doll. Then my brain burst in with Madeline squirming, her bunched up face. I don't want to. Come On.

I began crying and went out into the dim brightness of the kitchen, yellowish light from the ceiling bouncing off the brown cabinets that lined the wall. I was going to tell my mother everything, but when she asked why I was crying, I told her it was because I cheated on the book reading contest at the library. I didn't read all those dinosaur books, I lied because I wanted to be the smartest girl who read the most books, and I won the Crayola make-your-own-cup kit, where you colored pictures on a long strip of paper and slipped it into the clear plastic mug and it was yours. My punishment was to walk to the little branch library around the corner and tell the librarian, Joyce, who I loved so much I hated her children, that I was a liar, that I did not read all the dinosaur books. I tried but had found them horribly boring—there weren't any girls in them. Just mammoth lizards and scaly flying birds, all rendered in uninspiring shades of brown and green. I was crying as I made my confession. There in the library, the place I ruled. It was small as a corner store, with a smell that meant books. Joyce said it was okay, alarmed at the ferocity of my tears but not at what I'd revealed—she had known that I'd lied about the dinosaur books, and she had intended for the Crayola prize to induce this exact flood of guilt. Joyce let me keep the Crayola mug set but made me read all the dinosaur books. The tar pits and pterodactyls and the tiny front arms of the Tyrannosaurus rex. And I still felt awful about kissing Madeline. Nights later I did it all again, the tearful stumble into the nighttime kitchen, squinting against the hurtful brightness. I was let down by my mother's face as she looked at me crying. I wanted her to be alarmed, but parents are so jaded. They see kids crying all the time. I told her I played sex with Madeline. That we kissed. It got my mother pretty upset. There was the reaction I'd wanted, only now I didn't want it anymore. It was too real, the flickering ceiling fluorescents, my mother's horror. I thought you didn't know about sex! she insisted. I Don't Know, I said. I was confused. Was Gene Simmons on my bunk bed sex? Was Madeline as Erik Estrada real sex or just play, was fake play sometimes real sex? Fake dead wasn't real dead, though it was sick, sick and morbid, and now I was sicker than the sickest game of dead.

Eventually my father came home, late from work at the post office and after-work at the labor union, and I was cast into my bed of shame so that they could fight over whose fault this was. I hadn't gotten anything out of my confession. I had hoped to return to my room feeling holy and renewed, like one of God's children, all of it washed from my skin like a sacrament that made me new. Instead I was just kind of pushed into the corner, like the part of the dust pile you can't manage to get into the dustpan. My parents had an amazing fight. Dad decided it was all my mother's fault—she watched soap operas in front of us, cable TV, the Movie Channel. Just the other day he'd come in and found us watching Dracula, the Frank Langella one. And it's true that we had played Dracula. I told Madeline to bite my neck while I pretended she was enormous and evil. But really I got most of my inspiration from regular television, from the Fonz in his grease and leather, the leggy models of Blansky's Beauties, from Charo on The Love Boat and Charo on Fantasy Island. Do This, I'd instructed Madeline as we stretched out the necks of our nightgowns and pulled our arms over it, the collar tight beneath our armpits, the little sleeves empty and dangling. We sat back in my bed, the covers pulled up and our bare arms and shoulders exposed like the couples in bed on The Love Boat. My mother came in. What are you doing? Playing Love Boat, I said. Don't do that, put your nightgowns on right. I felt the dull plunge in my gut that meant getting caught. It had seemed glamorous to me—the lounging, tanned shoulders of the minor stars of The Love Boat. I didn't pick up its obvious implication, that the two had just screwed, but my mother's adult eyes recognized it and delivered a short reprimand, like when she'd caught me playing dead, my eyeballs stuck open and creepy. And what I finally brought to her—that I shoved my tiny self on my tinier sister and forced her into Sicko game playing—was so much worse than fake deaths and the stretched-out necklines of nightgowns. Of course my parents' fight was huge, as huge as the night.

Of course the Sicko games with Madeline stopped, right then and there, as I promised God they would.

It wasn't until we'd both gotten out of Chelsea that we grappled with the idea of abuse. Incest. Did I Molest You? I asked my sister.

Madeline would stomp across the game board when I was trying to play Monopoly, kicking the red and green hotels and all the cool metal figurines acrossa the linoleum. I would make her kiss me. It all seemed like one thing. Dying girls on hospital cots and dying girls with vampire bites, bloody throats and bruises. No one got sick and died and no one got kidnapped, but who makes it out of childhood alive? Later the world would open up into a sea of people who had possibly molested us. Maybe we would have a memory. About Mom, about Papa, about each other. Who knew what was lodged in our brains, waiting to pop. You think you know some stuff for sure, like the contents of your own mind. Just wait.

TRIPE, KIELBASA, SHELLFISH AND BEER

Dennis is my father and Louisa my mother. Louisa's name I've changed, because she is a good woman and horrified that I sit down in bars and coffeehouses, scrawling out the history of this family. Dennis remains himself, a darkly Polish man, mustached, always eating weird gross foods that he'd hoard, keep all to himself as if anyone in the family would want to take a bite. Tripe, for starters. What is it? I think it is intestines, but when I was little it was blubber, whale blubber, which I'd read about in school. How natives used it for candles and cooking grease. It seemed that my father liked to eat it. Long, bubbled strips of it quivered on the kitchen counter. I think he boiled it. It trembled, it was alive, like the Blob. It made sense that my father ate disgusting and mysterious things, because you are what you eat, I'd learned that, too, and my father was a mystery, one you didn't exactly want to figure out. Let him stay in the kitchen on a bright weekend, his day off, preparing his special foods with a can of beer gleaming beside him.

Kielbasa was a Polish food, and that was only for him, too. Like a hot dog, but the skin was so hard you had to pop it with your teeth, which was frightening. It was like you had to kill it a bit to eat it. You knew that the food Dennis ate used to be alive, used to be an animal. It really seemed like dead stuff, unlike hamburgers, which just seemed like hamburgers, not dead cows. Sometimes Dennis's food *was* still alive when he brought it in the door. The snapping crabs and lobsters that lived for a bit in the bathtub, attempting to scramble up the porcelain slope, then skidding back into the basin. Thick rubber bands binding the lobsters' claws. It was like the zoo had come into our home, or the zoomobile—like the bookmobile but with small, strange animals instead of books. It had parked at my school once, and one by one classes were allowed to leave the building and climb on board to view tarantulas and lizards basking beneath heat lamps in little aquariums.

Dennis brought live animals home, into this house where there were no pets. A parakeet, for a minute, but it was loud and screechy, and would jump into its dish of seeds and run in place, scattering the tiny grains all over the place. The parakeet wanted out. It would stick its hooked beak through the bars and bite your finger. A ferocious little bird, lemon-limey, we got rid of it. Now these hard-shelled things clambered about in our bathtub. The scuttling crabs and the lumbering lobster. They'd go into the pot. When water began to boil and bubble, Dennis, like a witch, would drop them into the stew, and they would die there before us. We'd watch, me and Madeline, having been called into the kitchen to see it. I thought of Bugs Bunny in a roiling tub, carrots bobbing in the water like bath toys, how he'd outwit Elmer Fudd and be free again, not dinner. But the sea animals, we watched their shells redden and their eyes grow dull and smoked. They'd be dead then, almost ready to be eaten. Once, it was a lobster, still alive, its stiff tentacles whipping above the water like the limbs of a drowning man, and Dennis took the pair of metal tongs, the ones used to lift sweet ears of boiled corn from the pot, and he dipped the pinching tips into the blue gas flame and heated them, then clamped them on the lobster's twitching antennae. *That's the most sensitive part of the lobster,* he explained, enjoying this last, extra bit of pain before the creature expired. Later, he'd split their shells with a crack and tug out the puffy, white insides. He gutted the entire body—even the clattering claws were smashed open with the metal nutcrackers we used during holidays. He removed a long, slender bit of meat that had fit the shell of the claw exactly. It was like pulling fingers from a glove. Dennis mashed it up with mayonnaise and kept it in a Tupperware bowl in the fridge. He ate it on soft slices of Wonder Bread. It was for him and him alone. Dad food.

Dennis was Polish but from where in Poland I have no idea. His parents, my grandparents, were creepy, old-world novelties. They were the oldest of the old and I was scared of them, saw them only in rare photos. Dennis hated them. It was an alcoholic family, they all mostly hated each other. Dennis had a host of brothers—some I never met, some I saw sporadically. When Dennis was drenched with booze he'd get nostalgic and plan for a reunion. Then there'd be some new Polish men, all alcoholic, all rotting away slowly from various alcohol-related diseases: cirrhosis, diabetes. My family called it "Sugar." Lots of divorces in these men's lives, children who refused to talk to them. Eventually Dennis wouldn't want to either, and the men would vanish again. Once, I met a girl, a couple years older than me and with all the coolness those few years can lend.

Her hair was daringly short, it was feathered. Her name was Debbie. She was my cousin. My Cousin? How? I was mystified. How could I have random cousins out there strolling about, cousins I'd never played with as a tiny kid, cousins who never came to my birthday parties?

Dennis would take us shopping, me and Madeline, to the special shops that sold his oddball snacks. Stop and Shop was good enough for normal stuff, but Dennis's strange palate required trips to butcher shops, where the hacked-up animals were splayed on ice: schools of dead-eyed fish, watery chunks of red, red meat, some with rocks of bone jutting out from them. The floors were wet and slippery, the air cold and heavy with a bloody smell you could taste, clammy on your lips. Dad's blubber would be laid out, too, like ribbons for a ghastly princess. A tank jammed with angry-looking crabs and lobsters, crawling around on each other. He'd point out his choices to the butcher, who would lift them, dripping, antennae flailing, and package them up. It was so weird to be back in the car with them, the shifting, moving packages. Live food. He'd take us into Martinetti's, where only bottles were sold. Row after row, and many enchanting—the glass extravagantly long at the neck, corked with wax, the labels old-looking, European. Dennis went to the back, to the refrigerated part, hauled a couple of six packs from the frost, and we were on to the next stop. Tripe, kielbasa, shellfish and beer.

MICKEY MOUSE ACID

There were certain things I could think about a lot, switch on like a TV rerun and let the drama spool out into my brain. Mickey Mouse acid was one of those things. The LSD announcement came over the school loudspeaker, or else on a mimeographed sheet of damp and flattened paper that stunk of a mild, chemical ink. You would imagine that an intercom announcement concerning tabs of acid meant for schoolchildren, for us, would have sent a roar of excited panic through the classes, but we attended a Catholic school, and our spirits were too broken for any real outbursts. There were three Catholic elementary schools in Chelsea: the French school, the Italian school and the Polish school. The Polish school was beyond obscure, St. Stanislaus—I never met a soul who went there. It was tucked on the outskirts of town, between the gangland squalor of Bellingham Square, where cops had just installed surveillance cameras on the streetlights to bust drug dealers, and that lonely stretch of engineering that led the brave into Boston, the Tobin Bridge. It was a real no man's land, the place that St. Stan's withered. St. Rose was Italian, as evidenced mainly in the teenage girls who came over from Italian East Boston to attend the adjacent all-girl high school. The elementary school was mixed, lots of Puerto Rican kids attended. St. Rose was run-down, on the edge of the square, a hop up from public school. Assumption was the French school, Assumption was mine. I think it was founded by a league of French nuns, hence its reputation as the French school, but only old ladies called the Catholic schools by their ethnicities anyway, old ladies like my Nana, who seemed to categorize everything that way.

But, the LSD. We were informed that it could look like candy, like a block of Pez or a sugar button peeled from a paper strip. It could even be a tiny square of paper, stamped with a picture of your favorite cartoon character. Druggies who hated kids wanted to sneak it to us, so that we would flip out. We would flip out and turn into druggies like them, and give them our money and our bodies, and our lives would be ruined forever. I was flushed with the idea of it. It seemed like even thinking about it could be trouble. I had a certain fantasy, it began with the school bell ringing at the end of the day, when the doors of Our Lady of the Assumption came open like a jostled pod, an insect colony, subterranean and sunless. All of our pale, plaid school-bodies like little bugs—some stunned from a day that had knocked them on their beetle backs, some winged and willful like angry things blessed with stingers. We would flood the cement schoolyard that pooled around the Assumption compound like a moat. Recess was conducted in the larger back schoolyard, flanked by the segregated dormitories of God. On one side, the nuns' white convent, with lace hung in the windows. The austere brown rectory was on the other—home of a Brother, a Father and the Father's two wheezing pugs. Occasionally, Father would make a recess appearance with his twin leashed dogs, and all the real kiss-ass girls would crowd cooing around their snarfling, nervous bodies, their dog eyes bulging and tongues lolling like they were slowly being strangled to death from the inside. Father would take them on a little drool parade through the schoolyard and then return to the dignified house. A round, Irish Father, Father O'Casey, with a big face, pink and cold like a loaf of bologna, and his own bulging eyes, runny like the dogs', watery blue, the face of an old alcoholic, really.

It was only Father O'Casey and the enigmatic "Brother" in that roomy, brown-shingled house, while the smaller convent was packed to the gills with women, a henhouse. The principal, Sister Rita, was all thick, dark lines—strong, horn-rimmed glasses perched on the beak of her nose, fuzzy eyebrows and slick vampire hair peeking out from beneath her black habit. A bitch, no surprise. Sister Terese, her sidekick, was meek and sweet. It was her job to hand-crank the alarming mimeographs. Sister Doris, thank god, would have a stroke before I reached the class she taught, but she would be replaced by the creepy, vacant Sister Lorraine, eyes like blue sea glass washed up from the deep. Her favorite project was dipping crayons into the tip of a candleflame and making these polka-dotted Crayola murals, all textured and waxy. She looked like a witch, Sister Lorraine, with her wide, smooth face and those eyes staring into the fire. Sister Maria, who had led the class in relaxation—nice, only occasionally violent, and never to me, so I loved her. Sister Gertrude wore bullet bras and no habit on her curly head, kind of a slutty nun. They all lived together like a sorority sitcom. I didn't get the nuns. On one hand, it seemed cool, like never growing up. You got to live in a clubhouse with no boys allowed, and you never had to get a real job, or squeeze out kids, or do anything that made me nervous. How did one become a nun? Could you knock on the convent door like a stray dog or pregnant virgin, and ask to come in? Did you have to prove you were good? How did you prove that? I knew that I wasn't good, and so the nuns filled me with a defensive insecurity. How neatly they cut off the world with their washed-out little castle and hairdo-proof habits. How easy it is to be good when strangers aren't trying to trick you with LSD that looks like cartoon stickers, when you lock yourself away from a world conspiring to trip you up and laugh at you.

In my fantasy I'm walking through the narrow front schoolyard, the one that exits onto Broadway. At the end of every school day I would exit through that schoolyard because my house was, can you believe it, directly across the street. The school sat there all day and all night, locked in an eternal showdown with my home. A big stone Mary that jutted out from the church and blessed the street below. There was nowhere to hide from the red-brick glare of Our Lady of the Assumption. You'd bump into the nuns all the time, even when it was the weekend and they had no right to you. Sometimes you'd see them in a car, which was freaky. Nuns drove cars. It seemed like they shouldn't be allowed, like the Amish. Or they were perhaps too simple, doddering and old-fashioned. I think I just suspected that they weren't equipped to deal with the real world, that's why they got locked up together in a benevolent institution, the convent. A sort of holy old-age home.

In my fantasy I'm just across the street from my house, which was a color I could never quite figure out. Maybe the color of an Irish alcoholic who is just about to vomit. No, that's too pink of a color, the squiggly mosaic of busted blood vessels lending a boozy radiance to the cheeks and the nose. The house was a sickly greenish-white—a sallow, ill color, food-poisoned. Probably it had seen more vibrant days, but the New England weather had oppressed it. In my fantasy the blanched house is before me, the huge and glorious house of God is beside me, and behind me is the school, still leaking children from its gaping doors. Beneath me on the ground is a little picture of Mickey Mouse. I see it when I crouch down to pull up the navy blue knee socks that slide down my ankles every frigging step I take. Suzanna Magno puts rubber bands around her calves to keep her socks where they belong—smart!—but my mother said no way, it cuts off the circulation and your legs will wilt like flowers in a dry jar and then doctors will chop them off. Maybe in my fantasy my socks do not sag but cleave nicely to my scrawny, bony-maroni legs, but another tragedy occurs—the weak buckle of my lunch box slips loose, sending a thermos and a baggie of bread crusts crashing onto the sidewalk, releasing a fuming cloud of musty milk-stink like a fart into the air. I bend down to grab my thermos, and there is Mickey Mouse. On a little piece of paper like a stamp. I reach my tiny hand out to it, there on the grimy pavement of Chelsea. It is so bright and clean beside the dusty bits of broken glass and dry weeds sprouting miserably through rips in the cement. My hand, a six- or seven-year-old hand, with fingernail tips I like to chew off in curving strips, then wedge the jagged crescent between my two front teeth and wiggle it with my tongue. I enjoy the quiet click it makes inside my mouth as the raw point of my tongue flicks it. My fingernails are framed by shreds of skin I'd also peeled away with my teeth, some fresh, some turning as hard and chewable as the nails, soreness and scabs. On my hand is a ring that is not round but very dented because I like to take it off in class and slam my desktop down on it, working it into new shapes, a triangle, an octogon, I'm a metalsmith, a jewelrymaker. This is the shabby little girl hand that reaches for the Mickey Mouse and ruins her life. All you have to do is touch LSD and it's got you, like electricity, a finger in the socket. One touch and it's on the inside of your skin.

Immediately the world goes funhouse on me. My home is just across the street but now it's flipped into the sky so I'll never be able to enter it, not ever again. It's a crazy twisted sky-house, huge in the air like a balloon in the Thanksgiving Day parade. The street is all in motion before me, and it's not just the cars. I mean cement like a river, rushing. The whole city is running away from me. Slowly, people, other kids, the crossing guard in his neon orange plasticwear, see that something is wrong. With me. *She touched the LSD!* They back away in horror, into the swirl of reality. They can't see how everything behind them has become a quick soup and they're about to become the meat and the veggies. I grip the chainlink fence that borders the schoolyard, encircling the empty lot where some houses burnt down. For a little while the houses had stood there like a mouth of rotten teeth, black and splintered, and then they got bulldozed, and a ring of chain-link was strung around the rubble. In my fantasy I grip that fence and scream and scream. I'm on serious drugs. I'm flipping out, screaming, peeing myself because the inside of me, the part you can't see, has gone berserk. One clenched fist still holds the little LSD-soaked shred of cartoon. Like electrified metal, I'm stuck to it. I leave the fence and lurch up Broadway, a shopping-cart monster-man, a crazy, even though I'm just a little girl. A drug-crazed little monster-girl, alone forever on the streets of Chelsea.

Our first house was on Broadway, owned by Chrisco Ariello, the firefighter who lived upstairs and had so many teenagers the place was like *Eight Is Enough*. I would go up to their apartment all the time and sit under the dining room table and dream. In the winter I'd play with the elaborate snowy village scene that curled beneath their fake Christmas tree. That first house was the biggest score, with an actual swimming pool in the back-yard and Chrisco throwing barbecues all summer and the yard full of teenagers who would talk to me and ask me questions and tell me I was cute. During one BBQ I was being punished and had to stay in my room crying, while outside my win-dow Madeline sucked on fat wedges of watermelon and told all the teenagers I couldn't come out because I'd asked Allie Leland next door to pull her pants down. Maaaaa! I shrieked, Madeline's Telling! My ass hurt from getting spanked. Allie was really Madeline's friend, and out front of the house they'd been tit-flashing all the cars zooming down Broadway. Cut It Out, I said. They giggled spastically, yanked their shirts up and stuck their pot bellies, their no-boobs, out at the world. Cut It Out, I tugged Madeline's shirt down over her chest while Allie ran around in circles, delirious. Okay fine. I lifted my shirt up at the honking cars. I was about six, they were four, it felt great. Flash, the air hit my skin. I dropped it back down, thrilled. It got old pretty quick. Pull Down Your Pants, I ordered Allie. She had thick blond hair streaked with the sun, it was wiry, strong hair. Allie was always filthy. *They let their kids run wild,* my mother said about the Lelands. Larry Leland was slightly older than me and beat up my little boyfriend Donnie in the dirt alley that led to their backyard. Larry left him in the gravel broken glass pigeon shit and took me upstairs for an ice cream sandwich. Michael was even older and would eventually sell coke on the corner down on Washington Street. More eventually, he would die in a car crash, and Allie would win one million dollars in the Megabucks lotto and dyke out. Once, me and Madeline slept over at Allie's and her mother was drunk and lip-synched to "Do Ya Think I'm Sexy?" with a hairbrush, in her nightgown. It was fun staying at Allie's house but there was a real feeling of no one keeping an eye on things and it made me anxious. It felt like you could do anything. It was too much. When Allie slept at our house, she peed the bed, she sat on my legs and had Madeline tickle my feet till I wanted to die.

Outside on sunny Broadway I told Allie to pull down her pants, and she looped grubby thumbs into her waistband and tugged her shorts down. She wasn't wearing underwear, the skin of her belly slid down her body and ended in a couple of fleshy nubs. We howled. Later it was dinner and Madeline told on me. What an incredibly jerky thing to do. I wanted to kill her but she started wailing like a red-faced bug when she realized how badly she'd fucked up. She got me in so much trouble. *Why did you do that?* It was my father, the mustache man. Dennis would show up on the scene erratically, working so late and leaving at dawn the next morning. I could go days without seeing him, and when he appeared, it was jarring. He was so different than me and Madeline and Ma. A big man, and we were girls. A certain female vibe would erupt in his absence, and the three of us would groove on it, just doing our things, and then Dad would come home and the needle came off the record with a scratch. Who was this foreigner who seemed to rule our house? He'd drink beer from cans and occasionally would allow Madeline a sip. I didn't want any, beer was gross. Bitter like a tin can.

Dennis hustled me onto his knee, he smacked my ass a million times while I screamed bloody blue murder. I was not a stubborn or dignified child, I had hot red lungs, I was a siren. The whole neighborhood would know I was getting hit. A peripheral glimpse of my mother in the doorway, a nervous hover. I yelled at her about it years later, when I yelled at her for everything. *It's what I thought we were supposed to do. Don't go acting like we beat you, we never beat you.* His big hand. I remember my mother guiding me to my room, where I stayed. I lay on my belly with my cheeks cooling—where was my underwear? I wrote, *I am so sorry I am so sorry,* over and over like a grammar school punishment. Sister Maria would have been satisfied with such an effort. I slid the pages under the door because my mother had ceased coming when I called to explain myself. Just Look On The Floor, Ma, I hiccupped. You know how when you're a kid you can just cry forever. Till your body shuts you down with shudders like an overheating car. I tested whether one foot in the hall, one in my room, was okay. It wasn't. Both feet had to be in the room, door shut. Outside was the backyard with the big teenager party and Madeline, much better now, telling everyone I'd looked at Allie Leland's privates and was locked up. The sun got slinky in the sky and the tiki torches were lit and I grew more anxious because there was only so much time left for my mother to forgive me and let me into the yard to talk to the teenagers. They played rock music on radios, and I sat at the window and hoped someone would notice me. I was a princess in a tower, in the pages of a book. I thought somewhere, someone was reading my story and feeling sad for me.

Chrisco's daughter Debbie got pregnant and we got kicked out of the house on Broadway so she could live downstairs from her parents with her new baby. We moved to the next town, Everett. A real ascent from shitty Chelsea, though we soon moved back. Bunches of kids lived in Everett and they all had these kid legends. Leah's father was a magician and gave her mouth coils, spools of colored paper you tucked into your mouth and unraveled dramatically, your eyes spinning as you pulled the colors from your lips like a toy. Leah's mother let her watch anything on cable, even the R-rated movies. Her brother was a teenager and his friends were all assholes. They played Pink Floyd's *The Wall* and I really got it, the creepy mumbles sliding out from their radios. I didn't understand how, if they got it too, they could be so mean. Throwing cups of water at us and calling us names. That song was about injustice toward kids, about the grown-ups who want to squash us, but those kids were just as bad, worse. Once we were riding bikes and Leah got stung by a wasp and was really freaking out and I knew you were supposed to put mud on it so I hopped off my bike and ran up into the courtyard of this big church, over to a ring of shrubs that circled a statue of the Virgin and, *boom*, there were two teenagers lying in the dirt on top of each other like me and Madeline, squirming around. I ran away. There's Teenagers Doing Stuff In There! I screamed to Leah. She was in too much pain to care—her sting was a hot mound on her arm, you could see it pulse. She wailed, Leah was a baby. Once, when a tough girl beat me up at the park, Leah just took off. I ran home alone with my blue satin jacket ripped at the shoulder.

Then there was Tracy, she had a blob of shiny hair that swung on her head, and her father was scary, his face a mess of rough folds. He'd gone to jail for holding up the curtain store on the highway with a knife. I wasn't allowed in Tracy's house, just in her yard, which was fine because she had a cherry tree and that was exotic. Behind her lived an old woman with a big German shepherd. Jenny. I'd read enough books from the young adult section of the library to know that Jenny was a witch and her dog her familiar. We would creep around the rusted fences that separated Tracy's yard from Jenny's, we could see her falling-down house, practically a shack. I told Tracy I saw skeletons through the dirty windows, told her the reddish roots that looped out from the dirt were Blood Roots and it meant someone dead was buried there.

I told Renee and Kristy next door that aliens had landed in my backyard and spoke to me. Renee and Kristy's parents were pot-smoking bikers and the girls didn't have proper blankets on their beds, just, you know, sheets and some other stuff. No pillowcases. It was like something had happened to their family, like they were recovering from something, but it was the way they lived. When it rained, their yard would flood and you could run through the deep puddle like it was the beach. We laid towels beside the pool of dirty water and tanned, floated toys in the muck. Kristy had squinty eyes and buck teeth and looked like a rabbit. Renee, a little older, had grown into a similar face and looked cool, wore bandannas tied around her forehead like her dad. At some point they were the kids not to like and we stole Kristy's Strawberry Shortcake purse and cut it up with scissors and everyone got in trouble and our parents had to pitch in to buy her a new one. I liked it better when they were our friends because Renee was much more willing to play my games than my sister was. Renee was a vampire, and I lay on the cool cement floor of my back porch and she bit my neck and arms and stomach till I felt tingly like when Ma or Nana brushed and braided my hair.

There were so many kids on that street in Everett. A couple of boys around the corner, so poor they only got a calculator for Christmas. I gave them my stupid *Battlestar Galactica* spaceship that was definitely not the *Star Wars* space toys I had requested. The *Battlestar Galactica* toys were crummy—a blank white spaceship no one had bothered to paint, mottled figurines in uniform, orange, no girls, no Princess Leia. Those boys were nice, they had a good shed to climb on and hide inside if it wasn't stuffed with trash bags. One time I'd gone over to find them and they were gone. They'd been evicted, stuff out on the street and then shunted away to who knows where. A new boy was there, he backed me up against the wall and made me kiss him. It was terrible, his lips hit mine and my hands shot out and I flung myself out of the shady alley that led to that home, back out into the sun, heart pounding. I was wearing a wraparound skirt, blue denim with the words "The Best" embroidered over the little hip pocket. A Boy Made Me Kiss Him, I told people. No big whoop, it didn't seem to faze anyone, but it had made me shake. I thought about saying that he had hit me, to see what would happen then, but I didn't want to lie.

There were lots of shitty boys around. Ricky Charmin, at whom I'd yell, Don't Squeeze The Charmin! till he stole my skateboard. The older kid with the moped who ran over my toes on purpose, Tony. I have no doubt I started shit with these boys. There was a certain thrill to provoking them until they did something, smacked you, one boy dumping a box of loose roofing shingles over my head. Something lightly violent would happen and then I could yell scream cry and they would get in trouble. Girls on television were always getting attacked by awful guys, but then there would be justice and the girl was so much more special somehow, for having lived through the pain. Someone fell in love with her, a cop or detective.

At my cousin's birthday party I harassed a boy until he punched me, not even hard really, but I flung myself to the floor and pretended to be unconscious. All the younger kids, who watched TV too, knew the scene well and started hollering until parents came and I roused myself slowly and began to cry. I hated that kid. All these boys were little jerks, it's like they were on the verge of starting shit with you from the beginning and I think I just wanted to get it over with. Put it all out on the table—you're a jerky boy and I'm a good girl and if you fuck with me you're in trouble. A tiny basket of power. I got brought home from the party, and my grandmother and aunt petted me and talked about what a little bastard the boy was. Eddie. He had a dirt bike, he was a really tough kid with a shaved head, a crew cut. I remember sitting on my front steps with him after he'd hit me at the party, my father between us. *Eddie do you like baseball?* He did. My father gave him a baseball hat, the Red Sox. It was new, it was supposed to have been mine. He hit me and he got a hat? *Leave Michelle alone.* That was that.

After Everett we moved back to Chelsea, to Spencer Ave, with the most enormous backyard, which was so good for riding bikes. Lots of pavement and also big patches of splotchy dead grass for you to sit in, though it itched your legs. Grasshoppers that spit brown shit into your palms when you caught them. All the kids would play ambulance. Someone would ride a bike onto the grass and pretend to crash, choreograph a dramatic fall to the ground and lie there all sprawled out in a phony coma. The other kids would ride up on ambulance bikes and administer first aid. I liked being the crash victim, hearing the fake *whoop-whoop* of the siren and the flurry of excited kids hovering above me, touching my head. *I think she's dead.* I'd flutter my eyelids and let out a small moan. *No, she's breathing, we've got to save her.*

Patti would come to my yard to play, rolling in on her wheelchair because she'd been hit by a truck a long time ago and couldn't walk anymore. Her legs were skinny soft things that hung like noodles from her body, her knees were a mess of scabs and runny wounds. She couldn't feel it when her skin ripped, and she'd crawl around my yard pulling herself with her strong little arms, cutting up her legs on the pavement. Patti's family didn't take good care of her. She had brothers and sisters who ran around wild, and nobody cared for her hurt knees to make sure they didn't get infected. I sat in Patti's wheelchair once, tried to spin myself around the yard but I just couldn't make the chair go like she could. My mother watched me through the window, said to me later, *I saw you in Patti's wheel-chair,* in the embarrassing after-school-special voice that she used to talk about meaningful things like divorce and marijuana. *What did that feel like? You're lucky to have two good legs.*

Other kids who came to my yard were Terri and Tammy, wild twins with shaggy blond hair. Lots of kids in my neighborhood were wild, you could feel it coming off their bodies like humidity, and it made me want them to like me. I told Tammy and Terri that I was a witch and brought from my house a Tupperware bowl filled with a little of everything in my bathroom—shampoo, shaving cream, cologne. I stirred it with a fat wooden spoon and said it was my potion. Tammy and Terri laughed. They didn't believe in witches. They ganged up on Madeline once and I chased them out the gate, ran screaming crazy at them down the sidewalk. I was such a chicken really, but I knew that Madeline was mine to protect and it was freeing to understand I didn't have the option of being scared. I absolutely had to fight them, but they ran too fast and got away.

Tammy and Terri had a brother named Joey and he was my boyfriend for a minute. Then he was in my yard with these other boys, wild animals all of them, and he pulled out his dick, so I had to break up with him. I was at the dinner table eating a bowl of Chef Boy-R-Dee ravioli with the image of his fleshy little thing still in my head and I felt compelled to tell my mother about it. *Why didn't you make him leave?* she demanded. *Don't let him in the yard anymore. You should've kicked him out.* She was mad at me. I couldn't kick him out, he would have laughed at me and not left, and then what would I have done? I did not know how to handle public school kids. They really were from a different place. Joey eventually killed someone, this boy named Kevin who was actually pretty nice for a wild kid. He used to ride me around on his bicycle handlebars. They were having an argument, something about football, and Kevin called Joey a faggot and Joey went home and got his father's gun and came back and shot him. This really tough girl named Melinda slipped a joint into Kevin's pocket at the funeral because he'd always said he wanted to be buried with a joint in his pocket. He was about thirteen.

All the different parts of my yard were separate to me, and they all had names. The line of trees at the back was Pine Row even though they weren't pines, they were just really tall and green. Those skinny, ugly trees that look like plastic. The front yard was a thick tangle of shrubs and weeds and mysterious vines that blossomed with curling purple flowers that bumblebees adored, and later in the fall grew small red berries. We would use them as weapons in our fights. They were poison and smelled weird when they hit your skin, bursting open and leaving bloody little smears like you'd been shot. The yard on the other side of the house never got sun, so the grass was cool and green and it was named Strawberry Fields after the song. A lot of the yard was named after Beatles songs. There was a little path of concrete named Lennon Lane. I loved John Lennon. I was so mad that he was killed right when I discovered him. At Lechmere my parents let me and my sister each get a record, and I bought a forty-five with "Woman" on one side and some awful screechy Yoko Ono thing I didn't understand on the other. My sister got "Shaddap You Face," which wasn't a real song, it was more like a dumb joke. My parents loved it and thought it was so funny and they'd all dance around to it while I sat in my room sulking and being real, listening to "Woman." I thought it was very deep and beautiful and it even made me cry. I'm sure I was just flooded with fresh hormones. I wanted everyone to stop prancing around to my sister's stupid record and come sit with me and cry about John Lennon. My mother had liked the Beatles too when she was younger, but only the poppy sing-along stuff when they wore those suits and dumb matching hairdos. *They started doing dope and their music got weird,* she said with a scrunch in her face. My mother, right before I was born, worked as a secretary or clerk in Boston, ate her lunch on a bench in the Common and watched the filthy hippies splash in the fountain. She had given up John Lennon and so he was mine now, his dead grey face coming off on my sooty hands as I chopped him out of the *Herald American* and taped him to my walls.

HARD-KNOCK LIFE

On the television set in the living room, an entertainment newsmagazine show was backstage with the orphans from *Annie*. A gang of hyper little girls lacking the sluggish malnutrition and deep melancholy of true orphans. If Broadway hadn't wanted them, it would have been Ritalin city for that bunch. Pretend orphans, in foppish dresses tailored to look like rags. They were telling the reporter about how they'd become orphans, the tryouts, their moms and their schools and all the things that kept them "regular kids," studying their spelling backstage, a book cracked open on a makeup table. When they arranged themselves before the journalist and burst into a whiny chorus of "It's The Hard-Knock Life," I wanted to die. The smallest, cutest orphan, the sleepiest one in the floppiest dress, she was almost six years old, and I was eight already. I watched and thought: It's Too Late. Some toilet inside me clogged with despair. I wanted to be an orphan so badly. Not even a main orphan with a solo line in a song, I would have been totally happy being just a mute orphan, a dumb prop, anything. Anything, God, Anything, I prayed, displaying my noble lack of greed like my mother praying for a lottery win: *I don't need to hit the big one, even five hundred dollars, even two-fifty*. We didn't want to offend God by dreaming too high, my family. Oh, I wanted to dance and sing with those orphans on the stage, I wanted all the people in the audience to love me. And it couldn't ever happen. It had to take years to work your way up to being an orphan. I mean, unless you were totally lucky and got discovered. You had to take children's acting classes at one of those places in Boston, and that cost money. You had to get lots of pictures taken and build a portfolio, you had to find an agent and I bet they would want some money, too. And even if I had all the money to do it, and went to the casting calls and waited in a huge line all day, even if I then ended up being a good kiddie actress, by the time I got it all together I'd hardly be a kiddie anymore, I'd be too old to be an orphan. My eyes brimmed with an angry heat. You had to start the process so young, before the desire was even there. Someone else had to have the desire for you. All I wanted was to be an orphan. I knew I could do it. I could be one of those girls. It wasn't fair. It was just like the year before, when I read in a kid's magazine about the youngest girl ever to write a book. She was five years old. I gasped and moaned. I had myself been planning on being the youngest girl to ever write a book, but I was already seven and had no connections, and some five-year-old jerk with a mom in the publishing industry beat me to it. Time was slipping away, I would never be the youngest kid to do anything, I was too old already. Once, when I was three years old, I got my picture in the *Chelsea Record*, on the cover. For being the youngest kid to know the Pledge of Allegiance by heart. I'd been in Gorin's

Department Store, hanging out by my grandmother's cash register, pledging. A reporter happened to be near my chant, I guess you could say I was discovered. But it stopped right there. It didn't open any doors. I knew there was more stuff I could do, but where did I go to do it? Who did I talk to? I needed another reporter, but I knew that stuff like that only happened once. It only happened once, and I wasted my big chance on the Pledge of Allegiance.

When it finally became too much to watch another shrill second of the grinning orphans having the time of their lives, the merciful camera swiveled over to Andrea McArdle. There, on the carpet, I relaxed. Andrea McArdle I loved. Andrea McArdle did not fill me with rage or call feelings of doom into my tiny ribs, because I understood that there was only one, could only ever be one, Andrea McArdle. It was her, she was lucky, I was happy for her. She was Annie, there was only one Annie. There were so many orphans, a plague of them. Up on the stage with Andrea, they were an orphan-colored backdrop she shone against in that famous red dress. Her shaggy dog and her rich, bald dad. Andrea on the TV being swarmed by a thick cloud of orphans, hugged on every side, bum-rushing her with all the gratitude a gang of rescued orphans from Newton, Massachusetts, could muster. They got to hug Andrea McArdle, their arms around that red dress. The smallest, most lovable orphan was six years old, and I was eight already.

We went to see *Annie* because all I did was play the album and torture my family with attempts at "Tomorrow." Imagine anyone trying to sing like Andrea McArdle. I was really working on it. The theater was in Boston, In the *"combat zone,"* my parents laughed, and I expected to see proof of war, bombed-out buildings and busted streets, but everything was pretty much okay, just dirty. We ate before the show in a tiny pizza place that had a video game. I'd heard of video games and thought they sounded cool. This one was called Galaga. I played it for a quarter and couldn't figure out exactly what I was supposed to do. Something like an electronic spider web stretched across the screen, changing colors.

In the dark theater we sat way up in the darkest part, up high, and Andrea McArdle was a red whoosh on the stage, the orphans pale and indistinguishable in their nightgowns. I felt frantic. If we were closer, if we were sitting in, like, the front row, maybe some-one would notice me. Someone would notice how orphan I was, see it in my face, how true I was, how good I could be. I would sing along to "It's the Hard-Knock Life" the way I'd been practic-ing, and someone would overhear and say *Would you listen to that? Grab that little girl!* Someone important would grab me, not a Sicko but an important person any parent would be thrilled to have their little girl grabbed by. Maybe there would be a part in *Annie* when they pulled kids from the audience onto the stage. They did that at the circus, at the Barnum & Bailey Ringling Bros. Circus. I have a fabulous memory of being lifted into a golden coach full of clowns and taken on a little spin around the ring, but I think it is perhaps a memory I invented. Maybe I saw some other kids lifted into such a coach, at the circus or the Ice Capades, and as my heart sank while watching the wrong kid carried away by clowns, I stole the kid's memory. The orphans never pulled anyone up on stage anyway. It was nothing that easy. It was hard work, serious work, and you had to have a demanding stage mother on your side, one with debatable judgment, like Brooke Shields's mom.

For the school talent show, the "Variety Show," I was an orphan. Back in first grade my grandmother had dressed me like a farmer and I'd sung a song about a donut. It was such a big hit that the following year I dressed like a farmer again and sang "There's a Hole in the Bucket." This year I would be a lip-synching orphan. I recruited Ruthie Caprizzio, who was not popular and therefore had no reputation to protect, to join me in this potentially dorky endeavor. Ruthie Caprizzio was the girl my mother consoled me with on nights that I could not sleep, kept awake by how ugly I was, kept awake with the dread that no one would ever love me, that I would never be a star and never be able to turn a graceful cartwheel. My mother would comfort me: *It's not like you look like Ruthie Caprizzio, she's a homely little girl, God bless her. Don't tell anyone I said that, she's a nice girl, it's not her fault.*

Ruthie was nice, if a little dull. I was glad that she did not seem to care about the very real possibility of everyone laughing at us. We found our most orphany outfits, and got sponges and a bucket of soapy water and mouthed the words to "It's the Hard-Knock Life" on our hands and knees, scrubbing the floor. I choreographed a few simple moves where we got off our knees and waved the sponges in the air, and a couple of hands-on-hips, angry-orphan marches. We practiced in Ruthie's room, which she shared with her about-to-be-married older sister. Ruthie's very Italian mother—*Off the boat,* my mother said—yelled at us to keep it down, all our stomping. We came up with a pretty good routine, but at the rehearsal Sister Rita started yelling. *No no no!* she yelled. We were crouched on the floor of the stage in the school auditorium with our squishy sponges, scrub scrub, our mouths exaggerating the words streaming out from Ruthie's little tape player. *Why aren't you singing?* Sister Rita demanded. *You can't do that, you have to sing!* She acted like we were cheating, trying to pull a fast one on her. It's Lip-Synching, I explained. An art in itself. A good lip-synching could get you on television, onto one of those lip-synch shows. *Either you sing or you're not in the show.* I guess it's unnecessary to explain how sternly she said this, she was a nun. Head-to-toe black, thick black polyester, weird pigeony women, all of them. And we couldn't use soap and water in our act because she didn't want us to get the stage wet. Our sponges could lip-synch, but we couldn't. *Sing,* she clapped. Ruthie looked at me accusingly, her face trembling. It had taken some convincing to get her to be an orphan with me. Her mother didn't want her to do it, something about theater and the devil, and I had assured her that she didn't have to learn all the words because it was just a lip-synch, all she had to do was move her mouth around. *Michelle,* she whined. It's Okay It's Okay It's Okay, I said. We Just Need To Practice More. The show was the next day. At the edge of the stage Charlie Agrazzi, who was doing a dance to "Le Freak (C'est Chic)" dressed as the Hulk in green body paint and shredded clothes, was waiting for his turn to rehearse. *Sing-ing!* Sister Rita repeated. It was like they had repetitive, mean little boxes in their heads instead of brains, the nuns.

The following night, me and Ruthie sang. Or I did. I would be the main singer since I knew the song beyond by heart, and Ruthie would do back-up, coming in on the chorus. We planned to keep our voices lower than our recorded accompaniment, but I got too into it and really let go with my throat, waved my dry sponge in the air, screamed for justice for orphans. Empty Belly Life! I shouted. Full Of Sorrow Life! No Tomorrow Life! It was like punk for kids.

I hurled it at my schoolmates, the plight of orphaned children. The deep pain and strength, I was feeling it, I was a beacon. Why couldn't there have been someone, anyone, in the audience? Someone not from Chelsea, someone who could see me and know, *That little girl, she's a star! Grab her!* It's The Hard-Knock Liiiiife! Me and Ruthie crescendoed and collapsed to the floor.

SUIT OF RUNNING WATER

Marisol Lewis lived in the projects down behind the Bradlees shopping center, a brick encampment the city flung down beside the oily creek that trickled along the edge of our town like a flooded gutter. The rusted corners of shopping carts poked through the sluggish current like skeletal shipwrecks, and trash bags bloated like slick, fattened jellyfish sagged at the shore. The trash bags intrigued and thrilled me, I was certain they held heinous secrets—a litter of soggy kittens, a butchered girl-body. What else would someone wrap in a trash bag and dump in a creek? Not trash. The creek's bank was littered with trash, though, faded plastic wrappers and millions of bottles, rotting tins.

I got so excited by water. Rivers and creeks in particular, they were old-fashioned and romantic, like nature, which didn't exist except in books about girls who lived a long time ago. These girls went to their river to do things like pound clothes on rocks and fetch water in pails. On trips out of

Chelsea I'd sometimes see the shine of a river streaming alongside the highway and it was like a flaw in time's fabric, where this old world had leaked through. It made me want to be beautiful and live along its banks, with the clean pebbles and the green stuff it fed. It made me want to be a girl in a book, beautiful in that old way girls don't get to be anymore, the kind of beautiful that needs to be fed by a clean river. I loved that dream of a girl, the Beautiful Girl, calm and wild as water. I loved her like I loved the Psychic Girl, another paperback myth, because she was a safe girl to love, a fantasy that I could own. When I grew up and began to meet so many different real girls. I met beautiful girls, calm and wild, who had grown up beside trees and pools of water and I hated them instinctively. They hurt my feelings. I had thought these girls were imaginary, but no, they were real, and I could have been one too, and possessed that water-fed grace. I didn't know who to be mad at for not giving me a river. The creek didn't count, the dirty creek that Chelsea had spun a fence around, kept cordoned off like the city dump, like a landfill. It didn't occur to me to visit the water there. It wasn't water, it was only wet. Creek versus river, dirty creek girl versus glittering river girl—I don't know why we had to be enemies but we were. I felt it in my heart, a piece of my body I could locate by its weight and frustration, hemmed in by all the other organs, bound by the veins running through it like rope, keeping it pinned inside me like a pretty winged thing that got caught. You knew where your heart was because you could feel where it hurt.

Marisol Lewis lived by the creek, but she wasn't like a long-skirted girl in a book. Probably Marisol only thought of the creek when the wind carried its moldy stink through her windows. The projects terrified me. They were like a prison complex, stacked and uniformly ugly, and the very poorest lived there, the poorest residents of a poor city. I didn't like to imagine the fuckups that brought these families to this housing institution by the polluted creek. Chelsea is the kind of city where hope of improvement is thin and minimal—you can hope to someday move into one of the neighboring cities, frayed places to be sure but cleaner, warmer, safer. You can hope for deliverance to Maiden, Medford, Somerville, but really you spent most of your hope on maintaining, on things not getting any worse. Hope for betterment later, when things evened out, but for now just hope that you don't slide away. In Chelsea, escape is less likely than a trip and fall into the projects, the place where people ended up, the worst-case scenario of Chelsea, the place where Marisol lived. Her mom was divorced, there was no man in the family, so I understood how she got there. My Uncle Joey, the only brother Dennis consistently liked, was there because he was a drinker, a drinker and a fuckup.

Maybe if Joey had kept his bad habits to himself and stayed away from other people, he could have had a normal apartment, led the bachelor life, but he involved himself with a woman, Janey, very Irish with her wiry red hair and freckles. Janey was sweet, which meant Janey was doomed. She married Joey, already pregnant at their City Hall ceremony, a business meeting really, a poverty contract Janey signed and some Chelsea official stamped. Thus began the drama of Janey's phone calls to my mother, when I'd get kicked out of the kitchen, where the telephone was, and my mother would hunch her head around the phone, her long brown hair soundproofing the conversation. Janey was in despair because Joey was drunk, Joey was an asshole, Joey was a Swankowski. My father would yell at Joey. *You're fuckin' married, Joe!* he'd yell. Things had to be bad if my father was schooling Joey on marital responsibility. If my dad was sent in to rescue him it had to mean that Joey was beyond help. I think he hit Janey, I think he fucked other women, I think it was the real bad stuff as opposed to the regulation misery of basic alcoholism, aggressively bad moods and distance.

When Janey was pregnant she would take my hands and place them on the taut ball of her belly and ask if I could feel it. The baby inside, little Joey Junior. Janey was delighted to be pregnant, her body was clearly a magical thing and she got to live inside it. *Can you feel it?* she'd ask, and I would become serious and still, the kind of focus I'd get when the nuns would herd us into church and order us to sit tight and listen for God's voice inside us calling out our True Vocation. I hadn't been very lucky in discerning my vocation, it was hard to untangle the voice of God from all the other voices and static that raged in my head like a radio between stations. But I felt the deep, fleshy ripple of a fetal foot, a presence becoming aware of itself. I gasped. I was happy to have felt it, it made me special somehow, like when an animal singles you out for affection. Embryonic Joey was feeling my good vibes and kicking out a Hello. The most precious connections in life were the ones that disregarded normal communication and went for the deep psychic pull, a cosmic recognition of mutual magic. Little baby Joey. In the hospital I looked at him through the glass in the baby lineup, the row of fresh product the baby-makers had created that day. He didn't look any different than the other pruny screamers, but I saw that foot, tiny and red, I saw it kick its kick, that dull kick into my open palm, and he was the Christ Child, a needy little miracle with his toothless mouth in a tight, heartbroken O. The air was all over him, pummeling his soft, soaked skin. It had to be terrible, being born. It had to be worse than dying.

Back in her room, Janey was propped limp in her bed, her face so white the freckles looked like flecks of paint you could peel from her skin. I was shocked to see that her belly was still so big. I thought it'd snap back to her hips like elastic once she'd evicted the baby. She saw me staring at it, all that flesh like an extra appendage. She laughed. *It's still there*, she said, pulling on herself like taffy. Probably I looked disturbed. *It'll go away*, she promised. Janey was so comfortable with the whole thing, none of the embarrassment-driven boldness I'd hear in the voices of women discussing the shame of their bodies. *My big fat ass*, stuff like that. It sounds proud but it's not, it's talking shit about yourself before anyone else gets the chance to. There was nothing shameful in Janey's changed and exhausted body, and though she was in a hospital she was not sick so there was none of the shame of illness, the dirt of time sullying your good machine, breaking you down. Janey was happy. She had a new baby.

One year later, Janey and Joey threw a birthday party for Joey Junior, a cookout in the project yard that they shared with countless other families. I think the projects scared me because I knew that if I had to live there I would get lost. The entrance to every building was identical, a dark maw in the brick face. You'd think they'd at least distinguish the buildings, give each one a cutesy name and bolt a plaque to the entrance, but there were none, just holes knocked into the walls that you entered like a mouse and roamed toward your family's compartment. I've heard that the housing projects of urban America were built by Nazi architects the government smuggled over after the war, the men who designed the camps and the ovens. This was their new vocation, building these monoliths for families to live and die in. I would look at the reddish compound and imagine myself trapped outside, not knowing which bare window held my mother. I would imagine running up and down the cavernous stairwells, pressing my ear to doors, straining to hear the voices behind the dense metal and rows of bolted locks. Joey Junior's birthday was a smoking hibachi and squat lounge chairs, adult asses sunk into the sagging plastic weaves. The ladies smoked cigarettes and the guys held in their fists wet cans of beer, pulled from the cooler with the clatter of tin and ice. Everyone was loud, shrill women and braying men. I joined a small pack of kids and ran through the maze of the buildings, mothers at our backs shouting, *Stay away from the creek!*

It was tempting for a minute, the thought of climbing the fence. I loved climbing fences, the sure insertion of a sneaker into a waiting link, up and up you went—it was easy, they were made for climbing. Later I'd initiate an elite club whose sole purpose and criteria for entrance was the ability to swiftly and fearlessly scale a fence, jump it, hoist yourself over the tricky pronged top that was so scary, pointing jagged metal at your denim girl-crotch. Alone I'd traipse through my neighborhood, scoping out good fences, fences that could deliver you to the roof of a shed, to a yard that held sweet lilac bushes. If I'd been special enough to live near a river, if I'd been a beautiful River Girl, I could have applied such talent and determination to trees and jumbles of rock, but I had only a dirty creek and the challenge and invitation of the fence that protected us from it. I don't remember the kids but I remember the feeling of being among them, a real mania, the rising unbound energy of all of us together, with the parents getting drunk off beer and greasy with hotdogs. We could do anything, we could do things we weren't supposed to—our hyperactive shouts and laughs drowned out the mom warnings which rang so loud in our brains while alone.

I'm Climbing The Fence, I declared. The kids got silent. The prohibitive weave of metal shone in the sun. Beyond it the creek oozed its muddy ooze. Maybe I could find something there, in the sun-fried grass along the bank. A prize to bring to the kids, something rusty, something cool. *It's electric. You'll get shocked.* The kid who said this lived here at the projects. He bragged his information, this was his turf. Really? *Yeah, you'll get an electric shock. They do it so kids don't go in the creek.* I looked at the fence. It looked like every other fence I'd ever climbed, an easy one too. No crown of rough prongs, the link stopped below a bar that you could slide your thighs over, no tears in your jeans. Fences like that were their own problem because they got so loose they billowed out like ship sails and made you get wobbly and lose your balance. But I could do it. Really? I probed the kid again. He nodded. *You'll get zapped.* He was almost encouraging. Probably most of them were hoping I'd try it. How exciting to actually see someone get electrocuted. I thought about it. It was a bright blue thought like a searing summer sky, the sky above our heads. Let's Run, I decided, and we chased each other through the projects. Maybe it could be cool to live here, people everywhere, kids at your fingertips. Maybe the tiny hives of a hundred homes actually expanded into one enormous home, everyone here together, everyone right above and below, right next door, everyone avoiding the electrified metal fence, staying close, and the kids a noisy pack dashing through the halls. Each building had two entrances, a front and a back, so you could run through them screaming and hear your voice rise up the stairwell, bashing against the walls. It was like going into a tunnel, the quick cool darkness, and then you burst back into the sun again. We were doing this. A ground-floor door opened and a girl leaned out, my age, perfectly blond hair, long on a long face. *There are old people who live here,* she barked. Like a kid playing school and she was the teacher. Tense and righteous. Then she broke it. *You all better shut the fuck up.* That was Marisol. Rhymes with parasol, those pretty, delicate umbrellas that keep sun, not rain, from the shoulders of sweet little girls who live in books and play by clean rivers. Pastel parasols with clumps of shimmering fringe hanging from each spoke. Marisol's mouth gaped open, ugly and pissed-off. Worse than a mom, she was a kid like us, stomping out the fun. Immediately I thought she could beat me up. She lived in the projects. All angry and glaring, tough about the old ladies. But I was high off the kids. This reckless pulse, I felt like the heart of it, I had almost scaled the electric fence. The day was a charged web and I was sprinting into its core. You Shut Up! I hollered and took off fast, the kids behind me, terrorizing all the old ladies dying there at the bottom of Chelsea. Leaving Marisol poking out her door like one of them, the angriest old lady with her cataract-blue eyes, her sunburn-red face, looking for a fight. She'd picked the wrong kids, we were there to play.

I don't know why my parents had such a big fight that night, but they did, the worst one save for the very last one, when my father kicked the three of us out, me, Mom and Madeline, all the girls, out on the front steps at three in the morning waiting for a cab to take us to Nana and Papa's. It wasn't that fight, but it was a bad one. Probably my father was drunk, can after can of Miller Lite at the cookout, bonding with the men, probably he wanted to keep going. He got sent home with the women, with the girls, the house of females that was all his fault, and he didn't want it, wanted only to drink with the guys and talk about, I don't know, the working man's life, the bosses and the unions, the union bosses who were just as bad. Talking about Polish Solidarity with the other Polacks, SOLIDARNO, a bumper sticker on the back of our car. Talking about how great it was that the new pope was Polish. When the Polish pope got shot a bit down the line, it sent Dennis into a deep depression. It validated his deep understanding that the world was impossibly unjust, that whenever something good happens—one of your own gets elected pope—something shitty has to creep out and blast it away, a bullet tearing through vestments. Normally, when Dennis arrived home, he'd open the door and proclaim, *Another day wasted*—his bitter salute to his slowly wasting life. Each of his days was a waste. When the pope got shot, Dennis didn't even say that. He didn't say anything, his bitterness had reached a new, mute level. It was bad enough that he slaved daily at a shitty postal service job, chronically unable to get elected into the esteemed union government. Now somebody went and shot the Polish pope. Dennis brought the *Herald American* with the story on the front page into his private den at the back of the house, and stayed there.

At little Joey's birthday party, Dennis was the party's humming generator, his gripes the loudest, his voice the crabbiest, his laugh the most joyfully sour. The men's cheeks reddened with sun and hops, and they laughed and laughed with my father. Of course he didn't want to leave. I know the sharp crack of a fresh can popped open that sinks you deeper into the glowing heat of conversation, you want it to never stop. I belong to my father, I'm his Polish daughter. I understand the liquid chain that strings the night together, how it feels like it could last forever and the pleading ache of just a little more, another cigarette, one more beer, let me finish this conversation. The sky softening around the perfect night, the night that went the distance, that drops you into an accomplished sleep. Alcoholics don't want to stop because the drinking brings them alive.

Our bedroom was a dark room that got darker at night. Sheets of wood paneling with pictures from *Sixteen* scotch-taped at the corners, Andy Gibb and Rex Smith and Rick Springfield. I had planted a paper garden on my wall, construction-paper-green stems and oval leaves and bright paper petals individually taped around the sunburst-yellow circle in the center. In the nighttime dark you couldn't see any of it, just the faintest shine from the phony wood that boxed me in with my sister and our beds and bureaus. The shouts from the dark beyond our doorless room streamed like the creek down our hallway and inside. No words, just tone, the loud barking dad-tone and slower choked mom-noise, the crying mom, the crying mom and from Dad a disgusted lowness to the voice, and the snap of a beer being opened. I knew my dad was bad and that he had started it. You don't know what dogs are saying when they growl and bite, but you know which dog is the sweet dog and which is the distempered bully, you hear it in the tone and pitch of dog-throat like the sounds that rang out of the living room. Then a shuffle, the shuffle and gulp of the crying mom down the hall to crawl into bed with her pups. Me and Madeline were already together, clinging to pillows and each other in my skinny kid's bed. We made room for Ma, wrapped ourselves around her, need and comfort.

Her brown hair was wet from her face and we breathed our jagged breaths in the dark. Where else does a mom go? Not into that bed that wasn't hers. There wasn't any reason why her bed should not have been her own but it wasn't hers any more than my bed and Madeline's bed were our own—they were all his, King Drunk, we were homeless long before he ever kicked us out. Wandering his halls, the smell that drifted from the bathroom, thick male dad-shit, the smoke of his cigarette burning a new brown smudge on the sink where it lay smoking as he sprayed short gusts of aerosol hairspray on his thin black hair. The Dry Look. The aerosol choke of deodorant sprayed into the scribble of his armpits, Arrid Extra Dry. The dry, dry dad, the dry stink of him in the bathroom and sometimes, another scent, the sneaky animal smell of my mother, a warm smell, humid. Where could the mother sleep? Not in the dad's bed, not on the couch where he sat, sunk in the cushions, his can sweating glittery beads on the silver tin, the dry, thirsty dad. Ma sleeps with the kids, in the girl-room. But no one sleeps, everyone cries. He Shouldn't Be Mean To You, I said into her hair, into the cloth of her shirt that smelled like cookout. A blue shirt, "Supermom" a shimmering decal across her chest. He Shouldn't Be Mean To You. *You go tell him that,* she cried. *Go tell your father.* Probably she'd had her own can at the party, her own can or two with the women. I climbed from my bed with the jungle animal bedspread and ran the dark house with bat radar. The smoking dad looked at me, black mustache, he looked like Sonny Bono, everyone said so. The school wanted him to sing "I Got You Babe" in the fundraiser talent show with a woman who looked like Cher. The joke was that the woman was fat, a fat Cher. It wasn't a bad joke because the woman knew it—*My big fat ass*, she'd say—but it wasn't funny enough to get my father onto a stage.

You Shouldn't Be Mean To Ma, You Should Leave Ma Alone. I'm as soggy as a kitten drowned in the dirty creek. But it feels good, standing here in the dim parlor smelling the yeasty rank of Dad's breath as he breathes and stares, and I know I've done something terrible and dangerous, the beat of my heart pounding all sleepiness away. I know I'll get in trouble but I don't care because it was true, someone had to say that to Dad and I felt good that it was me who padded through the house, me who risked something to fight for justice like any number of paperback heroines living on my bookshelf. *Get the hell back in bed!* he hollers, moving toward me, trailing me down the hall and into my room, where I fly back into the salty steamy girl-bed. Dad's at the door saying, *Don't you dare turn my kids against me,* to Mom, and to me, *Did your mother tell you to say that, did your mother make you say that to me? That's real nice, Louisa.* We can only see him when a tiny shred of streetlight from the window hits the silver cross around his neck. She Didn't Tell Me To, I defend. She hadn't, they were my own thoughts. I'd thunk them myself. *You're a real winner,* he says and leaves the doorway. I don't know if I'm the winner or if Mom's the winner but I know that really neither one of us is because he said it the way adults sometimes say nice things but don't mean them, mean the opposite. *You're not a winner.* It's all in the voice. Somehow it sounds worse than saying, *You're not a winner.* Maybe because we never thought we were winners in the first place, and Dennis's sarcastic awareness of this is the last thing we hear before sleep.

JOHNNA'S BROADWAY SCHOOL OF DANCE

Marisol Lewis, the girl from the projects, I saw her again inside the one-room dance schoolhouse that is Johnna Latrotta's Broadway School of Dance. Like Catholic school, after-school dance class was one of the few life-improving, social-status-enhancing options available to the children of Chelsea. If I lived by a river I'd be riding horses. Like Catholic school, Johnna Latrotta's Broadway studio was entirely white, despite the immigrant reality of Chelsea. Despite Puerto Rico, despite Cambodia. Puerto Ricans were swift and vicious, slicing tongues and illegal switchblades on their person. Take my word for it or take your chance and get cut. Cambodians ate dog. Everyone knew that. Keep yours in the house or smell it baking from your neighbor's window. It was a big problem that these people were here, in Chelsea. A bigger problem that they continued to think so highly of the countries they came from. Cars rolling through the square with the Puerto Rican flag hung from the rearview, or the antennae, stuck glittery on the bumper, Spanish music trilling out the window. It really bothered my family. *You like it so much, why don't you go back there?* my mother muttered. Not to their faces. That would be mean. It was hard to reconcile the God-loves-everyone line taught at Catholic school with this other sentiment at home. Somehow they coexisted, and everyone appeared comfortable with the obvious intellectual flaw. My grandmother sang, *Puerto Rico, my devotion, I wish it'd fall into the ocean,* in a Carmen Miranda caricature, thickly mocking. *You look like a Puerto Rican,* my mother'd shame me when my clothes were mismatched, too bright. Not Puerto Rican, but *a* Puerto Rican. That made a difference. We were Polish, Irish. Not a Polish, Polack, or *an* Irish—what was the bad word for Irish people? There was a catalogue of ethnicity in my brain. Polish, Polacks, they were dumb, that was the joke. What's a pimple on a Polack's ass? A brain tumor! But no one ever called me a Polack except the other Polish people in my family. I couldn't imagine the Puerto Rican families of Chelsea sitting around the dinner table bitching about the Polacks the way our conversation so often drifted bitterly toward them. Nobody seemed to care about the Poles. There was the abandoned Polish church in the city, Saint Stanislaus, St. Stan's. No one went to worship there except a scatter of little old Polish ladies who shopped sometimes at Gorin's, the department store in the square, where Nana worked a register. My Irish Papa, Mom's dad, would call me a Polack, sometimes a Dumb Polack, but he didn't mean it. He was fucking with me. I didn't know what to say back to him— Irish, who cared. This was Massachusetts. Oh, I knew they'd been persecuted a million years ago, signs in the window saying Irish people couldn't come in or couldn't get a job, everyone loved to talk about that long-ago oppression whenever me or anyone else sheepishly suggested that maybe the rampant hatred of the new Puerto Ricans or Cambodians was wrong. Or if someone, a black person, was talking about discrimination on a talk show, *Everyone gets discriminated against,* a familial adult would snap, annoyed. Trot out the stories of the downtrodden Irish of long ago. Who had been oppressing the Irish? It seemed impossible. Maybe the Italians? My grandparents didn't seem to like those people either, which made no sense to me because Italians were white. I mean, some were as dark in their skin as the Puerto Ricans, but still they were absolutely white, right? My mother's was the first generation to break out of seeing the Italians as somehow dirty, third-world. When she was young she'd been forbidden to date them, which was incredible to me. Italian boys were the cutest. You would hope for this to give my mother some perspective on the strange fashions of racism, who's in, who's out. Look how celebrated the Italians were now, both her daughters clamoring for their darkness, yet the darkness of the Puerto Ricans, the Cambodians—forbidden. And black people, duh. That went without a discussion, that was so ancient and obvious. The Italians, my grandfather still called them guineas. *That your little guinea friend?* he'd chuckle with a smoke after dinner. He was amused at the passage of time, how his granddaughter could now have a guinea friend and nobody would comment on it but him. He was the guardian of some slipping-away time.

Don't Call Her That, I'd snap. Everyone would giggle. Guineas, Polacks, spics. What about the Irish? They drank too much, this I knew. My grandfather sometimes drank too much. Supposedly, one of his drinking buddies was black. This unconfirmed fact was brought out by my mother or grandmother whenever Papa said something shitty—the N-word, stuff that flew out of his crinkled dry mouth and singed my heart, made something desperate and angry claw useless in my chest. I wanted to like Papa, I wanted to like my whole family, but they made it so hard. It was hard to like Papa once I realized you couldn't like people who said the N-word. Could you hold your family to the standards you held for other people? It seemed hypocritical not to, but it seemed terrifying as well, a mental process that took my family away, left me an orphan, loveless and lonely. Because if I couldn't like Papa then I could hardly like Nana, and I couldn't like Ma even, could I, she wouldn't let me go out with a boy who wasn't white, or even be friends with Puerto Rican girls, really, and my father had used the N-word and called the loud and fast-speaking families in the square "spics." I had yelled at a girl in my class for saying that word before, and she'd looked at me like I was nuts. *It's short for Spanish People in Chelsea,* she explained.

Once, Madeline started going out with a boy named Gino, who everyone assumed was Italian. When it was discovered that he was mulatto, our family made her break up with him. He was the captain of the Pop Warner football team and everything, but that didn't really matter since lots of black kids played on the football team and they were still black. *It's just the saddest,* my mother lamented, *the saddest, saddest thing, those mulatto children. They don't belong anywhere—the blacks don't want them and the whites don't want them. It's a sin.* Mulatto boys came from a "different culture." Who Doesn't? I asked. Our family would have huge, loudmouthed debates about it, turning the house into the set of a TV talk show like the one that featured the black mother of the scorned mulatto baby, or the one with the Black Power rappers on it, all puffed up in their big coats, angry at white people. *See, they don't like us, either,* Ma said triumphantly, watching the screen. The "family" extended to whatever neighbors happened to be over that night sucking down mugs of tea, it reached out to Nana and to Papa, and I felt that raging ache in my body and was spurred to pit my new way of thinking, knobby-kneed and weak, instinctive and emotional, against the rationales that had been passed back and forth and down the generations for years. It seemed like it would be so easy to explain why it was wrong, the way they all talked about black people, but when I brought it down to the most simple and true thing, They're Human Just Like Anybody, I sounded young and stupid, flaky too, and all the adults kicked back and pulled on their cigarettes and laughed great, smoky laughs at what a little bohemian Michelle was turning into. *Whaddaya, Nigga-lova?* Papa inquired. Later I'd cry. *Oh, he doesn't mean it,* my mother brushed it away with the flip of her hand. *One of his drinking buddies is a black guy, he's been drinking with him for years.* Apparently he was with this mysterious drinking buddy that nobody in the family had ever met during that one Christmas Eve binge that had knocked him out before the traditional festivities at my house. I cried again, it was Christmas, we needed Papa. *Call your grandfather, tell him you're crying.* Nana had the plastic phone in her hand, its smooth curve thrust to my little ear. Women's power is the children, that's not new. The power and the weapon, the bargaining tool. Papa answered the phone, a web of drink clogged in his throat. I yelled at him. Come Over Here! I yelled. It's Christmas, You Should Be Here At My House. The women beamed. *Your grandmother make you call me?* He wasn't mad, though. Papa was nice always, even when he was drunk. He came over, he'd had his disco nap and was cheery, drank the Seagram's 7 my mother bought every Christmas, especially for him. Christmas dinner also had special Papa foods that interested nobody else but had to be there for the Grandfather. Little white onions, wet from a can. Pale branches of celery in a glass of water. Seagram's 7 on Xmas Eve. A highball. *Ya missed me, kid?* A big red hug. It was better once Papa was there. He would call me a Polack, teasing me, and I was stumped. Drunk Irishman, I'd snap, and he'd laugh, dunk the corner of his buttered Wonder Bread in the spaghetti sauce on his dinner plate and laugh. Bread and butter was Papa food, soft, mushy bread folded into a little envelope. Also tomatoes sliced and salted, a little arc of them on the edge of your plate. Men, it seemed, always had special food needs. Drunk Irishman, I continued, encouraged, Drunk Irishman You Got Pee Stains In Your Underwear! Don't ask me how I knew the Irish peed in their drawers. Cause they're too drunk, right? *How dry I am, wet I'll be, if I can't find the bathroom key,* that was a drinking song, maybe an Irish one since Papa knew all the words and would sing it at me if I had the hiccups, like I was drunk too. I was, after all, Irish as well, though Papa seemed to believe the invading Polish genes cancelled Ireland out. Papa laughed so hard at the yellow underwear insult that I knew I'd said the right thing.

But back to the others, those odd and exotic races that wandered the streets of our city, ruining it. The Cambodians were more recent immigrants to Chelsea so people didn't talk about them as much, not like the Puerto Ricans. The understanding was that both of them, the Cambodians and the Puerto Ricans, had come to our city because they were lazy. As if they had all taken leisurely luxury cruises across their oceans to get here, just drifting lazily along, plotting how best to take advantage of all our noble slum had to offer. Maybe no one knew that American military had started playing dress-up in Puerto Rico. Maybe no one knew that the Cambodian families came here so they wouldn't be murdered by their government, maybe no one knew they almost died anyway in the getting here, maybe no one really cared.

I didn't know that the "Broadway" in Johnna Latrotta's Broadway School of Dance referred to New York City. I thought Johnna had fucked up and named it after the wrong Chelsea avenue, Broadway, the street that my Catholic school was on, instead of Washington Avenue, where her little one-room dance house sat. Johnna Latrotta's Washington School of Dance. It didn't have the same ring. It rang of presidents, lacked glitz. I wasn't down on Johnna and her school. I was actually quite excited to attend. I'd been in a dance school before. Eugenie's. Her part of town had gotten really run-down, it sat too close to Bellingham Square and the defiant displays of poverty that crept out from it like kudzu, promising to eventually wrap the city whole in broken glass and spray paint. At Eugenie's I'd worn a silver satin costume with a sequin star on the chest and a ruffle on my ass. I'd danced to *42nd Street,* the bumps and grinds that the audience loved on little girls, how they laughed with hands over mouths, *So cute!* Pretending to be sexy, it was like the orangutan act in the circus, cute, yes, but creepy. I danced to "Muskrat Love" with brown felt animal ears on my head. Later I was at Johnna Latrotta's.

Word on the street was that Johnna was a bitch—in a really admirable way. She just loved the kids she taught and was doing them a favor by being hard on them, pushing for greatness and perfect posture. It was Tough Love, and the parents were all right with her being so snappy to their kids. Johnna's studio was a storefront, and you could walk by the windows and look at the miniature studio portaits of last year's girls posing in their tulle and sparkles, satin caps bobby-pinned to a poof of hair, marabou trim or a hang of fringe that danced over an ass, glittered gloves racing to elbows, sequins in loops and stars. The girls in the photos jutted their legs out, and all the legs were the exact same color, Suntan. Arms were splayed, reaching, and a phony photo smile ripped into their faces. Lots of makeup, little dolls, spots of rouge on the cheeks and blue on the eyes, Easter egg faces. A splash of dark gloss on the lips. I couldn't wait for my photo to be up behind the glass, my private glamour exposed to Chelsea.

You arrived at Johnna's with your dance clothes underneath your regular clothes, and in the tiny foyer you pulled off jeans, velour sweatshirts, you stripped down to the polyester body suit and tights, and yanked grimy ballet shoes over your feet. The foyer was steamy with the anticipation of performance. In the next room was the insane clatter of smacking girl-feet. Johnna's voice gusted above the racket, *ONE two three four ONE two three four one two THREE four one two THREE four,* she was the conductor of an orchestra of feet, chunks of metal nailed to shoe soles that spanked the smooth floor with sharp clacks. *No no no NO!* Johnna shouted at some poor girl. The music stopped. It was always weird old music, show tunes, warbly-lady voices spinning out from a record player. Too heavy a stomp would cause the vinyl to skip. When class was over, the sweaty girls fled the mirror-lined room, hair unraveling from ponytails, dance shoes in hand. Flushed and happy, despite

Johnna's hollers, from an hour or so spent in their bodies, in front of the mirror, twirling and being girls. Unless of course you hated your body, always or maybe just that day, and had been forced to stare at its relentless reality in the mirror the whole time, distracting you from the pirouette and shuffle ball change and jazz squares. Obsessing on the way your arms fit awkwardly in their sockets, or how you couldn't locate your hips, though they were right there in the mirror, you couldn't *feel* them. It could get surreal if you looked into the mirror too long. That's my body. Watch the leg lift. *Smile!* Johnna cried above the song and shuffles, clapping her hands to the beat of feet hitting the floor. It was like the army for girls.

Probably Johnna was gorgeous. Parents were in awe of her, she was so self-possessed, a big, Italian body, big strong thighs. *A dancer's body,* they'd say, like there were different types of bodies out there and Johnna got that one. How lucky for her, being a dancer and all. She always wore black—satiny long-sleeved black bodysuits that really glowed where her breasts heaved against the fabric, shiny black tights and a little dance skirt tossed around her thighs as she moved, elegant. None of us girls were allowed to wear those skirts, I think Johnna was trying to keep the competitive fashion dynamic low, the focus on Dance, but we ached for our own as we watched it swish pretty from where it looped around her waist. A thin gold necklace with a sparkling cross, and thick black hair, full and shiny, Johnna was a shimmering jet-black muscle. Even her ponytail looked strong, like you could hook it up to a plow and let her trudge the land with those big dancer's legs.

Johnna had an assistant, Janice, who was older and taught sometimes, but mainly moved the mats and changed the records and did the sewing, sewed yards of sequins and appliqués, made satin bracelets for our wrists and fixed feathers to tiny headpieces. Janice was perpetually tan and, like Johnna, was in such good shape for her age. That's what the parents said, the mothers. It was like they were from somewhere else, Johnna and Janice, with their strong, elegant bodies and their age and their youth. But they lived right there in Chelsea.

The dance room was drafty, heated mainly by the motion of girls. You walked in and immediately you were damp with the smog of sweat the previous class had left behind. You arranged yourself on a mat before the wall of mirrors, and Johnna would lead stretches. The worst was the Scissor, when on your back you lifted your legs high and brought them down sooo slowly, excruciating, *Spread and cross spread and cross.* The sadistic Johnna, sleek as a horse, all flank and shine, would make us keep our legs an inch above the floor forever, the strain of it clenching our guts, pulling the cords of our bodies till tiny pearls of sweat popped and rolled on our faces. Finally Johnna, the great conductor of little girls' legs, would release us, and legs would collapse to the ground and my belly felt so weak, soft and runny as a clam, but I knew I was making it strong so it was good. Sometimes at home I would do them in private, forever, all the different exercises, all the stretches. I'd ride my body like a bicycle and drink glasses of water with ice from the freezer and think about how I was making myself beautiful. I could kick my legs so high, I'd show my mother. Watch, Ma, I'd shoot my leg up as high as my head. *Great,* my mother smiled.

It was a deep pain to me that high kicks were not so prized in Johnna's class. Some steps required kicks, and I would flood with excitement, feeling my moment to shine approaching, when Johnna would gasp in amazement and farm me out to the Rockettes, when she would call in the dance authorities—surely no girl had ever kicked so high so gracefully, with apparently so little effort. *Not so high, Michelle*, Johnna disciplined. Because the kicks were to be easy and decorative, all the girl-legs lifting in gentle synch, none of the athletic strain I loved, the gasp and yank of the stuff inside my thigh, beneath the skin.

The mirrored wall had a barre bolted across it, the ballet barre, we would pose beside it like real ballerinas, our hands clasping it for balance when we dipped so low, little frogs. I loved how wrong it felt to point my feet in the different angles, the tension in my hips. There were my hips, I felt them for the first time in the unnatural placement of my feet, first position, second, third. The ripple of tension stuck there in my pelvis, here was my body, finally. Sometimes it just felt grotesque, the animal squats. I could see my little belly in the mirror, the tiny triangles of new tit jabbing at the inside of my body suit. Weren't boobs supposed to be round? Mine were poky, fleshy pyramids. It seemed wrong, I flushed at the sight of them. And my hair was so greasy. Look at all the girls with nice, neat hair in barrettes and elastic, look at that one girl, Sharon, with tits round and hard as apples. You could see the stitching of her bra beneath her body suit. Sharon was growing too fast for her clothes to keep up, one of those girls. Puberty is hardest on poor girls. The lag time between your tits showing up and your mom rustling up the funds to accommodate them. You just hung around bursting out of your outfits. I could see the strain on the girls around me.

Next to Sharon was Marisol, the girl from the projects who had yelled at me in my glory as I disturbed all the old ladies. Seeing her, I felt the danger of the streets, the girls of Chelsea always wanting to kick your ass for no reason, girls you passed with your eyes stuck to the sidewalk, counting the black circles of old filthy gum worn onto the pavement, not looking up, feeling like a coward, their eyes brushing your neck, bringing up shame like goosebumps, feeling like shit, scared and not noble, not strong like at the barre with your legs showing muscle through your tights. These flat, bad feelings leaked into the good place of Johnna's studio, the place where you met the challenge of your body in the mirror, the tug of hidden muscles. That place got flooded with the bully from the projects standing in the mirror. Maybe I'd get beat up here, too. *Shoulders UP!* Johnna hollered. *I'm talking to YOU, Michelle,* she moved behind me and with a chiropractic tug yanked my shoulders out from gloom. She wrapped her hand around my forehead and drew my face up. I was at attention, a little soldier. Everyone was looking. But it was only the tiniest snag in Johnna's purpose, immediately she was before us again shouting, *Sashay, sashay!* We skipped sideways. *Sashay ball change!* We bounced on our feet, swung our hands and slid back across the floor.

Marisol didn't remember me at all. She actually wanted to be my friend. It was like that a lot—tough girls could smell the stink of fear, admiration and longing that my glands gave off in their presence, they rooted me out like a truffle, to beat or befriend me. But Marisol wasn't so tough, really. Marisol was perfect—tougher than me, but not a jerk. She went to the Italian Catholic school, Saint Rose. Since it was not as nice as mine I'd always suspected the kids there were cooler, and here was Marisol talking about MTV and cigarettes, whispering as we waited our turn to twirl across the floor. All the girls were in a line and one by one we cut across the floor, spun and kept going. *Sash-AY!* Johnna stamped her foot. She had the high-heeled tap shoes we couldn't wait for, a simple black pump, a thin strap across the foot's bony bridge, a cap of silver on the thick heel. We were twelve, about a year away from such glamour, trapped in our flat baby shoes, glossy black, wide and flat as a platypus bill, tied with a floppy ribbon like we were five years old and not *preteens.*

One by one the girls whirled like tops onto the floor, while me and Marisol huddled in our tights and grumbled, made fun of Johnna. What a relief. Someone to mock Johnna with. Everyone thought she was so great, yelling all the time with her special dancer's body. She did so much for the girls of Chelsea, taught them dance, taught them poise, sent them to camps to become student dance teachers, mini-Johnnas. She held retreats for all the moms in big hotels with Jacuzzis, she gave them facials. She threw citywide beauty pageants with real tiaras and trophies, and if you were good at all that stuff and she liked you, you could end up on TV like that one girl Stephanie who went on to marry Johnna's son. Stephanie made it all the way to Miss Teen USA, me and Marisol watched it together in my living room, along with Madeline, who just worshipped Stephanie, Stephanie the proven Best Girl of Chelsea, with her feathered black hair and straight teeth. But her nose looked shockingly lumpy on television, and she lost to Miss Teen Texas. It was sad, but it had been too much to imagine Chelsea winning a title like that, scoring the big tiara. It was enough that she'd made it to television at all, more than the city'd expected.

She's not so great, Marisol observed later that night when everyone was asleep and we crammed into the bathroom to smoke a cigarette together, the smoke of our breath encasing us like a heavy-metal band in a dry ice stage show. We passed the cigarette back and forth and it got damp and hot with our greedy pulls, the cherry a stabbing orange point like a toxic crayon. We flicked it into the toilet with a *zzzt* and opened the door. The smoke poured from the small room and joined the larger nicotine haze that shrouded the house, like a river emptying to the sea.

Johnna Latrotta's dance classes were broken up into tap, jazz and ballet. Every class you did a little ballet, fluid whirls where you sometimes held hands with the other girls, propelled each other with spins, tromped in a circle like maypole maidens. Tap was snazzier, you put on the special shoes and made some noise. It was all about rhythm, playing drums on the floor with your feet. Jazz was sexy, slinky, it was tap slowed down and extended. The outfits, the class leotards, were pastel pinks and baby blues or classic black like Johnna's. I had an electric blue leotard with dark purple tights, and sometimes I wore my yellow "Oh No, It's Mr. Bill!" T-shirt over the whole thing. One of the craftier girls at Assumption had brought us all into a new hair fashion by weaving thin ribbons into normal barrettes and leaving the ends dangling long in your long hair, or sometimes hung with beads at the end. Lelrine Thomas, the one black girl in the entire school, had brought us this fashion from Boston. She lived there, in Dorchester, a part of Boston we'd heard was all black people, where white people would get killed just for walking down the street, so none of us were allowed to visit Lelrine at her house. None of us girls at Assumption, Lelrine's classmates, all white. My parents debated it. My mother was strictly No Way about it, but my father claimed that if you were there as the guest of a neighborhood black person, they left you alone. Lelrine would weave us barrettes, I had a beaded pair clacking in my hair like those illegal balls on a string, Clackers. You weren't allowed to bring them to school because you could crack someone on the head with them and kill them. I had tiny, innocent beads clacking in my greasy hair.

What Do You Think? I'd asked Marisol. *That's cool.* I didn't know that the bathing suit wasn't a leotard. It looked multipurpose to me. I had somehow acquired it, a spaghetti-string one-piece with thick black and white stripes that ran down my torso like highways. Then a tiny frill of a skirt that wrapped my hips. It was very Go-Go's. I wore it to dance class, which we simply referred to as *Dance.* The white tights beneath it looked really odd. That's when its true function as a bathing suit became obvious. All that skin, neck riding into collarbone, a bit of sternum, and then weird white tights on my legs, scarred and bunched with runs and pulls. I felt a sprinkle of panic at the thought of walking into the fluorescent-lit studio in this outfit. Did I look like a slut? There was something slightly obscene about it. Did it look like lingerie? I twisted anxiously in the large mirror that curved above my mother's dresser. It was too late to change, it was time to go. My regular leotard was balled up in the musty wicker clothes hamper, the underarms carrying a new stink. I had managed to buy the striped contraption, and now I had to wear it.

Johnna Latrotta immediately pulled me aside. She was actually nice. I was prepared to hate her always, for her confidence and her power, the fast way she had of snapping at you and then dashing away like it was no big deal, like you were just supposed to bust out a few jazz squares and snap your fingers while your chest caved in and you tried not to cry, the whole time your obvious struggle lit bright as an interrogation room and flashed in the mirror for everyone to observe. I was afraid that Johnna would think I was bad the way parents—mothers—tended to think I was. Johnna's eyes were on my chest, the smudge of nipple a hazy target beneath the thin fabric. You couldn't wear a bra with it, not even the one strapless bra that was too small and sometimes flipped beneath my breasts into a useless belt that bisected my torso. I glanced into the mirror as Johnna glanced at my body. There was something gross about the way the soft chub of my underarms gathered into a visible fold when my arms were relaxed. Johnna told me not to wear it again. She wasn't mean about it. She was so gentle, I felt a brief, futile pulse of hate for her. *It kind of looks like an old-fashioned bathing suit, from like the forties, doesn't it?* I nodded. My bottom lip was stretched on the rack of my teeth. *Maybe, we can have a recital costume like it?* she suggested optimistically. *Janice could make a striped hat?* I nodded.

I wore the bathing suit one more time, to the beach with Marisol. Revere Beach. Revere being Chelsea's football rival made it a tense stretch of the Atlantic, but we only had the creek in Chelsea, and we had to find water somewhere. Most of the beach was sand like normal, but one chunk of it had been paved into a cliff of concrete. The Wall. It was perfect for lying out on your towel, no sand clumping the chasm between your butt cheeks, no sand sticking to your suntan-lotioned fingers and getting on your cigarette. Revere Beach used to be excellent, I heard about it all the time from the grownups in my family. It seemed impossible that there used to be a roller coaster, impossible that someone would tear a roller coaster down. Once there had been a coaster and glittery bumper cars and flying horses. You could sit on the carved wooden animal and feel like a princess being lifted up and down the golden pole. Back when the creek was cleaner, more like a river, there had been these other things, too. Now there was that Italian place with really great pizza. Slices as big as your face. There was Kelley's, which was great for squiggles of fried clams and oily hunks of scallop, and there were bars. One where girls took their clothes off, The Strip.

One Christmas Eve, when the adults were all suitably ripped from highballs and lowballs, me and Madeline were carried along in the excitement of lights and gifts and a gigantic tree in the house, manic with the red cheeks of the chattering adults like a contact high, me and Madeline started to dance. We put on a show and the adults loved it. Until Madeline got a little crazy. She was bumping and grinding in her little Christmas dress, red and green, velvety with bows, and the adults put their hands over their mouths, laughing like when the baby class—the youngest girls in Johnna's school—turn their backs to the audience and shake their tulled tushes. *She's too much!* cackled an aunt. Auntie Heidi. She always cackled when she drank. *Don't dance like that. Cut it out!* my dad barked. *She's gonna end up at The Strip*, laughed one of the guys. Madeline was maybe nine.

Older kids hung out on the Wall at Revere Beach. Cute boys, Italian boys from Revere, which was Italian, and their girls, eternally hostile, high school girls whose tits filled out the cups of their bikinis. Me and Marisol spread our towels on the pavement and baked, rose occasionally to smoke a Marlboro. Revere Beach was a good place to smoke because you could relax and be dramatic about it, no one would see you. There was no one but teenagers and the nearly-teen, no parents, it wasn't even Chelsea. Once, the new fifth-grade teacher at my Catholic school was there, a pale glare of skin standing where the cement ran down like a ramp into the ocean. But he was gay, everyone knew it, so it wasn't like he could get us in trouble. Being gay was so much worse than simply smoking. We ignored each other. I took damp, salty drags from my Marlboros, and he was gay with his gay friends and everything was fine.

I had that bathing suit on at the beach. The ruffle crinkled at my hips, the center of everything. All things mysterious lay beneath the hips. Things to be revealed in drips, soon, any minute really. Hopefully not while at the beach in this suit that was so thin that, when wet, felt like it could tear beneath your fingertips like tissue. We loved the Revere boys, me and Marisol. Both of us had professed our love for the dark boy, the Italian boy, not so much liking the blonds except for Billy Idol and David Lee Roth, who were bleach-blonds anyway, making a wrecked joke of the blond ideal, too blond, fried blond. The best way to be blond. Even naturally blond Marisol tarnished her gold with peroxide, an imitation of herself. Fake ruled. Dirty creeks and trashed amusement parks, concrete dumped over natural seashore. Me and Marisol constructed our crushes, selecting our desires and giving them identifying tag names: Orange Shorts. Gold Cross. The One With The Earring. We knew we were too young for them to consider, but it was impossible not to hope. We *were* mature for our age, me and Marisol. We had discussed it. We didn't even talk to the other girls in dance, I couldn't tell you any of their names, save for Sharon because her tits were so captivating. They were kids, safely spinning on the flats of their ballet shoes, but we were there for the promise of glamour, the display of our bodies glittered up at the grand finale that was the recital. We were there for the feel of our bodies tugging with every stretch and leap, a little more every week, we hoped to break.

We gazed at the boys on the Wall at the beach. Furtively, so their girls wouldn't notice and kill us. The air was thick with oily coconut and the sour fishsalt of dirty Revere Beach. Probably it was every bit as filthy as Chelsea's creek but there was simply so much more of it, it roared out to the sky, the waves smacking crashes at the horizon, mellowing out as it reached the shore, flopping like foamy puppies. The smartest civilizations were the ones that had an ocean, I learned this in Social Studies. It was all that promise, the next wave could bring anything, a ship, a mermaid. I smoked my Marlboro and watched the generous ocean bring trash upon the lips of its wave. Beside us the boys played with a fuzzy neon tennis ball and we tried not to stare. Behind us the ghost of an ancient roller coaster rose into the sky and left an imprint of rickety danger and thrill on the strip. We looked at the boys. We watched the lemony-lime glowing tennis ball fly from their hands and into the water. There was a patch of frothing algae like the sea had puked, and that's where the ball went. It lapped there at the concrete curb, bubbling and weird, no sand to soak into. All the boys hollered and cursed when their ball dropped into the disgusting ocean. *You get it. Fuck you, you get it.* None of them would get it, the water was gross. The boys leaned their bodies over the ledge, skimming the tip of the sludge with their fingers. Then they started looking at us. Finally. One came over and crouched beside our terry cloth, Gold Cross. His hair stood in spiky clumps from sweat and salt water. He smelled like summer, spicy and tropical, I caught a whiff through the yellowy stink of my cigarette. The charm on his chest caught the sun and sent it back in oily splinters. *Would one of you girls go get that ball for us?* A cheap grin, phony as peroxide but the only grin a boy had spit our way in weeks of sunbathing. A cute boy anyway, not the weird straggling boys or gross older guys with Sicko flasher vibes. Gold Cross was very tan, the ocean streamed from his mullet. He must have swum earlier, before the sea threw up. Marisol sat up lazily, drunk with sun. I was already alert and excited. This was the dare I was waiting for, the chance to display my bravery. The opportunity to flex for the boys like I flexed at the ballet barre, the wild recklessness of scaling chain link, wasn't that sex? The dash into the electrified metal, scorching your body to reach the water and the water was dirty, that was sex.

You Want Me To Get Your Ball? I asked. *Yeah, would you get it?* The others were looking over, girls too. I liked the boys who were tough, and I thought that if I could show them that I was tough too, that I was like them, then something would pool in their chest, something like love, an understanding that would draw them in and I would belong, finally, to them, to something, and it would be big and frightening and courageous. It would be gorgeous. I would be brave and respected and no one would want to beat me up. I'll Get Your Ball. I leaped off the towel. Marisol's open mouth leaked smoke. I took my body in its cheap, strange bathing suit to the edge of the Wall. I saw the ball bobbing in the mat of ocean scum, it looked like a boil on the sea's bad skin, everything the same bright, pukey green. I jumped into it, this patch of froth. I felt the splash, felt it land in my hair, I grabbed the ball and dove beneath the surface, away from the ick, dove down with the water warm and cold around me, the Atlantic Ocean. Dove like an otter, like a mermaid, my feet spanning out like the fins of her tail, feet in first position, the pull and tense of my body and air held in my lungs like a jewel.

I pushed through the water, I swam, broke the surface away from that nest of rot, triumphant. I had the ball. I was a dog. The stupid and eager dog that plunges in after the tennis ball. Everyone was howling. The boys and the girls but mainly the boys, and perhaps the girls were worse with the simple repulsion cresting on their perfectly made-up faces. Water had not touched those paint jobs. They were there to tan. *Eeeew!* the boys were shrieking, hopping around. *That's whale sperm!* They screamed. *You're gonna get pregnant! She went in the whale sperm!* I padded over to the ramp that led from the water back up to the Wall. The place where the new gay fifth-grade teacher had been splashing his ankles earlier. I had their stupid ball, soggy like a wet dog's mouth. I tossed it at them, and it fell heavy to the concrete and splattered the girls. *Eeew!*

Hey thanks, said Gold Cross. He'd just been yelling with the rest of them. He gave me that cool nod you give someone when you don't really want to say "Hello" or anything friendly. He folded himself to the ground with the rest of the boys, a ring around the girls. After a while the sharp laughter faded and I relaxed in the sun, smoked a cigarette. *Why did you do that,* Marisol said. A statement, not a question, so I didn't have to answer. We shared the last Marlboro and packed up, hauled our stuff blocks away for the bus back to Chelsea. A long, drowsy ride, bumps jolting you out of your heat-daze. Past that record store with the Kajagoogoo poster in the window. That seemed like a cool place, someday we'd go there. For now we poked each other awake for the bus's rumble past the enlarged photo of Limahl and his impossible hair that spanned the storefront, his cheekbones and thin eyes. Thin the way eyes get when they're smogged with cigarette smoke, or squinting in a hazy kiss. The heat pulsed in our cheeks. We were sunburned, me and Marisol.

PUPPIES, PAPERBACKS, PIROUETTES

Marisol didn't live in the projects anymore. She'd been moved with her brother and her mother into the apartment above her grandparents. It was on the street behind the library, Library Street, not so far from my own. In Marisol's bathroom we snagged a jug of Noxzema and slathered our hot skin with the stuff. We'd laid out on the Wall for hours, our skin pulsed with it. The Noxzema was heavy and white like frosting, we sculpted thick waves of it across our thighs, our cheeks, everything. We splayed our bodies over the furniture in her living room and felt the cool of it sink into our skin. All propped up like rich ladies getting pedicures, the grease of the Noxzema was part of the larger procedure of beauty, tending to the wound of the tan. The sharp eucalyptus stink seared our noses. Marisol's mother smelled it as she entered the house, heaved herself upstairs to the flat. *We're sunburned*, Marisol announced proudly. We'd done our time at the beach. After the soothing first coat faded we felt the heat rev back up. The pain of the oily lotion and the burn was terrible, but with the television we endured. Marisol's mom was amused. At least she didn't think we were stoned, like usual. Marisol's mom was great because she was broke and single, so supremely casual, would joke with you in that almost mean way grownups did to let you know they were cool, on your team, and you took it with a grin because you got it, they *were* cool. *Look at ALL THAT eyeliner, Michelle,* she inspected the Crayola blue rings poking out from my Noxzema mask. *You look like a real toughie.*

Marisol's brother had her same horsy face but without the feminine decorations that softened it, a length of hair falling loose all over the place, a roach clip clamped onto the roots, chunky feathers dangling from suede cords. Boys were so pared down, you got the stark core of their face and nothing else. Short brown hair, boring, quiet boy, younger than Marisol. He never spoke. Marisol and her mom ruled. They were both so loud, and they fought. Once, because her mom had won the lottery, *hit the number,* that rack of special digits she'd been playing every day for a million years, like all the parents did. *Play my numbers for me,* she'd tucked some dollars into Marisol's palm, and Marisol promptly forgot all about it. The one day that Marisol's mother's numbers all came out. They picked the numbers every night before the five o'clock news, some kind of air machine that blew the balls around in its belly and eventually hawked one up and the attendant gently turned the ball in her fingers and showed it to the camera. Marisol's mother's numbers flew out of the machine one by one. She was crying, her face in an incredulous twist. She was finally out of Chelsea. *Bring me my numbers!* But Marisol didn't have them. Shit went flying all over the house. The mom went tearing through the trash because

The Chelsea Whistle

88

Marisol, terrified, lied and said she'd lost the slip. Crap all over the linoleum, chicken bones and empty boxes and the mottled slop of canned vegetables scraped from the plate. Marisol was crying too. She admitted that she never even bought the thing, and her mother made her leave the house so that she wouldn't be tempted to beat the shit out of her. My mother understood, told me she would have had to ask me to leave, too. *All that money,* my mother clucked when I told her. *That's a sin.* When something really unjust occurred it would be deemed a sin by the women in my family. *She's raising those kids alone, too.* Marisol had a dad somewhere in the world, maybe in the South, Kentucky. She stayed with him a few weeks each year and went to amusement parks with her redneck cousins who she assured me were gorgeous and wore red bandannas over their hair, the way Marisol would for weeks after she returned.

Usually Marisol and her mom fought because Marisol's mom always thought that Marisol and whoever happened to be with Marisol were stoned out of their brains. *Let me see your eyes!* Her hands would seize Marisol by the chin and yank the knobby bone of her face close for inspection. Marisol's eyes would squish shut as she tried to squirm free but her mom would bark, *Open them!* The bizarre part was that her mom would often be stoned, barking scratchy cotton-mouthed orders with a certain spaciness in the eyes, trying to train her blurry focus on her daughter's face. That Marisol's mother smoked pot affirmed her coolness, it was unfortunate that the herb brought out this violent paranoia, inspired her suddenly to be the most *uncool* mom in the world, clutching Marisol's face with her fingers. *Leave me alone!* Marisol screamed. When her mom's hand relaxed, she pulled her face away and ran into the bathroom, kicking the door shut behind her with a clunk.

Marisol's house was really clean. They didn't have a lot of stuff, so there wasn't a lot of crap strewn all over the place like the obstacle course of debris in my own home. And they had animals. Marisol was a Gemini and she alternately loved and abused these pets. She abused them in a playful way, how little kids pull the tail of a cat, like she'd discovered a new, neat way to play with the toy that was the bird or the dog. The bird I think belonged to her brother. A plump green thing, it huddled in its cage like an old lady hunched in a tropical muumuu. Sometimes they let it loose in the house, which was thrilling, but it never zoomed through the air the way I wanted it to. It would simply find a perch up high on a curtain rod, and brood there in its feathers. Marisol would scoop its little body into her hand, its wings folded snug, little bird-face expressionless, and she'd hurl it at the pillows on her bed and let out a whooping cry. She was happy. The bird would hit the cloth with a muffled sound, then the flutter of it rearranging itself on the bed. I think that it was an old bird, resigned to Marisol's occasional cruelty. Sometimes she would simply fling things at it as it sat calmly up by the ceiling, watching us. Once, she threw a pen that hurt its beak and she got in trouble.

Marisol's dog happened because of me so it was my dog too, sort of. I came home from school one day and found it on my steps, dying. I don't know why it came to my house to do this, but there it was, all ribs and tits, racks of bone curving against its dull fur with those sacks dragging obscenely. I'd never seen a dog with boobs before so of course I could only stare and think of women, like the dog was a sick morph of girl and animal, those Greek myths where some poor maiden pisses off a god's wife and gets turned into a she-bear, graceless pelt and clodding feet, lots of drool. But the dog was so sad, it was dying. It was all in her eyes and you know how dogs' eyes are so heartbreaking anyway, and this dog had puppies starving somewhere and was about to croak. I stepped around the morose curl of her and ran into the house to call Marisol. There's A Dog On My Steps! What a mystery, how terrible that it couldn't speak. I'd seen television shows about dogs who walked the globe to return to their home thousands of miles away, dogs who pick up the tiniest speck of salt in the air and follow it to the ocean to die on the sand. Marisol came and took the dog home. Her mom was like that, you could just bring an animal inside and it stayed. We named it Nikki after Nikki Sixx because its fur was black like the stiff blackness that rose from the scalp of the admired bassist. Marisol took Nikki home and fed it and it got better, its tits shrunk back into its belly and it was a normal dog again. Then Marisol discovered that when you yelled at Nikki, the most mournful whine would stream pleading from her throat and she would huddle close to the floor like she was trying to hide herself inside it, tail tucked beneath her. It was a show. Marisol would yell at it in a dad's voice, *Nikki,* low and threatening, and we would watch the animal shrink and fold like a fortune-telling fish on a sweaty palm. Marisol, I'd scold, but my voice was soft with a tinge of awe. Something about cruelty, that flavor of cruelty, like a mystery drawer accidentally slid from a desk. It was hard not to watch. I felt the exhilarating pull of right and wrong in my chest. The spectacle of the frightened dog and Marisol's glee at discovering its secret. It had been abused, it had to have been. All Marisol had to do was thrust an accusing finger and raise her voice and the dog would go into its act, preparing for a blow, begging it away. It had been trained, and I wondered if Marisol had been trained as well, to assume her own posture at the sight of something whimpering. Later she'd nuzzle it with love, scratch the shine of its head. *Where's your puppies, Nikki?* She'd coo. *Your babies are dead, Nikki,* singsonging sweetly, lifting its silky ears to rub the crook of fur beneath. *All your little puppies are dead.* The dog laid its head on her lap.

Sometime later Marisol had real puppies in her house. I don't know how, they weren't Nikki's. It was a legion of them, soft and bumbling, fenced off in a spare room where they snuggled and yipped on piles of blanket. I went to look at them in the morning after a sleepover, leaving Marisol sleeping in her bed forever, never waking up until the house was saturated in light coming in the windows, the day in full roar. I got up early to visit the puppies. I didn't get them, the mess of bulky fur that littered the room. Cats I understood, they had a focus and purpose about them, but dogs were loose, constantly bewildered. One lumbered toward me, its lumpy head the color of cookie dough. It sniffed at me. I had my nightshirt on, Garfield on my chest with a plate of lasagna. It bunched up at my thighs where I crouched and the puppy brought its crumpled face to my crotch and sniffed me there. I was frozen. The same freeze of shame and fascination that rooted me to my spot as Marisol triggered Nikki into one of her panic attacks. The house around me vibrated with empty quiet, Marisol knocked out and nobody else home. The puppy bumped its nose against the fabric of my underwear, and then the blunt brush of its tongue. I was still.

I'd read about this before, women and dogs. My mother's book of women's sex fantasies, it sat in the bouquet of her underwear drawer, that humid adult smell mixed with little sachets of potpourri tucked into the shiny nylon folds. It acted like a sociology textbook, that paperback, like anthropology or psychology but really it was straight-up porn. Page after page of all the crazy, dirty things that get loosed inside the secret brains of women, it wrapped me in its yellowed pages and pulsed with me, sweating, heart and cunt racing in synch as I waited for the sounds of parents arriving, when I would hurl the book back into the fabric and slam the drawer. My parents' bedroom was the largest room in our house, it was a dim place that hung over the stump of our dead-end street. It was always kind of messy, which was okay in our house. Bedrooms could be disheveled, but the rest of the house should be kept decent. Ma's room had a slightly musky smell, a living smell, like you had just walked into some moist nighttime part of the natural world. I believed it was the smell of grownups, of grown-up women. Her skin was like a plant releasing chemicals into the shadowy forest of smells and pillows, unmade bed, clothes tossed around. Occasionally I'd find the underwear drawer empty and would crawl beneath the bed, feeling around for the chunk of the book, a fat paperback. It had that exploded look books get when they've been around a while, been urgently read by everyone in the house, I'm sure. Madeline had read it.

There was one day when we had the privilege of walking home from school with Jenn Capoletti. There was something about her, you wanted to be fused to her side. All the coolest things came to Jenn, and they would come to you too if she allowed you to hang out for a while. Jenn was very hot and cold with me, excited about our friendship sometimes, and then just icing me like I was the biggest dork, straight out of nowhere. I never saw it coming. When she liked me I would sleep at her house, in her room papered with Sylvester Stallone pinups from teen magazines. Glowering from walls like a big oiled-up blockhead. Jenn thought he was the sexiest ever. It was hard to sleep at Jenn's house because she slept with the radio on and I needed quiet. It was another cool thing about Jenn, how rock 'n' roll kept her company all night long, a kind of subliminal study of the world, beamed into you at night when your rarest parts bloomed like secret flowers, soaking in the music and all its magic. I couldn't reach over and shut it off. The simple excitement of sleeping at Jenn's house, and on a school night, was enough to keep me awake even without the radio's distraction. I would lapse into deep nighttime fantasies that carried me through the hours in lieu of rest and dreams. I'd get that shirt at the mall, somehow I would. The one that looked like slick black leather but was only an enchanted cotton, with real zippers instead of seams, a zipper slashing across the chest, too. I'd wear it with Jenn to the roller rink and get a boyfriend. We'd hang out together in parking lots and sneak cigarettes and I'd look so great in that tough shirt. We were going to become vegetarians together, I'd eat only pickles and tomatoes, I'd look excellent. All night long Jenn snored beside me, until the rising sun snagged her braces and filled her mouth with morning gleam. She'd spring from her bed well-rested and rattle off some cheerleading cheers, practicing in her mirror. Jenn was head cheerleader for the Chelsea Pop Warner football team. She had all the arm movements, the bent elbows, strict little claps, the slap of a heel. I would be racked with panic, the kind of panic specific to insomniacs, dread and doom as you tallied the number of hours you lay awake having freaky daydreams about the mall. I calculated in time to Jenn's stomps, one, two, three, four—did I really lie awake for eight hours? Surely I slept a little. Did I really just lie there for eight hours, the tinny, synthetic noise of eighties songs, "hits" that were dead before they hit the airwaves, haunting the still room? It was popularity penance. It was a punishment that could have been plucked from any of my own negotiations with God: if you let Jenn Capoletti be my best friend, I'll lie awake all night long and not sleep a wink.

Meeting Marisol had seriously reduced my obsession with this girl, but clearly not enough. If only Marisol had gone to Assumption and not to St. Rose, but instead I was tortured daily by the social whirlpool that sucked me down into Jenn's little queendom. So I was mortified when, walking home with Madeline and Jenn, my sister announced that our mother owned a book that contained stories describing women having sex with donkeys and dogs and bunches of other creatures you weren't supposed to have sex with. *Your mother has a book about doing it with donkeys?* Jenn gasped. *Yeah, goats too,* Madeline continued, scrunching up her face. I felt like a security system had been triggered inside me, lights and bells. Jenn was a fickle gossip, and I knew how the telephone game of Assumption worked. Someone spotting a tiny dried-up cat turd outside the litter box in Charlie Walker's house turned into Charlie's family being so poor and filthy that there were huge piles of shit scattered throughout his home. I knew in about a week the whole class would be whispering about how my mother fucks goats. I was surprised that Madeline had found the book, I had thought it was my very own secret, my book. The one about the woman forced to take the entirety of donkey cock up her, the one about the little girl straddling her puppy in the woods behind her house. I scrunched my face up too, and thought of Ma. She did her best, she hid the book away like you were supposed to do with dirty things. I thought about her room smells again, warm and human, the smell of a heart baking like bread inside the rib-cage oven. A being alive smell. I did not want Jenn to think my ma was a Sicko. There's Other Stuff In The Book, Too, I said. Not Just Animals. *You read it too?* Jenn asked, big-eyed. Yeah, I shrugged. It's About, You Know, Sexual Fantasies. I knew sexual fantasies were okay and normal. It said so inside the sexual fantasy book. I believed it, it helped me not feel bad when my privates burned at the tales of women being tied up and attacked and raped by men, by gangs of them sometimes. It didn't mean I wanted that to happen to me, the book assured me. It was a sexual fantasy.

When the house was really empty, I would hunt down this book with the flower on the cover. I would sit as close to the front window as I could without filling it, without being the dirty girl in the window, mouth slack, hurriedly poring over the pages, rereading my favorites. I clamped my hand over my underwear and pressed. My coochie burned. It never occurred to me that this was only the beginning, my body ringing the service bell. I thought the burning was the point. I read the book to feel the singe. Eventually a car would come coolly up the street and I would fly up like a freaked-out bird, stash the book back in its nook, hoping I remembered correctly the angle I'd found it in, the exact way the bra had been draped across its cover. Slam the bureau drawer and zoom back into the living room. It was like breaking the surface of water—brighter, disorienting, with that nagging thump in my crotch.

One time I brought it out of the bedroom and into the bathroom, because I had to pee and I couldn't put it down. And my parents came home. I was stuck in the bathroom with the pilfered pornography. *Hellooo!* My mother's cheery call into the house. Hi, I croaked from the bowl. I could hide it in the wicker hamper stuffed with damp towels and pajamas. But what if she did laundry? I stashed it under the tub. I had no idea how regularly my mother consulted this book, what hours she kept with it, but it moved between the underwear drawer and under the bed regularly enough to make me nervous. I racked my brain for a reason to have been in her room. Had I left her dresser open? *We're going to get subs for dinner, what do you want?* Tuna! I shrieked, thrilled. *Okay!* My mother laughed. *Be right back!* The door closed behind them. I wiped my crotch and left the bathroom.

Later I discovered another level to the burning. I'd heard about it in different books, books by Dr. Joyce Brothers, other books like *Nice Girls Do—and Now You Can Too!* Orgasms. Women had them. For some reason, I just figured I didn't. Like, other women did, but not me. I wasn't sad about it. I had a fine life without this mystery. But then it happened. One night in bed, playing back the stories in my head, under the covers. It was too much, it seemed I would hurt myself, like my body could not contain the roar that was pouring into it. It was so sharp. When I was little and had a kidney problem, pain in my abdomen, the doctor asked, *Is it a sharp pain or a dull pain?* This wasn't pain, but it was weirdly similar. So sharp. My body took it. The sharpness thrashed me out. I felt like stories I'd read about young girls inhabited by demons. Maybe this is what struck them. It felt foreign enough. I didn't know who I was in the moment that had seized my body, I lay in its aftermath and breathed like a drowned girl yanked from a swimming pool. After that, whenever I heard the car slide up the street, I'd fling the book into the drawer and dash into the bathroom to rub it all away. A demolition derby of shame, fear and thrill in my cunt, me on the toilet, my legs flexing tense against the narrow bathroom. Soon it would become too much, and I'd wipe myself with a puff of toilet paper and flush the moment away.

Johnna Latrotta had selected our recital costumes from a glossy catalogue that featured a billion smiling blond girls posing in a variety of satin and spangle. She brought us up to the rickety desk in the chilliest corner of the studio and one by one slung a yellow tape measure around our waists, clamped it with the tusks of her fingernails, and reported a measurement over her shoulder to dutiful Janice, who recorded it in a lined book. The tape measure got looped beneath our damp armpits, over the tiny swells of our tits, the slope of our pelvis. It was embarrassing, but we were rewarded with the photo of our costume in the catalogue. This one was beautiful, the very best one. Pink—no, fuchsia—with bronze sequin trim and, Johnna promised, a sash of pink marabou that Janice would sew across the chest. Because Johnna taught the three classes—tap, jazz and ballet—the costume would have a series of ornaments to be applied and removed, making it different for each dance. Ballet was nice, a skirt of pink chiffon, like the scarves my grandmother would knot gauzy beneath her chin, webbing her hairdo. *Babushkas.* A skirt that would receive the wind of our movements, make visible the air that our earnest grace stirred, a lovely pink swish around our hips. A bit of marabou for our heads, to waver like an undersea animal with tentacles caught in a current. The tap accessories sucked.

Tap always seemed too jokey, kind of slapstick for girls, and to confirm this suspicion that we were in fact dolled-up clowns, Janice the seamstress took yards of white satin dotted with hideous pink and green polka dots and cut them into cuffs to be pinned to our wrists, with a matching dopey round hat stuck on our head, held there with elastic that ran beneath our chins. I thought we looked like a bunch of organ-grinder monkeys, the elegance and flash of our gorgeous costume destroyed. But the jazz outfit was perfect. Just the hot-colored shine of the costume, with its modest spangle and fluff. Johnna benevolently decided that we were mature enough to dance in adult jazz shoes. Beige pumps, shoes with heels, heels that lifted our legs into a tough-sexy flex, that showed our muscle. We were all ecstatic. My entire career in tiny-town dance had been propelling me toward this fabulous moment when I would finally be allowed to dance in heels, a grownup. We were finally young women.

Johnna announced that we had no song for our jazz number, she was having trouble locating the music that would be the backdrop for our carefully arranged sashays across the stage, the bouquets of girl-hands rising and falling in generous arcs, the restrained kicks. We were a chorus of showgirls. I knew that we had to dance to the Go-Go's. "Our Lips Are Sealed" would be perfect. It was all pink and girly, sassy and capable, like our dance. I begged Johnna. She bent her head down at me and heard my plea, she was some sort of Italian statue of justice, all polished and solid, she listened. Johnna had to give me something. Because of that bathing suit incident. She had taken something away, had said no, and now she had to say yes to something. I'd been so good about it, hadn't pouted or argued, and I'd been so humiliated. The glow of my nipple beaming out from the fabric, we both knew it was there. I'd returned to class forevermore with a dense coat of polyester and a dumb, useless bra beneath. I'd been good and now I needed my song. The Go-Go's. *Doesn't matter what they say,* the song went. It went, *Can you hear them? They talk about us. Telling lies, well that's no surprise.* Like God was a big sister chirping her word to me through the airwaves, finally, after all those wasted years in church.

As hormones began their defining trickle from purses of glands, as personalities sharpened like cheekbones beneath the melt of baby fat, I saw not so much where I belonged but where I didn't. Chelsea, the whole fucking town, everything I could see, the whole world, for all I knew. That awful time when difference first marks you is understood mainly in negatives. Not like that not like her not like them not like not liked. I had Marisol, thank god. She wasn't like anyone either. And there was radio. Casey Kasem's American 40. The bottom of the list, the thirties and forties, those were the best. Songs burst out like fireworks, a dazzling explosion that left a brief sparkle in the sky and was never heard again. The cannonball smack of "For Those About to Rock." I first heard the Go-Go's there, "Our Lips Are Sealed," and through the radio observed its rise to popularity. Higher and higher it went till even the popular girls liked it. I watched resentfully as the normal and well-adjusted fell into the singsongy bounce of the music, missing the point. It was *my* song. *Can you see them, see right through them?* I could.

I brought the forty-five to Johnna like a chalice, gleaming in its little envelope. The band was shrouded in towels and Noxzema, the secret process of girlness, the behind-the-scenes exposed and revealed to be as fabulous as that supposed end result—a girl in a dress, nice skin, clean, *Seventeen* magazine. It was like they were factory workers in the industry of Girl, they should have had gloves on their hands, work gloves. I loved them. It surged from my chest. I had found my girls. Please, I said to Johnna. She placed it on the turntable, brought the needle to its groove and we listened. It was perfect. Psychic choreography, like all along Johnna had been conducting our bodies to the beat of this song she'd never heard. It worked so well, and the girls of course loved the song, my song. Our feet skimmed the floor and our bodies took on new emphasis. *All right,* Johnna declared. I was so excited. It was perhaps possible to be Chelsea, the thing I'd been helplessly born into, and this other new thing, the idea of cool, something Chelsea couldn't touch, I was the alien daughter of the two, proudly sashaying in my pink to the voice that taunted the normal—*They have no shield, no secrets to reveal*—and soothed my adolescent anxiety—*Doesn't matter what they say.* And it didn't. It was my performance. The others were simply dancing.

The dance recitals were held at Revere High School, and the bustle backstage was incredible. I have spent the rest of my life trying to recreate it, to find an atmosphere capable of shocking me into submission by the simple power of a billion stinging sequins, daggers of glitzy light stabbing you in the eyeball, the manic energy of a hundred little girls scared to dance and bursting to perform, to display the miracle of their girl-bodies, bedazzled and as set to twirl as the plastic ballerina in a tightly wound music box.

The helpless baby class was corralled in their small area, tended to by a small gang of mothers armed with bobby pins and pots of rouge, boxes of safety pins. Little girls dumb and hyper as puppies, offering their mouths to wands of shiny gloss. The older girls more calmly receiving dusted brushes and the tugging mom-fingers lassoing chunks of hair with elastics. The suck of a girl-belly deep into her ribs as a length of fringe was pinned around a waist. Blasts of hair spray, the chemical smog of backstage. Mothers smoking, tense as the girls. Tenser. Me and Marisol in a corner, in our heels, running through our number, counting the beats out in soft breaths, *One two three four one two three four. Remember to smile.* That was Johnna's final order. Big clown smiles, nerves and joy, finally we would display to all what perfect girls we were, how great we were at being such animals. I loved it so much. Enduring the dig of the bobby pins, the shine of makeup heavy on my face. We'd worked all year. What if we fucked up, forgot our steps? I dreamed of boys, faceless. Who would be out in that audience, who would fall in love with me? The recital presented every possibility I had ever yearned for. Love and fame and understanding. A certain pair of eyes somewhere out there beyond the glare of stage lights that blinded you, someone I could not see would be watching me, singling me out from the girls I kicked and tapped with because I had Something.

I knew about Something. I heard about it on television shows, when hosts of experts were hauled in to discuss the crazy popularity of, say, Brooke Shields. *She has Something,* the experts would say, still delightfully mystified as to what that Something was. *She does have Something,* a more thoughtful critic would offer. And then, *She has that Certain Something.* The elusive Something, captured and defined at last. It was a Certain Something. The interviewer would nod, understanding. Everyone seemed to understand what Something was. I thought maybe I had it. What else could this angry bubbling restless shameful difference be? What I needed was someone who understood the Something to catch me in action and see that I had it. That no one in Chelsea seemed to recognize this quality in me only made me more sure that it was true. Chelsea was a Certain Nothing.

Besides the order to smile, Johnna had instituted a couple of additional backstage regulations. Suntan tights. Suntan being an actual color recognized by the pantyhose industry, the shade of a Caucasian leg after being left out in the sun. We all were Caucasian. Chelsea, city of Puerto Rican girls and Cambodian girls with skin naturally the color of the nylon we stretched across our legs, careful not to tear. Johnna advised everyone to keep a spare pair backstage, just in case. Everywhere girls were hunched over, naked, carefully coaxing the material up their calves. No underwear was Johnna's other rule. I was old enough for this rule to be potentially horrifying, old enough to find rules of any kind seriously suspect. What If, I demanded of Johnna. You Have Your Period? I didn't have mine yet, but I was expecting it soon, any minute. What if it came during the recital? What if a fantastic twirl revealed the seeping splotch of blood on my ass? Johnna looked at me like, you do not have your period yet. She said, *You can talk to me if that's a problem.* So like the others, I crouched with bared crotch and carefully yanked the hose around my naked waist. It mushed around my crotch like around the mug of a burglar. Swiftly I tugged on the satin costume, and went to work on the fun part, hair and makeup.

Standing at the edge of the stage, all in a row, mercifully stationed next to Marisol, who had found my hand in the dark and was giving it a damp, clutching squeeze. I squeezed back, the ridiculous polka-dotted cuffs glowing in the dark at our wrists. We had to be very careful not to move or squirm, lest the taps of our shoes carry out into the audience, or distract the moves of the class currently occupying the stage. It was a group of older girls, high schoolers, dancing improbably to Gary Numan's "Cars." They wore gold lamé costumes and waved bouquets of gold Christmas tinsel. I squinted at the girls as they sashayed into my line of vision, searching for the one who had known the cool, robotic song, the one who surely had brought it to Johnna's attention much the way I'd captured the Go-Go's for my own class. But all the girls looked the same, more or less. Hair, blondish or brownish, piled onto their heads and subdued with bobby pins. Blue eyelids, reddish-pink mouths, swaths of blush streaked down their cheekbones. Boobs, snug behind the shine of their costumes. They were indistinguishable from each other, especially in the blur of their movements. I wondered if I looked equally as uniform, my hair, dull brown, pinned back beneath the humiliating monkey hat. I gazed at my class in the dim light. With the exception of the irrepressible shine of Marisol's hair and the ever-growing bulge of Sharon's boobs, we all did look alike. I felt a twinge of panic, and calmed myself down. The Certain Something is inside, I counseled myself. It slept inside me like my heart, beating. I'd heard fashion designers on television talk about Inner Beauty, apparently all their models possessed it. It seemed akin to the Certain Something, perhaps they worked in synch. "Cars" began its fade-out, and I watched the neat line of golden teenagers spin offstage. There was a pause between songs as the audience applauded and certain female names were shouted by newly deepened voices. My class tightened, waiting for our cue. I felt a sparkle rise into my chest, it pulled me from the wings and out beneath the hot, blinding lights of the stage.

BROKEN HOME

In a Catholic school the classes are small and the same kids stay together for the entire eight years, so like a bad family the roles are well established and proven by time. It was around sixth grade, when personalities were really taking shape, that Jenn Capoletti and Krista Joel emerged as popular. They stayed that way until graduation. Jenn had super-long blond hair, straight and thickly fine like a Barbie's; Krista's was the same, only brown. Krista had thin squinty eyes, and Jenn's were round and watery blue, almost bug-eyed. They wore their long hair back from their faces with metal barrettes, and thin wisps they called "baby bangs" would escape and swish lightly on their foreheads. Sometimes I hung out with Jenn and Krista, and sometimes I hung out with the less popular girls. The less popular girls were fun because there was no pressure, they still acted young even as they galloped over the threshold of puberty. But Jenn and Krista were exciting. They always had boyfriends, public school boys in tight jeans. First Jenn went out with Mark Baker, who was tall and blond, then he asked her if she was a virgin so she broke up with him and went out with Ron Giordano, who was short and Italian and played hockey, the popular sport for boys.

I drank my first beer with Jenn, a brown bottle of Budweiser we split behind the apartment building of this young couple she baby-sat for. The husband wasn't there very often, but when he was he would give Jenn beer. The wife was pretty and blond, and she would talk with us about sex. This couple treated us like adults, and so we loved them. One morning the woman, Jessie, cooked us pancakes and told us about having anal sex with her husband. She didn't like it, said it actually hurt, but her husband liked it a lot and that was part of being married. They were newlyweds. Jessie inspected the naturally blond locks growing from Jenn's scalp and informed her that when her pubic hair came in, it too would be blond, which was lucky because *Playboy* paid a lot of money to girls with naturally blond pubic hair. She told us that she smoked pot even when she was pregnant, and that's why her baby was so calm and happy. He was a really easy baby. I would baby-sit with Jenn and she would stand on the first floor and I would stand on the second floor and we would send the baby up and down in the elevator.

It was Jenn who first showed me how to smoke, turning me on to Marlboros and teaching me how to inhale by pretending I was getting caught and gasping—Huuh! My Mother!—pulling the smoke in with my startled gasp. But it was Jenn's mother who saw me smoking, and consequently forbade Jenn to hang out with me for a little while. It was so unjust, Jenn always did everything first and then corrupted me, but I always had lousy luck with parents. Krista was who I first smoked pot with, on the train tracks with all these older public school kids who lived in her neighborhood. I really liked it, it made everything kind of slow and dreamy, and silly. I giggled a lot, and felt very close to all the kids around me on the tracks, like we were all really good friends even though I didn't know any of them. Me and Krista tried to start a secret club one summer, with an entrance test and an initiation. It was my idea. The test was all these questions about your period and wearing a bra and stuff about boys. There weren't any wrong answers, it wasn't a test you could flunk. It was more like an interview. We only put one girl, Renee Welch, through our process. Renee was another girl whose mother wouldn't let me hang out with her, because she had heard me say "frigging" once. The Frigging Bus Driver Drove Right By Me, I said, walking into Renee's house, shaking off my wet raincoat, and there was her mother, right there. We had Renee answer all the questions, and then for the initiation we blindfolded her and made her eat a bunch of stuff. She was scared. Her lips were a tight, impenetrable line. Come On, Renee. It's Not Poison, We're Not Going To Kill You. What did we feed her? Jam, mustard—dijon mustard, straight off a spoon. Milk, a hot pepper, mayonnaise. Whatever was in the fridge: A.I. Steak Sauce, prune juice, cottage cheese. A cookie. A shot of whiskey from the bottle in the cabinet. Renee puked. She said she felt sick so we took her blindfold off, and she ran into Krista's bathroom and puked. She stumbled home crying, but she was in the club. She was the only one because no one else would consent to the food initiation, so the whole thing just fizzled out. Jenn and Krista were best friends, they both had older brothers so perhaps that was why they carried themselves with such masculine confidence, and knew which bands were cool and what radio stations played them. WCOZ was rock n' roll, and in my bedroom I listened to it on my scratchy radio like studying. The Police was a band that Krista liked, so when the DJ announced "Spirits in the Material World," I cranked it up. It was such a creepy song, I was alone in my bedroom with Sting's eerie disembodied voice and I got scared and shut off the radio. But at least I had heard the song.

This was at the very beginning of my parents' divorce, when they would fight late into the night and I would stay awake with my radio on so soft, one ear pressed against the plastic web of the speaker, the other anxiously following the argument's progress. Soft Cell's enchanting, spooky "Tainted Love" lapsed into Rick James's "Super Freak," and soon a parent, usually Ma, would come get me from my bed and we would leave. We went to her friend Anna's house, they were nurses together. Anna was divorced too, or perhaps she had never been married at all. If Anna had been a kid, she would have been a public school kid I wasn't allowed to play with, and I did not like my mother playing with Anna. She had two boys, red-haired little motherfuckers. I remember Anna yelling at them to leave me and my sister alone. She had to keep yelling at them. We slept in their little room, which held a record player and a pile of AC/DC records, *Dirty Deeds, Highway to Hell.* I had never seen the band before, what they looked like. A bunch of leering longhaired guys sneering out at me from the record cover, devil horns on their heads. It looked like something I was supposed to stay away from. Once, Anna had some friends over—Will and Frankie, orderlies at the VA Hospital where Ma worked, and a random frosted-haired lady. They sat crowded together in Anna's small, shag-carpeted living room, talking in low adult tones that made me nervous, while I sat in the boys' room spinning records and Madeline and the redheads ate cookies in the kitchen. Will sauntered into the boys' room, where I was shuffling through the stacks of cardboard and vinyl, an impressive tower for a couple of kids. *AC/DC,* said Will approvingly, watching me place the grooved disc onto the turntable. *You like them?* I shrugged and said, Yeah. Will was a big guy with a ski hat and an earring. He had the kind of acne that never goes away, just becomes a part of the face, like his eyes, his almost translucently blond eyebrows. A red guy, friendly. The earring impressed me—lots of guys in Chelsea still thought only fags wore earrings, but Will had his single gold stud glinting modestly in the correct, non-homo, ear lobe. He stood in the room for a moment, bobbing his head to the guitar streaming out of the speakers, then nodded at my yellow T-shirt—Rick Springfield, my true music of choice. I had sent a construction-paper heart to the address on the back of his album, with a chunk torn out and replaced with a picture of his face, smiling charmingly as Dr. Noah Drake on *General Hospital.* You Fill That Hole In My Heart, I wrote on the back. Please Write Back Soon. *Rick Springfield's a fag,* Will teased. I looked at the AC/DC cover again, the mean sneers and raggy clothes. They could've been any pack of scary boys smoking cigarettes on a Chelsea corner, taunting, *Jailbait,* as I passed by in my Catholic plaid. I looked down at my shirt, Rick in a pink suit, a skinny purple tie. Maybe he did look sort of faggy. Will would soon become my stepfather, as soon as Ma was through divorcing Dennis. I left Will, walked into Anna's living room with the dim seventies lighting that made me anxious. It was the eighties now but just barely, and Anna's apartment was still sleazy seventies with low lamps and muted tones, fake bamboo. In the dimly lit living room Anna smoked a very small cigarette with tweezers, and my mom hopped up and scooted me back out the door.

Those were Egyptian cigarettes, Anna told me later in the comforting fluorescent light of her kitchen, but I was no moron. *You don't like me, huh?* I guess she was stoned. I Like You, I said. *You don't have to lie,* she said. Anna had a short arm from polio and it was hard for her to make hospital corners on the beds at the VA hospital. It was called the Soldier's Home and was a great arrangement for Chelsea mothers in bad marriages who would soon have to leave their husbands. The hospital's nursing school was free, though the books were expensive, and you could get certified and everything, but you had to take care of the vets when you graduated. My mother had worked hard, studying all night, scratching awful-looking equations into notebooks as me and Madeline scurried around her in a kind of awe. It was like she was becoming a real person. When she graduated we threw her a big party, and Dennis had acted so proud but really he hated it. Whenever he got home from work, she'd be on the couch, as excited as a girl to talk about her day at school. Which teachers were bitches and how the doctors all thought they were God. *Every night I get home it's like fucking* General Hospital *around here,* he'd snap, shutting her up. Dennis came home from work each night later and later, leaving me more anxious time with my radio, spinning the dial from WCOZ to WBCN, all the way down to Kiss 108. Eventually the fight would come, we would get in a cab and go to Anna's. And it was true that I didn't like her. I shrugged helplessly in her kitchen.

That night had been the final fight, when Dennis kicked us out for good. It was around Christmas—after Christmas, because the toys had been moved into our bedrooms but we weren't bored with them yet. The Barbie townhouse was in my sister's new room, Dennis's former "den," his office. What had gone on in there I did not know since he'd forbidden us to enter it. I knew from thrilling peeks that there'd been a couple posters on the walls—one that said something like, "If You Want to Soar with the Eagles, Get Ready for a Lot of Bird Shit," and another with a bunch of frogs smoking cigarettes that read, "If You Don't Like My Smoking, Go to Hell." I was afraid that the swear words in Dennis's posters would prevent him from getting into heaven when he died. Our family would be split in the afterworld, with the girls winged and in heaven and Dennis roasting in hell, talking labor politics with Satan. It made me anxious. Dennis was a cloud of bad energy, but he was still my dad, and I didn't want him cast into hell for all eternity. I'd wish for him to take the offending posters off the walls and repent. I don't know what happened to the posters when he relinquished the room to Madeline. They were replaced with Barbie and Strawberry Short-cake and Care Bear paraphernalia, the centerpiece being the thrill-ing display of cardboard architecture that was the townhouse. It was tall, magnificent, with a plastic yellow elevator that you pulled with a string. When it reached the floor you wanted, the Barbie would topple onto the cardboard floor. I always wanted the big Bar-bie accessories, the pools and the cars and the houses, but really they only illuminated how plastic and lifeless Barbie really was. It was like these accessories were the magic Barbie needed to really come alive, but of course she would only sit there, still and empty in her outfits. When we were playing Barbies, I insisted that all the clothes had to be placed in a big jumbled pile, and one by one we had to close our eyes and plunge our hand into the pile and randomly select an outfit. Otherwise I feared Madeline would grab all the best dresses and hog them. She always wanted the beautiful filmy one with the lacy halter top and the skirt that flowed with gauzy pastel color like something Stevie Nicks would wear. The older I got, the worse my Barbies behaved. They would be prostitutes and lesbians and they would be on drugs. I'd play with these awful Barbies and I would get so turned on my cooch would throb as I smooshed their naked molded plastic bodies together.

The day of the final fight me and Madeline were playing with the Barbie townhouse, and our Barbies were models. In the other room my mother was sobbing hysterically and my father was shouting at her. Me and my sister kept playing, tugging the elevator up and down the cardboard building, delivering Barbies to different parties and important meetings. My father came into the room, the small, new bedroom at the front of the house. There was a phone in the room, leftover from when it used to be the den, and Dennis grabbed it and with one strong and horrible tug pulled it out of the wall and hurled it onto the floor with a smash and a ring. Me and Madeline kept playing like nothing had happened, dressing and undressing and then dressing again our hollow dolls, the dead phone smashed in the corner behind us.

My father was so obsessed with the postal workers' union, always trying to get elected into different union positions and always losing. He said it was a popularity contest, and really he did just want to be Popular. He was a Leo. He took me and my sister to the annual Labor Day union breakfast at a fancy hotel in Boston, in a ballroom with chandeliers like huge diamonds twinkling above our heads. A bunch of ladies got up on stage and sang "Look for the Union Label" and then we ate powdered eggs and bacon and juice. The tables were round and, once, Michael Dukakis sat at ours and asked me if I liked my eggs. I didn't. The union also volunteered at the Easter Seals Telethon. I got to answer the phones and take pledges, until someone found out that a little kid was taking the pledges and they kicked me off, which wasn't fair because I had been doing a good job. I talked forever to old ladies about how brave the Easter Seals kids were and how sad it all was. They made me go sit at a table and sort things by zip code, it was really monotonous and I hated it.

The night that my father plucked the phone from the wall and slammed it to the floor he was supposed to go to a union meeting. He called all the union people and told them my mother was crazy and couldn't be left alone with the children, and then he ripped out all the phones so she couldn't call the people back and tell them it wasn't true. Eventually me and Madeline went to bed, and soon after, Dennis came into my room and said, *Get up, you're leaving.* I lay in my bed in my paneled room and I wondered what shirt I should wear. Then he came in again and really yelled so I got up. I put on my yellow Rick Springfield shirt. It was the last night I slept in that house that had been mine that afternoon, but that night, as I listened to AC/DC in the horrible boys' room, it wasn't my house anymore.

Krista's parents were divorced but Jenn's parents were still together. They got married real young, Jenn's mom had gotten pregnant the same exact time as Jenn's grandmother and that's why her uncle and her brother were the same age. Krista's divorced dad was a bartender at the French Club, and would fix us Shirley Temples if we came by after school. I remember being in the schoolyard at recess, waiting in line to jump rope, I was behind Krista and I wanted so badly to talk about divorce. I said, Krista, Do You See Your Father

A Lot? and she shrugged and said, *Yeah.* She was sucking on a Jolly Rancher stick in this really cool way that she and Jenn ate their candy, like it was a cigarette or something tougher than sugar.

Jenn and Krista would both take ten minutes at the start of recess to pull their Jordache on under their uniforms, then pull striped boys' tube socks over the ankles and then put on their leather Nike high-tops. It really cut into their recess time but it was worth it, because they looked so good jumping rope. It was a great look and no one else could wear it because they had thought of it first and you couldn't copy. You could only stand and look and be jealous. Do You Like Your Father? I asked Krista, and she shrugged like I was weird and said, *Yeah.* You're Lucky, I said. My Father's An Asshole. Krista turned and hopped into the rope.

Dennis had talked to me and Madeline on that last night, as he threw us from his house. He told us that if we ever saw him walking toward us, we should cross the street, because he would not say hello to us. He would not be a part-time dad. Me and my sister listened and nodded dumbly. The awful acceptance of childhood. I miss nothing about it. All I could ever do was nod and stare blankly and ask for more toys. Me and my mother and Madeline moved in with my grandparents, in a house that sat across the street from a cemetery that we used like a park because it was the worst part of Chelsea. We weren't allowed to go to the real park because everyone was afraid we'd get beat up by Puerto Rican girls. We slept in a little spare room, on a cot, and my mother would have nightmares and wake up urgent and confused, thinking that the house was on fire.

It was awful how little money Ma had. She was trying to save up from the job she'd just started at the hospital, but all this shit kept happening. The time she climbed up the stairs at six o'clock crying because she'd lost her wallet. Then the mean landlady who wouldn't let us play in the yard realized a small family had moved in upstairs and doubled my grandparents' rent. At night when my mother got home I would dial up KISS 108 and dedicate songs to her. The DJs loved it. *We gotta little girl here who wants to send a song out to her mom.* Listen, Ma, Listen! Eventually our cousin Colleen who was nice rented us the first floor of her house on Heard Street. The walls were kind of patchy like they'd just been tossed up, and me and Madeline shared a side room, bunk beds. And Ma started dating Will with the earring who liked AC/DC. One weekend we went out to a cottage by a lake that a nurse from the hospital owned. It was summer and my mother walked around with Will a lot, and then they went out on the water in a canoe. Just the two of them together on the lake where *On Golden Pond* was shot. That was the legend. They looked like a Hallmark card, both of them out there on the still water with the setting sun illuminating their blond hair. It looked romantic. I watched them from the shore, damp sand mudding the ass of my shorts. They're Going To Go Out With Each Other, I told Madeline. *No they're not.* She hated that. I didn't think it was so bad. Will wasn't just an orderly, he was an artist too, and he played drums. I was old enough now to identify cool, and Will was cool. I had not thought that my mother was cool, so I didn't understand why he liked her, but I was glad he was around. They worked on the same floor at the Soldier's Home, and Ma loved to tell people how she had been scared of him at first, thought he was a thug with his earring and the inky jailhouse tattoos bleeding green onto the skin of his wrist and fingers. But really he was such a nice man, and wrote poetry and liked her kids. He painted a village of Smurfs on the wall near Madeline's bed, and a unicorn and a rainbow on the wall by mine. The unicorn was white and had these feathered bangs that I wanted for myself, but my mother would not let me get a hairdo. *You have to really keep up with a hairdo like that,* she said, waving her hand in dismissal. MTV was still new, and I was watching it and wanting a hairdo. I watched Kim Wilde singing "Kids in America." It was dangerous and exciting like I imagined New York City to be, and I wanted her hairdo. When she sang *There's a new wave coming I warn you,* I believed her. I was waiting for it. Adam Ant was softer than the girls on MTV, and all the more dangerous because of it. I watched him and tried to wedge a safety pin into my ear. It wouldn't go all the way so I left it hanging half out of my lobe until my mother made me take it out. I tried to emulate the fashions I saw on the videos, but I didn't have the resources so I just looked weird. Like a child prostitute.

After Will painted the village of Smurfs and the unicorn and rainbow on our bedroom walls, one night Dennis came and knocked at our front door. I was in bed, but the house was so small it was almost one long room. There were no doors, light from the lamp in the living room spilled into my room and the television was on. He knocked at the door and my mother let him in. He said he wanted to see her new house. He had heard she had a TV, how did she have a TV? Did her boyfriend buy it for her? My father had a big black trash bag full of beer and he dragged it clinking into our living room like a sick Santa. He sat down on our couch and refused to leave. He just cracked open his beers and drank them and insulted my mother. *Call the cops, I'm not leaving.* So she did. Two cops came into our house, walkie-talkies on their belts sputtering nonsense and static. *I wanna say goodbye to my girls.* He came into my room and I pretended to wake up. *Bye bye,* he slurred. *The police are going to take your daddy to jail. Mommy's having daddy arrested.* He bent and kissed me with his scratchy mustache that stunk like beer. He looked at the Smurfs on the wall. *What's that?* He squinted in the dimness. *Oh that's real nice, that's nice. Who did that?* His voice was bitter. We had a cousin named Albert, a fag who cut hair in Boston and the only member of the family I could think of as an artist. Albert Did It, I said. We barely ever saw Albert, my father knew that. *Albert,* he said, looking at the wall. *Let's go, Sir,* the cops said from the doorway. They put handcuffs on him and took him out the door. In the living room I sat on the couch and it was very late. I figured I wouldn't have to go to school the next day, and I figured it was okay for me to swear. He's An Asshole, I said, He's A Frigging Asshole. My mother was crying. She went into the kitchen and got the phone and called Will. *Michelle's swearing up a storm,* she wailed, then, *no, I have not been drinking up a storm!* Will came over to our house and sat with us in the parlor. One of them said, *Just because this happened, that doesn't mean you can swear.* And I had to go to school the next day, too.

TO MARKET

Goldstein's Market way up on Washington Avenue sold hamburger and cheese and other stuff you couldn't just grab at our corner store, Heinie's. Heinie's was run by an old woman named Heinie, maybe we were related to her, nobody seemed to know for sure. Heinie's was a dark, Polish store that sold mostly candy and packaged pastries. It felt very Brothers Grimm—dim, the haunted-house sound of creaking floorboards, hunched-over Heinie, ancient and glaring in a raggy dress, the counter full of candies gleaming in their crinkly wrappers. It was a creepy errand to run but so preferable to getting sent up to Goldstein's. Walking to Goldstein's was always worst when the sun was about to go down and the sky was dusky and sinister, like clouds passing over the sun as the final nail was driven into Christ's ankles. The Chelsea dusk made martyrs, it was a certain test.

There were two routes you could take to Goldstein's. The longer route was straight up Heard to Washington, and then all the way down the slow bend of the boulevard. That took me past Aunt Stella's house with her yard of gnomes and lawnjockeys and chipped Madonnas and little painted squirrels and stone ducks. Past the brown house where there lived a woman whose husband had gone crazy on her, he had turned nuts and wandered Chelsea's streets, but often he came back to this brown house to sleep in the bedding his old wife kept for him on her porch. Washington Avenue was at the top of my street, and the length of it held the homes of many horrible boys, big porchy homes that could accommodate many of the horrible boys' horrible friends. At the corner of the Washington Ave block that held Goldstein's was the Sparta Spa, another dusty relic of a shop run by old cranky mean people, selling time-faded packages of things people didn't buy anymore. There was a lunch counter inside the shadowy spa and you could still get fries there. A wire-grated basket of them crisp and raw was drowned in the bubbling oil, then removed all golden and oily and hot to burn your tongue. You could get a fizzing Coke in a curving glass, and you could get your ass kicked. A snarling pack of horrid boys congregated outside the spa, despite the owner's constant threats to call the cops. He had a scoop of white hair on his old head and a splattered apron wrapped around his wide body. It was so fifties, this old bitter meanie dashing out of his store waving his spatula at the boys, the greasers. I hated all of them, the boys and the man and the inside of the Sparta Spa that felt like falling backward into a slow, grainy long-ago time. The toadish old people whose backs were permanently hunched from leaning over the lunch counter and into their coffees. The one lady who smoked Mores, those skinny brown cigarettes. It looked like smoking a long, elegant turd. The spa had an old-fashioned phone booth with a glass-and-wood door that shut out the hum of the ghostly lunchroom, and sometimes I would step inside to use it and the big aproned man would stand stiff and hostile and wait for me to steal something. The geriatric lineup at the counter would stare curiously, silent, expressionless, they were like some terrible gallery of the nearly dead, and they spooked me as I dashed into the wooden phone box. But they were not worse than the boys who clustered outside the place, because the old people were simply odd and ugly and irritatingly judgmental, but the boys would smack you, trip you, hurt you. There were often girls there, too, showing off to their boys that they could also kick ass. Oh yes, girls kick ass, yes they do. Mostly the asses of other girls. Although this route was clearly dangerous, Washington was a main street, one of the two main streets in Chelsea, and there was traffic, cars idling at red lights, and people walking around, normal people, adults who didn't want to break your face and maybe, in an emergency, would step in and save you if your face was being broken.

The second route to Goldstein's was much quicker—the back streets. The speed of this winding path was important because no matter how quickly you walked to the grocery store, the sun would be quicker, sliding down the sky like a bit of food that somehow ended up on the kitchen wall, butter or tomato sauce or jelly skidding down the wallpaper—that was the sun and you had to beat it. You didn't want to be outside when it finally collapsed and the yellowy streetlights buzzed on, at least I didn't. The back streets were a fast track but they were deserted, the light there denser, almost a fog in the Chelsea dusk with no car lights or streetlights or storefront lights to warm your little walk and make you feel safe.

Another variable in this Goldstein's problem was the little sister Madeline. Walking to the store with Madeline: good or bad? I wasn't sure. Maybe she really did repel potential attackers the way my mother, a fan of safety in numbers, believed. She did help carry the bags. Both of us fought over who would carry the arm-breakingly heavy gallon of milk, its damp plastic handle freezing your hand off and leaving a sour stink on your skin. Mostly Madeline was simply someone else I'd have to protect, a weak spot in a fight when I already had so many—long hair, limp wrists, fear.

One night, with Madeline, I took the back streets. There was a boy on a bike hanging around this big, poor house where all the poorest kids in the neighborhood lived. It was so Mother Goose. It was the old woman who lived in a shoe, the house was like that. The sole coming off, the tongue torn, the laces frayed. It looked like an orphanage, but a single family lived there, a single mother and her two million grubby kids, a menagerie that included many boys who enjoyed hurling things at your head as you passed their rotting porch, sometimes even glass or chunks of brick from the house's crumbling walls, but at least they stayed on their porch. The big poor house with no front door and shit all over the yard, sheets blowing in the windows—what made it so bad was that each rotten boy somehow managed to find friends, friends as rotten as he was, as rotten as the wooden steps that led to the doorless front door of the big poor house. Wooden steps cracked in the middle, a gap wide enough for a kid's sneaker to slip through. Wooden steps with wood that melted away in the rain.

The kid on the bike, the boy, he was familiar to me. He had liked me once in a girlfriend way, and for a minute I liked him back, played with being that girlfriend. I really loved the idea of boys. The idea of them, the hot, glossy notion of them was enough to occupy me for hours as I rolled atop my top bunk bed, daydreaming, scheming about how I'd improve my looks, appear both prettier and tougher, scheming about how I would snag these wild boys popping wheelies on their dirt bikes, sagging against a brick wall, kept company by their shitty little radios, their boom boxes, their ghetto blasters. Dented plastic and metal on the sidewalk beside them blaring Ozzy and Run-DMC. I loved the dreamy boys who floated like macho gossamer through my mind, but the shock of their bodies in the real world sent my insides roiling, made me feel like beef stew. The boy on the bicycle hated me because I wouldn't be his girlfriend. He had been so nice back when he was trying to convince me to like him, but since it hadn't worked out he now felt comfortable enough to shrug off the nice-boy suit and reveal himself in all his bastard glory. He cornered me and Madeline there before the poorest house in Chelsea. Against the splintered fence that contained the creeping tide of debris, the boy ordered me to kiss him. I'm Not Going To Kiss You, I huffed. It was hard to gauge how I came off in situations like this, being cornered. If it was a girl blocking my path, I'd try to negotiate, because she was a girl, and surely there was inside of her a shred of girl goodness—I only had to locate it, and coddle it, and then everything would be all right and I would be permitted to pass and maybe we would even be friends. Of course, this only sometimes worked, but with the boys, I understood there wasn't any goodness, none at all, not the tiniest bell of kindness to work a chime from. I could only hope I sounded as gruff as any twelve-year-old girl could hope to sound in the face of a bastard boy who was about to twist a sour kiss from you.

Get The Fuck Out Of My Way, I ordered. We Have To Go To The Store. For Our *Mother*. We had a family waiting for us, did that mean anything? We had an adult, did adults still have any power over this boy? It didn't seem likely. I rolled my eyes like he was playing a dumb and boring game. I shoved his dirt bike, the glinting, grimy handlebars. *Don't touch my bike,* he growled like he thought he was the Fonz. I felt the stingers of tears behind my eyes like a nest of tiny bugs. *Fucking crybaby.* Let Me Go, I demanded. I Got My Sister With Me. *So, I'll kiss your sister too.* Poor Madeline, little Snow White. Dark, dark hair, coal black hair on a milk-white head, so pale my grandmother thought she was anemic, told my mother to feed her iron. The boy lunged. The big poor house behind us was quiet—was this good or bad? There was a girl who lived inside it who was okay and didn't want to kill me, maybe if she were there, she could help us. But nobody was anywhere and we should have taken Washington Ave, where at least a car would have passed and I could've flailed my arms in the head-lights like an SOS. The boy lunged, and he lunged at Madeline, he had to duck to get her but she ducked too, so mostly he got splintered fence and she got her knees banged up by his bike. Madeline scooted away, she was little, and we both ran, our animal instinct, up to the relative safety of Washington Ave. Fending off the boy on the bike had taken so much time, the sun was done, switched off like a TV and now we'd be late getting back home. Ma would worry and her worry would turn angry and we'd be in trouble when we got home with the hamburger. *Why?* she'd ask. A Boy Stopped Us. A Boy Wanted To Kiss Us. Telling it never showed it right, never gave anyone the appropriate feeling, the feeling that you were going to get killed, murdered by these boys.

Two blocks from Goldstein's, the boy on the bike was behind us. It was suppertime throughout Chelsea, but probably nobody fed him. He was riding his bike into my leg, the treaded tire snagging my knee sock. *Cut The Shit!* He rammed into me. *Cut The Fucking Shit!* I stopped walking. Electric lights were sparkling all around us, we were dolls hung in a Xmas tree. We were all on a movie set. I was the heroine and the boy on the bike was actually a nice boy, a handsome actor who had to pretend to be an asshole because that was the actor's job, pretending. I said my line grandly: Go On! I pointed to the red-brick sidewalk before us. Go Ahead! He smirked and pedaled forward. Then I knocked him down. They call that improv. When you bust out with a move not in the script. I could have let the entire terrorizing affair come to an end, maybe not a triumphant end, but still, The End. But there was something in the wobble of his back tire as his legs bore down on the pedals, as he strained for some momentum, wobble wobble, it looked *vulnerable.* Is that what I looked like making my way to the store? Wobble wobble down the darkening streets, my body straining for some momentum to rush me quicker to the fluorescent-lit safety of Goldstein's, for a reprieve and some shopping before, wobble wobble, I make my way back home? So obviously shaky that it was childhood, boyhood, instinct to try to knock me down? That was the way my foot shot out, fast and unthinking, and kicked the back tire and knocked the boy down. His dirt bike tipped and toppled, his splayed starfish hands scraped the ground and went bloody at the palms, his feet slipped in their sneakers. He was tangled in the spinning wheels and inky chains of his machine. *Fucking bitch!* he yelled, recovering quickly. I could see, up ahead, where light from Goldstein's windows spilled buttery onto the sidewalk. I could see women walking with their plastic Goldstein's bags bulging and sagging, tearing against the sharp cardboard corner of a cereal box. I could see the boy's corduroy ass landing back on the saddle of his bike as me and Madeline sprinted the rest of the way to the store.

Inside Goldstein's we breathed the cozy smell of burnt air, warm, blowing out from cobwebby vents in the wall, the smell of scattered sawdust piled up and over the sweeter smell of broken glass and jelly. Milky smells like lunchtime breath, and the wet and bloody tang of the deli case and its various meats. One pound of hamburger, the cheap stuff. Or, half cheap, half better. A pound of bologna and a pound of American, both sliced up by the whizzing machine. A box of Hamburger Helper, a gallon of milk, a two-liter of Pepsi. Bring it all up to the register, dump it on the slow black belt that creaked your purchases up to the lady who punched in the price and dumped it in a hag. A crazy, skinny guy was in line at the register next to ours. *I am a millionaire!* he was screaming. *I am a mill-ion-aire!* His mouth was wide open and happy, but something about his face looked askew. I Think He's Crazy, I whispered to Madeline. *Yeah, go back to ya' mansion, then!* some bitter wise guy quipped, and everyone laughed. *I will go back to my mansion,* the crazy man vowed, his eyes darting around to find who said that to him, *because I am a millionaire!*

The boy on the bike was now inside Goldstein's, behind us in the checkout line, sans bike. He kicked me. It gave me a stark, white feeling, like all nice feelings were being sucked out my feet and all I was left with was a manic, electric rush. The millionaire had just left and the shoppers were busy making fun of him and nobody noticed the angry boy with the bloody hands kicking the Catholic-school girl with the hamburger. This Boy Keeps Bothering Us, I said to the cashier lady, and pointed to the bike boy. Me And My Little Sister. I pushed Madeline forward by her shoulders so the cashier could get a good look—yup, that's a little sister. Will You Call The Police, Please? Because He's Going To Follow Us Home, He's Trying To Beat Us Up And Kiss Us. *She knocked me off my friggin' bike!* he screamed, holding up the raw palms of his hands, skinned, the torn, thin rolls of straggling skin, sidewalk grime caked into the blood. I was so grateful that no one had ever taught this boy not to swear in front of grownups. Not to swear loudly in public places such as grocery stores. *Hey!* the checkout lady chastised. Miss, I tapped her, I Was Trying To Get Away From Him. *We* Were, I shook Madeline like a little doll. *You buyin' somethin'?* she asked the bike boy. He wasn't. *I want you outta here,* she said to him. Are You Calling The Cops? I asked excitedly. *Don't make me,* she said, still looking at the boy. *Fucking bitch,* he muttered, to me or the lady. She turned from him and dumped our food into a plastic bag. The boy pushed himself out the glass doors.

How would we ever get home? It was dark out now, nighttime for real. The boy on the bike obviously had nothing to do but follow us around, getting madder and madder. He was probably out front waiting, maybe with other boys, maybe they'd all make us make out with them. Madeline clutched her bag with the box of Hamburger Helper and the bottle of Pepsi. I had the bag of meat and cheese in one hand and the icy curve of the milk jug aching and numbing my other. Nobody was going to call the cops for us. Ma didn't have a car to come pick us up. And she was tired. Tired from working all day, tired from divorcing my father and tired from having married him in the first place. I couldn't ask her to walk all the way up to Goldstein's and collect us like a couple of scared cats. Come On, I said to Madeline, and we burst through the glass doors. I had no plan except to walk Washington Ave. There weren't any bikes or boys that I could see, just streetlights and darkness and cold wintery air that seared the inside of your nose with each inhalation.

Mom, There Was A Millionaire At Goldstein's. My mother snorted. *Yeah, so why's he in Chelsea?* she asked, pushing clumps of our half-and-half meat around in a frying pan with a wooden spatula. I loved the sizzling stink of it, how it clung to our kitchen curtains, the faded blue and white checks, the march of ribboned ducks. But He Said He Was A Millionaire, I insisted. I wanted him to be. *Yeah, I can say I'm a millionaire, too,* Ma said, and dumped a packet of orangey spices into the greasy meat.

INTRODUCING UNCLE MARKIE

Uncle Markie was my mother's little brother, and his story starts with the toy garage my grandmother demolished in front of his little blond tomato face, nineteen-fifties adorable and screaming. He was playing with the garage on the kitchen floor while all around him my grandmother was trying to make spaghetti without having a panic attack, because my grandfather was out with his "drinking buddies" and would be home any minute, rosy with scotch, and the dishes would fly. She'd be tossing them. Though Papa of course was not a drunk but a *drinker,* and a happy one—jovial, making up drunk-dad dances, shuffling on the linoleum. Still, my grandmother hated it. She'd asked Markie eight times to please clean up his goddamn toy garage, and he hadn't, so she smashed it. Hopped up and down on it like a crazy woman mashing grapes between her toes, making wine from the shards of cardboard and plastic. The little toy garage dead beneath the pumps of God, the foot of Armageddon stomping out Markie's little world.

Like most Biblical victims of wrath, he had been warned. And now he stood in the doorway and cried. All Markie liked were cars and trucks and garages, and it's all he would ever like. He sucked at school, the words on the page swam and scrambled when he looked at them, fucked with his head, so they put him in the dummy class, because it was the fifties, and nobody'd heard of dyslexia.

Uncle Markie was on drugs and all his friends were on drugs too. *Buncha pips,* Papa would grumble when Markie roared off with them on his Harley. I'd gotten a ride on it when I was five years old. I'd been lifted and plopped on the wide leather seat as my mother and everyone else stood bunched around the house where Markie would live, with his parents, forever. Everyone was standing with fingernails lodged between their teeth, waiting for the eldest daughter to die. For Markie to return from his spin around the block without even realizing Michelle had slid from the back, that Michelle was sprawled in the street around the corner, her cracked skull spilling into the gutter. But Markie brought his bike to an elegant sputter at the curb and I was lifted from the machine and deposited onto the ground, grinning a big numb grin from all the air that had pummeled my face. I loved it. *She loved it!* Uncle Markie crowed, *Di'ntcha, Shell?* That was the summer that Elvis died. All the ladies on my grandparents' street lounging into the evening on the front steps, "sitting out," it was called. Like, *You going to sit out tonight?* On your wooden stairs with splinters that would launch into the skin of your ass if you got too heated up with your gossip and shook it in an excited wiggle. On your cement stairs with the pebbly surface that dented up your cheeks. *Elvis Presley died,* said the lady next door, smoking on her steps. Butts were piling up on the sidewalk. I was sobbing. Not because of Elvis, whom I didn't really know about then, but because it was time to go home and I never, ever, wanted to leave the lazy comfort of summer on Chester Avenue. Across the street was the cemetery that was the closest thing we'd ever have to wilderness, growing unruly greenness everywhere, birds that weren't pigeons flying up from the trees, the sky taking its sweet time out night. All the chatty ladies with their soft packages of cigarettes, the gritty *click click* of rusting Bics, the sulphur tang of matches floating on the air. I held on with all my might to the wrought-iron banister on my grandmother's steps. Her front yard was a thick tangle of roses, tiny pink ones with more thorns than smell. It curled angrily up and over the fence, like a child scribbling outside the lines. My mother was pulling me like I was a tough piece of rope in a game of tug of war, I would not budge. I was red and howling. I may have never been so bad, at least not yet. Just screaming to blot out the world with my sound. It would either work, this new and terrible behavior would impress upon my mother how important it was that we stayed with the ladies, or else I would be in more trouble than ever. When I was finally pried off the banister and taken home, my hands were stiff like the hands of a dead girl, cramped and red and white, sore meat and stuck bone. I hiccupped all the way home, sucking in my breaths like a fool.

Uncle Markie's hair was worthy of a lion. It was gold and long and thick like his mustache, it was tough like his leather vest. The word "Mark" was tattooed on his wrist, with an inky little flourish beneath the deep green letters. *So he don't forget his goddamn name,*

Papa growled absently, his eyes stuck down on the *Herald*, smoking a Pall Mall, too disgusted to look up, but really he was Markie's best friend. They called each other Charlie. *Hey there, Charlie, howsabout you lend me ten bucks? Hey, Charlie, you having some spaghetti?* Ma, I tugged, confused. Why Are They Calling Each Other Charlie? *Oh, I don't know,* Ma sighed, maybe a little irritated.

Markie lived in the room off the kitchen in my grandparents' rented apartment. He hung framed pictures of eighteen-wheelers on the walls, Peterbilt. Trucks had to be Peterbilts the way motorcycles had to be Harleys and the electric guitar on the back piazza had to be a Les Paul. Even though it was broken and missing strings and Markie couldn't play it anyway. His friends were all in a band, they played Three Dog Night covers at a bar in the square. Markie did drugs with his friends in the band, and then he rang our bell at three in the morning because there were bugs all over him, biting into his skin, all tangled up in his hair. He rang the bell so late and woke everyone up, and at the front door there was yelling, and then Markie left with his bugs. Coke bugs. They were blue, he said. Imagine thousands of little bugs chewing you up beneath your skin, where your bones and blood were. *Not real bugs,* my mother explained. *The drugs make you crazy, make you think there's bugs all over you.* Invisible bugs. I got it.

Uncle Markie never had presents for anyone at Christmas. Just a card with a serial-killer scrawl at the bottom that everyone gathered around to decipher after he left. Even though Markie drove his Peterbilt all over the East Coast, picking up boxes and dropping them off states away, even though he lived with his parents and paid no rent, he never had any money. He even owed money, to the Mafia. The thing about owing money to the Mafia is, you got to pay them seventy-five dollars a week just to keep yourself alive. Just to keep the goons from breaking your legs or dumping the chopped and bloody horse head in the sheets while you snore, zonked and oblivious from whatever drugs you spent all your Mafia-money on. Drugs you probably bought from them, too. That weekly seventy-five-dollar payment did not go toward your outstanding Mafia balance. That debt was to be paid in full, one lump sum. It took you forever to come up with it, since all your spare change was going toward keeping your body out of the harbor. For Christmas Uncle Markie would give that card with the unreadable ball-point scrawl, and the promise of a gift in the near future. And sometimes a toy would "fall off the back of the truck" and I'd get it, a toy I grew out of years ago, a doctor's kit, something from Playskool. It was like Markie didn't know how old we were. Stuff was always falling off the back of his truck and finding its way to our house. Once, it was a couple cases of mango Tang from the Philippines that lay on our pantry shelves for years. Gross orangey powder in plastic jugs caked with dust.

Uncle Markie would come into our house to use our shower and then stretch out on the couch in front of the TV. When I got home from school, he'd be there, trying to get me to do his laundry for a dollar. A Dollar, I'd scoff. Get Real. *Don'tchoolove your uncle?* he'd moan. *Gota tha store an get me a packa cigarettes, you can buy yaself somethin' too.* I Don't *Need* Anything, I'd retort. If it wasn't Markie trying to get you to wash his ratty T-shirts and buy him smokes, then it was my mother wanting me to make her a cup of tea or buy *her* cigarettes, or Madeline wanting me to go into the kitchen and pour her a cup of Pepsi or lug her wet laundry down to the dryer in the cellar. I swear. I never asked anyone to do anything for me, except maybe Will, who I'd ask to make me a raspberry lime rickey when he came over to visit with Ma. Ma was real careful about bringing Will into the house, initially for dinner. *Is it okay with you if Will comes over for some lasagna?* she asked. I was thrilled. I loved having visitors. Especially a visitor who once played drums for Billy Squier at a party, back before his house caught fire and melted his sparkly red drum kits into amorphous, glittering lumps. Will told the story with a chuckling bravado, and I felt an odd comfort at how he laughed so lightly at his own misfortune. His big, football-player shoulders shrugged it off. It was all just a story now, and a good one. I wanted to be like that, sitting casually at a strange family's house, wiping the Ragu from my lips with a paper towel as I continued . . . And Then The Cops Came And Dragged My Dad Out Of The House. And I Had To Go To School The Very Next Day! I'd shake my head at the absurdity of life and take a sip of Coke, while my audience lingered on the last of my words, clucking their tongues, marveling at the insane life I'd survived, and the ease with which I'd let my tragedies roll off me.

Will was a reformed criminal-type, used to get wasted and fist-fight in the square, buying drugs, maybe selling them—once, he got pushed through the plate-glass window of a shop downtown, because of some drug buy gone awry. Another time he was stabbed with a switchblade. It was all so deadly and exciting, like having a personified cop show at your kitchen table. Probably Ma didn't love Will revealing so much of his seedy youth to her kids, but it was clearly far behind him. He had survived his violent teens and twenties, had arrived safely at thirty. Now he hefted the elderly war vets gone bonkers with Alzheimer's, he pushed them around the ward like big babies in adult strollers, swaddled in their blankets and hospital gowns. Maybe she was as dazzled by his tales as we were. Who doesn't love a Bad Boy, especially one gone good, employed in a caretaking profession? Will came to visit more and more often. He'd spend an hour sketching in a notebook a tripped-out, psychedelic, Escher-like spelling of my name, each letter a labyrinth. When it was done he'd tear the artwork from the spiral wire and I'd tape the ragged page to my wall, above my bed. M-I-C-H-E-L-L-E. My personality swelled when Will came to visit, my loud voice getting louder, getting braggier as I listed off what bands I thought were cool, all the rock trivia I had amassed from my hours plopped in front of MTV, or crouched beneath the covers with my radio. I drummed to the beats of songs on countertops, on the kitchen table, jostling the crumbs, hoping Will would notice how constant I kept the beat, even hard ones, the fast ones. Maybe he'd suggest I should become a drummer, like him. Maybe he'd buy me a drum set, metallic red. But Will didn't have any money, not really. What he could offer was food, pots of chili, an exotic, spicy mess of a meal with beans and crumbles of meat, all globbed over rice to soak up some of the heat. *Five-alarm chili,* Will boasted, proud at what his mouth could withstand. I claimed to like it hot, too, though it made dinner feel more like an athletic event and less like a meal. He brought us lime rickeys, another special concoction prepared with lime syrup and raspberry ginger ale, with halved and gutted limes bobbing with the ice inside one of those giant plastic cups you got free with a large drink at McDonald's. Like Dennis with his tripe and Papa with his holiday can of baby onions, Will had his preferred foods too, but they weren't gross, they were adventures. And instead of hoarding them, he seemed to get a great delight from delivering them to us, presenting the red mound of chili on its steaming lump of rice, delivering a clattering plastic cup that gave off nose-tickling fizzles as you brought it to your face to drink.

But back to Uncle Markie. I loathed coming home from school and finding him passed out in my actual *bed,* my shades drawn against the cheerful and sunny world outside. Ma, I'd whine. His face slack on my pillow and all his grubby trucker clothes, work boots and everything, rubbing into my sheets. It was already so hard for me to keep my things clean, I didn't need Uncle Markie making it worse. Now I'd have to wash my sheets, something I tried to do only a couple times a year. One time Uncle Markie had scabies. We found out the day he'd spent an afternoon power-napping in my bed. No, I moaned. My family. Ma, I cried accusingly, pointed into my room where the unconscious Uncle Markie slumbered. *Wake him up, then.* She didn't want to deal with him either. Her little brother. Markie Get Up, I jostled his shoulders roughly. *Aww, Shell, jus let me sleep. Justa little longa.* Markie, This Is My Room, I said stubbornly. You Have To Get Up, I Have Homework. *Do it in the kitchen,* he begged. *Come on, Shell. Justanotha hour.*

Nobody ever knew if he was crashing off amphetamines or nodding off on heroin—he wore long-sleeved thermals even in the summertime to hide the scabs in the crook of his arm—or just honestly exhausted from an overnight run, the way he always claimed he was. His scruffy, bearded face burrowed itself deeper into my pillow. I left, slammed my books onto the kitchen table, where my mother was plunking gobs of chicken meat into a bowl of egg, then a plate of flour, then twirling them in bread crumbs and flinging them into a sizzling pan of oil. *Chicken fingers*, she said brightly. I loved them. Pretty much every night my mother cooked dinner. For everyone. What a drag. All day she spooned mush into the uncomprehending mouths of demented old people, then came home to fry up a bunch of stuff for us. I wasn't ever going to have kids. I knew I couldn't hack it. The kitchen was bright, fluorescent, warm and oily with food. Sometimes Ma would go on strike. Because she was tired and cranky and the house had been too messy for too long and nobody helped her. *Fix yourselves something.* Frozen planks of Steak 'Ums, cans of ravioli, boxes of safety-orange macaroni and cheese. Ramen. There was always stuff in the pantry, beneath the endless mango Tang. Markie lurched from my bedroom like an overgrown teen. *Gota tha store fa me, Shell?* He croaked. *I'll give ya a dolla.*

DENNIS DISAPPEARED

To be fair, there was a moment, a scant blip, when Dennis tried to be our dad. He'd bucked up to the humiliation of being a dreaded "part-time dad," a silly phrase I'm sure he'd heard on a human interest segment on the five o'clock news. A segment that no doubt also interviewed real-life latchkey kids, like me. I wore my house key on a piece of shoelace around my scrawny neck, like a good statistic. Tucked beneath my shirt like a Catholic scapular. I loved being a latchkey kid. I loved the ring of the house when it echoed nothing but my own sneakers, and the backup scuff of Madeline. I loved no parents around, a comfy freedom. I didn't even do anything bad, unless someone had forgotten a pack of cigarettes on the coffee table. Then I would take one in the bathroom to savor, to exhale erotically—up my nose and out my mouth—like Catherine Deneuve in *The Hunger*. I imagined my second-hand smoke was the tulle springing off the chic hat she wore, wreathing my face in mystery. I liked the pouch of my mouth as it sent the plume of smoke into my nostrils. French inhaling.

Dennis drove up to our new address on trashy Heard Street, and we climbed into our childhood car, the Maverick, and were driven back to the house we'd been kicked out of. My old bedroom was empty, just sitting there like the inside of an empty box. It was weird to be in the house. How quickly it had become foreign, so not mine. It felt like some creepy museum of myself, or a place I'd lived in a dream. The furniture was mostly gone—we'd gotten to keep it, though Dennis had seized my mother's hope chest, the polished wooden trunk where a bride-to-be stores the precious miscellany of her future. Cups and saucers, folded sheets. The bottom drawer had been stuffed with stacks and stacks of photo albums, albums with quilted covers and gold spiral binding. Photos of me and Madeline, from birth all through our childhood. Dennis was hoarding them— no doubt they just ended up in a dumpster somewhere. It was pure spite. My grandparents donated their own enormous snapshot collections to my mother, with Dennis's face scissored neatly from the pictures. Smiling me, smiling Ma and Madeline, and then a gaping oval. No more pictures of Dennis. We'd gotten the couch and the armchair, sagging wool lumps in an autumnal floral pattern. The coffee table, scarred with waxy rings from teacups. Dennis had refurnished his newly vacant home in real bachelor fashion, buying first a bar with a couple of stools, and then a bizarre couch-bed covered in orange fun-fur, long-haired, sitting right in the middle of our old living room. Aimed at the television. When we spent the night that one time, me and Madeline slept together in the wide bed my mother once slept in, and Dennis bundled up in the funky new sofa-thing. We'd gotten a bucket of wings from Kentucky Fried Chicken and watched TV. It felt so strange, like we were an incom-

The Chelsea Whistle

138

plete replica of an old family. When we were all together we would do this, me and Madeline glued to *The Love Boat* or *Fantasy Island*, Ma and Dennis on the couch behind us, or in the kitchen shaking a pan of popcorn in oil above the blue gas flame. It felt pathetic, or blasphemous—surely new rituals should have been enacted for this new phase of our family life, but Dennis, incapable, plopped us in front of his TV with some fried wings, and sat behind us on his play furniture, restlessly drinking a beer.

Another time, he took us to a mall that played whispery "Major Tom" on the sound system, and the stores all had cheap post-Halloween sales and I got a tube of roll-on glitter that became my new fashion staple. Another time, he took us to the union office, where he held some minor position, not the coveted General Secretary-Treasurer he'd never been elected to. The telephones in all the rooms had strange curves of plastic on the receivers, to be nestled into the crook of your neck while you typed or shuffled papers. They looked like swoops of vanilla frosting. Me and Madeline ran from office to office and called each other on the phones, bought bags of potato chips from the vending machines, got bored quickly.

That was about it for Dennis. He stopped coming to dance recitals, and didn't show up at my Confirmation—the bizarre ritual of the priest slapping your cheek and making you an official Catholic—or graduation, though he insisted that he had been there, lingering in the back against the wall. Just long enough to watch me accept a certificate and then dash out the church doors. I would go to his work when I snuck into Boston with Marisol, in hopes he'd give me money, and he would. Five dollars, ten dollars. He sold postage stamps at a big post office downtown. It had taken him forever to work his way up from sorting packages in the back, to this esteemed position behind the counter, serving the public in his blue shirt. Then one day he wasn't there anymore. Nobody knew why, or where he'd gone, or even who he was at all. Just, *I don't think he works here anymore.* I left him messages on his answering machine at home, a place he never seemed to be. Shy at first, growing angry, until finally I yelled, and then he called me back. He yelled, too. *I am still your father, you don't talk to me like that, ever.* You're Not My Father, I cried hoarsely. Fathers See Their Kids! We hung up on each other. Then his phone was disconnected, and Dennis was gone. Ma scavenged scraps of information, he was seen here, seen there. At the funeral for a newly dead aunt I'd never met. Drinking at Max's, a bar down the street from my school. Drinking there a lot. He'd been fired, Ma had divined, for being drunk, and on drugs, too. He had plans to move to Florida. Uncle Joey had all the information, and he wasn't telling. *I don't think he wants you all to know,* he said uncomfortably on the telephone. Child-support checks, always erratic and preceded by an angry telephone conversation with Ma, stopped. I thought she should take him to court, but Ma bristled. *I don't need his money. I don't want his money.* I did. When the five o'clock news did specials on deadbeat dads, I thought of Dennis somewhere, drinking a beer and watching the news, thinking of us.

THE CHELSEA WHISTLE

Rita Blanchetta lived down the street, and there were reasons why I couldn't hang out with her. My mother tried to blame it on Rita being older than me, but she wasn't all that much older, she just looked it. Will stuck up for her. *Never judge a girl by the size of her boobs,* he said one afternoon as Rita left our house, her giant teenage tits held tight and buoyant beneath a glitter-decal T-shirt. Yeah, I chimed in, but in my heart I knew my mom was right. I was out of my league with Rita, and her boobs were only the most obvious indication.

I was wild that summer, or the summer wanted me to be wild, called me to be wild like the kids who played chicken on the tracks across the street, seeing how many times they could dart across the rails before the big dark train plowed them down. They gripped the candy-striped board of wood that hung down to keep the cars at bay. When the train was gone and everything was safe again, the striped board would rise to let the cars through, and the kids would be lifted into the air, their legs kicking in their jeans. Sometimes the board would crack, jagged wood splintering sharply from big kids trying to hang on. I had tried it once, back in the winter when the sky got dark so early. The wooden board was lowered and the warning lights flashed like cigarettes as I sprinted across the dark stripes of train tracks. The train was a circle of light in the distance that grew brighter as the earth began to rumble and shake. This boy who liked me grabbed me before I could try to run across again, held me in a tight hug, and I felt dangerous and beautiful like the girl from *Footloose* when she straddled the windows of the two speeding cars, a semi charging toward her middle. I wanted the whole summer to be like that moment, beating the train and landing in a pair of arms that understood that I was an animal, wild. That summer I would pull my stereo into the hallway, drag the speakers onto the front steps with the mismatched lions on either side. I would play the Go-Go's, and Rod Stewart, Human League. I turned the white plastic stereo up loud on the street and I sat there, aching. Every time my mother said, *Too old for toys, too young for boys,* I wanted to kill her. I was thirteen years old and after the summer I would be in eighth grade. I had gotten my period, and after the initial Judy Blume-esque excitement waned, I learned how disgusting it was to have a goopy, crusty mound wedged between your legs, always afraid someone could see it. My mother didn't even want to discuss tampons, there was something disturbingly sexual about them. You put them in a hole. Where was the hole, exactly. It had to hurt.

I was not too old for toys. There was a big black plastic trash bag in the closet me and Madeline shared, the bag was dusty and torn from the stabbing plastic legs of Barbies and all their jumbly furniture. Inside the bag were dozens of dolls, and a slew of outfits.

I still loved to snap the clothes on them and tie the tiny sashes, pull the shiny synthetic hair into tangled ponytails. Soon I would start butchering their hair and coloring it with magic markers, but for now I still enjoyed the fall blondness. And I wasn't too young for boys. Johnny was a secret because even though he wasn't Puerto Rican he looked like he was and my mother would kill me. Johnny was Native American. *Indian*, he said. His hair was fine and slippery black and long for a boy. I saw him riding around on a pink girl's Huffy and I said to my friends, That's A Girl's Bike. I Bet He Stole It. *It's my sister's bike*, he told me, and I relaxed into the idea of Johnny as a nice boy who wasn't dangerous, even though he looked tough and went to public school. We would walk together on the train tracks that led to the shitty little park with the tall weeds and graffitied plastic jungle gym. Walking the train tracks always felt like accepting a dare. You entered in the sunlight, walking board to board or atop the dully gleaming iron rails that you could leave a penny on and wait for a train to squash into a smooth blob of copper. There was stuff on the tracks. Railroad spikes were cool, heavy and greasy with flakes of rust crumbling into a fine brown dust on your palm. A dog got hit once and there were bloody chunks of fur and bone scattered up and down that stretch of rail that led to the park. It was a blond dog, and we found its severed head in the shady part of the tracks, where they ran beneath the bridge. It was there against the concrete wall, where spurts of green weeds grew from the cracks. Kids poked it with sticks. Underneath the bridge that blocked the sun was the most thrilling stretch of the train tracks. I saw a lot of dick there. Men hung out on the bridge rafters, reaching into their pants and yelling, *Hey*, or making those squishy gross kissing noises, and when you looked up they had their cocks in their hands. It was a good place to sneak cigarettes and also to stash your pack, safe from the rain, hidden in the weeds like that dead dog's head. The train tracks were a short cut to the park or the mall, but I wasn't allowed to use it because it was so desolate, and I could get whacked by a train. Me and Johnny, who in less than a day became my boyfriend, would walk the tracks to the run-down park and sit together on an orange play structure. Boyfriends just occurred out of nowhere when everyone was thirteen and horny with no social skills. A boy I had never seen before would decide he liked me, and a friend would be sent over with a message: *He wants to go out with you.* I'd say okay. Suddenly I'd have a boyfriend. Me and Johnny did not make out in the empty park. We talked a lot, I remember talking, and thinking, Johnny's Deep. I thought it was because he was an Indian and all of his people were gone. They'd all been killed, by white people like me. I was upset that it had happened, and Johnny didn't seem to hold me responsible but it ended shortly anyway.

After Johnny I got another boyfriend, Paulie Cannessa, a good name. He wore a hooded sweatshirt, the hood tugged over his head and his eyes burning out from it like the grim reaper. He lived down the street and I had first heard about him from Nora, who lived in the red house across the street. Me and Nora were friends, which was also a problem, because Nora was sixteen. *Why would a sixteen-year-old want to hang out with you?!* My mother demanded during one of our Nora fights. Oh, Maybe Because I'm Nice, I fumed. Because I'm Smart. Because I'm Funny. My mother drove me crazy. I could only assume she thought I had no personality. Will was more direct with his concerns: *Sixteen-year-olds have filthy mouths,* he said. *All they talk about is sex.* Well, that was true. That was why I loved hanging out with Nora. To my mother's credit, something about Nora was a little off. I was a mature thirteen-year-old, but she was an immature sixteen-year-old. We fixed her attic up into a sort of clubhouse, and Nora put a blue light in the window that looked out onto ragged Heard Street. *Blue lights mean you're having sex,* Nora informed me, and I loved when people let me in on the secret codes. I knew there must be lots of them. Life was a joke, the punch line went over my head and I knew it had to do with sex. If I could just understand that part then everything else would fall into place.

Nora had a boyfriend named Stevie, who was a jerk. He had short hair that was kind of colorless, and bad skin that was not rugged. He was a bully. I was always having to tell him to shut up. Stevie finger-fucked Nora on the train tracks, and she told me it felt good. Really? *It felt really good,* she told me and I didn't believe her. Nora told me Paulie Cannessa who lived down the street was going to ask me out. Who Is He? I asked, bewildered. How Do You Know? *Say yes,* Nora urged me. *He's cute.* So Paulie came to my door and asked me out in this mumbly way that was sexy on boys. I said yes and went back in my house. I had a boyfriend.

Me and Paulie hung out after school. He was kind of an asshole. He would run up to people and hop on their backs and yell, *Turbo!* He would also bend his elbows and move them back and forth and thrust his pelvis out like fucking and go, *Up the bum!* and spit a raspberry, that farting sound you make with your lips. It was gross. One night me and Paulie and Nora played Spin the Bottle. It was so stupid. Basically me and Nora took turns kissing Paulie. And it wasn't a bottle, it was a stick of roll-on deodorant. It didn't bother me to watch Nora kissing Paulie. I mean, I understood that it was weird for Nora to be kissing my "boyfriend," but I didn't feel anything about it. I thought Nora was ugly. Her body fit her like a too-big pair of pants that chafed when she walked. And her hair was dumb. She couldn't put on makeup any better than I could, but she was sixteen. When Nora kissed Paulie she closed her eyes and their lips moved around on each other like they were eating. It sounded wet. I spun the Ban Roll-On and its smooth round head landed on Nora. I spun again and it landed on Nora. I spun it until it landed on Paulie. He had his hood up like always with the drawstrings dangling and ratty where he chewed them, his hands shoved in the pouch on his belly. When he put his hands on me I shivered. His mouth was full, and it sucked my lips in like little bits of food. His tongue poked in and wiggled around and I decided I didn't want to go out with Paulie Cannessa. Certainly this would be the start of something. He would expect me to tongue-kiss him again, and he would want to finger-fuck me on the train tracks. Forget it. It was easy to break up with these boys because the whole thing was so vague to begin with. Me and Nora got in a fight on a Saturday when we were supposed to go ice skating and when I tried to talk to her she said, *I'm not going to fight with a thirteen-year-old!* All of a sudden it counted that I was thirteen. I went across the street and didn't hang out with Nora again.

I think that when you want things so badly, it shows on your body. When you're young like that, it's when you want things the worst and you don't even know how to hide it. You don't even know that it shows, like your slip hanging out from the hem of your skirt. The lump of your pad on the ass of your jeans. I had a reputation as a slut before I ever kissed anyone, and I understood even then that being a slut wasn't really about what you did, it was about who you were. Something invisible that wrapped all around you. It clung to my skin like the wet summer air, and I didn't know how to shake it. I sat in it on my front steps, playing my music, my legs bare and skinny, jutting out of my shorts. Boys old enough to drive rode by in cars, windows down, their own music spilling onto the street, yelling something out the window as they rolled past, their voices lost in the hot, thick air. Everything was slow motion in the humidity. Rita Blanchetta was outside on the corner. She always was. Her hair was blond, a dirty blond. The sides flipped back and there was a patch at the bottom that was bleached a perfect chemical white. It looked like a feather hung in her hair, and Rita did wear feather earrings. Her eyeliner was blue and thick and smudgy, eyelashes were stiff black bristles. Girls in my Catholic school who didn't wear makeup and had the right modest outfits would fool around with boys and no one called them sluts. Rita and her friends looked like the biggest whores and certainly they did things with boys and no one called them sluts, either. No one would dare. I didn't understand how these different girls managed to protect themselves. Rita's jeans were so tight. They clung to the swell of her ass, folding beneath the curve when she walked, the denim there soft and faded like the spots on her knees. Her shirts were tight across her formidable tits, and she turned me on to putting fuzzy decals on the shoulders of your shirts, where men get tattoos. Rita always got *Playboy* bunnies, but you could also get lightning bolts and fat round hearts, at the T-shirt shop at the mall. If you were like me and found out late about this fashion option, you could bring all your old shirts down to the shop and for only fifty cents they would sear these symbols onto your sleeve. I had a baseball shirt with deep blue three-quarter-length sleeves and a shimmering Def Leppard decal on the front. A light pink *Playboy* bunny on the shoulder and my name on the back. My favorite shirt. I have a picture from that summer, I'm wearing the shirt and my hair is kind of feathered and very streaked from Sun-In. I would pump the stuff on my hair and then bake it in with a blowdryer. I wasn't allowed to bleach, but Sun-In was okay. It was natural, kind of. It actually turned my hair calico, lifting some locks to blond while refusing to budge from orange in others. And the roots stayed brown. My mother realized too late that Sun-In was more dangerous than she thought, and at Assumption I was yelled at for bleaching my hair. It's Sun-In, I defended myself, but the school made no such distinctions.

School let out like a fever breaking. That summer I could see that I would not end up like the Catholic-school girls, I would not learn to carry myself with their discretion, I would always just watch and feel dirty. Rita stood on the corner and I watched her smoke. She didn't hide it like the Catholic-school girls who cupped their smokes in their hands and crouched behind parked cars. Rita clasped the length of her cigarette between two thin fingers and took a long, showy drag. She was surrounded by boys like usual, this gang of older boys who lived on Heard Street. I hated when my mother sent me to the store and I had to walk by them. Jackson Smith was so cute, blond hair blue eyes, so sweet-looking, but he would bark at me and call me a dog when I passed. The Diaz brothers were older and seemed to be bored with harassment, they would ignore me. Sometimes Paulie Cannessa, my old beau, would be there, and he would nod at me coolly. There would be silence as I passed, and then when I was about a block away, an explosion of laughter. One of the boys was Rita's brother, he was okay. Darryl. He didn't bother me so much. His friend Ricky sucked, and Lenny was really bad, the worst. And he was cute, too, the cutest one, with squinty eyes and wavy hair. He looked like Huey Lewis. If he called me over I'd have to go, because he was so cute, and my heart would thump and I would pray inside my head to please let him be nice, let him do something nice, and he'd be holding something, a tree branch, in his hand and *whump!* hit me in the crotch with it. I couldn't cross the street when I saw them because they'd see me and would never let me get away with acting so scared. The best I could do was take entirely different routes that led me whole neighborhoods out of my way, but even that wasn't foolproof because those neighborhoods had their own packs of Lennys and Jacksons.

The city was a landmine of dangerous boys and Rita stood among them, fearless, swishing her long hair. She had a friend named Heidi who looked just like her only her hair was permed. Heidi had the same patch of blond at the end of her hair, more yellow than white because her hair was darker. She had the fuzzy decals on her sleeves and a round pin, black, with a white *Playboy* bunny on it. They stood among these boys and somehow they were safe. Occasionally they'd swat one, *Shaaat tha fwaaack ahp*—they had those voices, the accent I was trying to escape by carefully pronouncing my Rs, rounding out my words. *You sound like you're from Canada,* my mother commented. It worked. People always tell me I don't sound like I'm from Boston. But now I like the accent, and it's too late, it's gone. Sometimes when I'm drunk or really excited it comes back. The Rs take too long to sound out, and my tongue flies right over them. But Rita's accent was intense. I couldn't understand why she wanted to be friends with me. I guess she got in a fight with Heidi, her twin, and was desperate. It was just her and the boys, and she tried to pull me into that treacherous circle. When Rita first came up to me I was sure she was going to start a fight with me, and I was thinking quick. But she was nice. She recruited me into her fashion and for that I was grateful. First decal tip, then I soaked and soaked a clump of my hair in Sun-In, trying to get the feather effect she and Heidi had shared, but it just got oranger and oranger. *You gotta use bleach,* Rita advised, but I couldn't. My mother.

I slept at Rita's house once. I wore a pair of her baby-doll pajamas and slept beside her on top of all the covers because it was just so hot. The filmy curtains in the window above her bed were still, there was no breeze. In the morning her parents were there, they seemed like they used to be hippies, or maybe bikers, and Rita herself told me they used to smoke pot. Her brother Darryl was home, he couldn't leave the house because he was on some medication that gave him a rash if he went in the sun. Outside there was nothing but sun, glaring off the houses and making the street shimmer with heat. Lenny, that creep, came over and he was so surprised to see me there, inside Rita and Darryl's home. Drinking my morning Coke at the table, still in the fluffy baby-doll outfit. He could not say anything. I was safe, inside Rita's house. You could see it throw him off. He was having to reassess and reformulate everything. He scowled. I liked being with Rita, but it always felt like something bad could happen. We'd be out on the front steps and the whole troupe of boys would come down the street and I would fill with dread. I would figure out a reason to go home. Sometimes Rita would come along, and sometimes she would persuade me to stay. Amazingly enough, when I was with her, the boys would leave me alone. They'd play hockey in the slow street, scratching their plastic sticks on the hot pavement. Pushing and tripping each other. They had a special whistle Rita told me was the Chelsea Whistle. These boys would use it when there was trouble. Like if another group of boys started a fight, they would make this noise with their lips and boys would come from all around to help. It sounded magic. The Chelsea Whistle. Rita knew how to do it. She tried to teach me but I didn't want to learn. It wasn't for me. The boys it was meant to call were the boys I would need to be saved from.

Since Marisol was away in Kentucky that summer, visiting her dad and the legendary redneck cousins, my Catholic-school friend that season was Cheryl. Cheryl went to Assumption, but she was more like me, not like the girls who knew how to act good. She had long brown hair, thick and uncontrollable, and a pudgy cute face, a little smile, dark eyelashes and freckles. I tried to hang out with Rita and Cheryl together, but Rita would ignore Cheryl. She only wanted me. So Cheryl wouldn't come around if I was with Rita, and so Cheryl faded away. Rita always showed up quicker because she lived on my street. Once, I had specific Cheryl plans, and Rita came over first. Everyone was going pool hopping, *Come on, let's go.* Pool hopping at the Chelsea Pool, the big blue pool that cost a quarter, and I wasn't allowed to go in it. Because it was dirty, all the kids peed in it. Plus, I might get beat up. My childhood, a constant struggle to keep me away from my environment. But to go at night, to sneak in with all the big kids, to swim in the dark without all the little shits pissing in the shallow end and trying to dunk you. We would climb the fence, Rita said, or one of the boys would bring fence cutters and just cut the thing down. I was such a dork. I told my mom what we were going to do. I had a problem seeing my mother as an authority. She was just someone to report things to. I liked the idea of a parent who was more like a friend, so I would just pretend that that was the situation, and hope it caught on. Ma went nutty. *You know what'll happen?* she demanded. *You'll get arrested! You want to go to jail?* I scoffed. Cops wouldn't arrest a bunch of hot kids for stealing a swim! I really believed in the goodness of youth. The kids would prevail. The idea of scaling the chain link and plunging into the illegal waters was beautiful to me, so *Outsiders*. But none of these boys were Ponyboy. *You're not going anywhere with those punks on the corner,* my mother snapped. Okay. I thought about mean Lenny. Would he push me in? Would he dunk me and hold me under? Probably he would. In the dark, with no lifeguard but Rita. Maybe Mom was right.

After dinner I went to Rita's house with my bathing suit tight under my shorts. It was aqua and white, the top was two wide sashes that came up over your tits and tied behind your neck, creating a V that plunged down to your belly. It looked really Lolita on me, pretty pathetic. I had another bathing suit, intensely French cut with a *Playboy* bunny-shaped screen on the ass. When you lay on your belly in the sun, the bunny would get tanned onto your butt. Like the fuzzy decals, but more permanent. Kind of like a tattoo. Only the bathing suit sat on your ass a little different each time, so you ended up with this tanned blotch instead. I went to Rita's house to wait for the boys with the fence cutter, but they never came. *Fwaaack 'em,* Rita said. We did something else instead, and Cheryl came to my house and I wasn't there and so she didn't want to be my friend anymore. Then I didn't want to be Rita's friend anymore. It was just too stressful. I wasn't like her. I wasn't like anyone. I was supposed to go into Boston to see the Fourth of July fireworks with Rita and her stoned parents, and I didn't. I pretended I was sick and I lay on my bed and I cried. I Have No Friends, I wailed. The dark air outside boomed with fireworks. They were so gigantic, they echoed over the harbor and into Chelsea. I cried all night and my mother didn't even feel bad because I had sold Cheryl out for Rita and her *Playboy* accessories. *Maybe you should call Cheryl and say you're sorry.* I hated hearing it but she was right. I called and said the words and my chest ached and me and Cheryl were friends again, for a while. She actually ended up more like Rita than I ever was. She got this boyfriend who was tough but nice. Eric, long hair and denim. He was from California, supposedly he had been in this gang called the War Pigs. I found out from Cheryl that Eric sold pot to Will.

Will had married my mother while me and Madeline were off on a trip to New Hampshire with our grandparents. Somehow he managed to skip regular stepfatherhood, and become my actual father. The whole newly configured family had gone to a small courtroom in Boston, very early in the morning, sticky sugar donuts in our hands, and my sister and I told a judge lady that we loved Will and wanted him to be our dad. We got new last names and new birth certificates with Will's name on them, like the other guy never even existed at all. It was creepy. That you could stamp someone out like that, officially, in an official room using important documents. Was I supposed to act like my first father never happened, that Will had always been there? Or did I just then come into existence, there in the dark New England courthouse with an altered birth certificate reading "Michelle Tomacheski" in my greasy sugar fingers. It was so strange. Will simply was not my father, hadn't been there, had only just showed up. I didn't understand it except as a slap to my first father, who none of us liked so that was cool. It seemed more vengeful than anything. And egotistical. Will didn't like being referred to as a "step" father, second prize. I thought about Dennis not wanting to be a "part-time" father. These men were such babies. Their ownership of me and Madeline was a constant legal battle. But having Will around was good, even if he was being greedy about the daughter thing. We'd never had some-one as cool as Will inside our home—the blurry green tattoos he got in jail, his old life in the square, drugs and fistfights. It was okay to like these things about Will because they were his legend, not who he was now. Now he was good, though he still went drinking with his old friends, tough, weird guys, men who appeared to still be teenagers. But we saw them rarely. Will had settled down and we were legally his new family. He still smoked pot—bought it from my friends and asked them not to tell me.

I pretended I knew all about it when Cheryl told me about the deal in a buzz of excited whispers. I was so furious, I acted real whatever about it. I had already known that Will smoked pot. My sister found a joint once, hidden on top of the medicine cabinet. They tried to blame it on some carpenters who had been fixing the shower, but I knew the truth. It made Madeline really paranoid. She was certain our parents were doing cocaine. Oh Come On, Mad-eline, They're Just Drunk. I hated watching her cry and freak out. But she was right, Will was snorting coke and smoking pot and getting it from people I knew. Steve Elliot was a lot older, part of a group of boys who were about eighteen it seemed, and hung around outside Dick's, the bar where Will drank. Steve let me and Cheryl dunk our fingers in a tiny scatter of coke and rub it on our gums so they turned numb. We got a little hyper, too, but it could have been the excitement of being so close to something so illegal.

DRUGGIE

We knew that all that crap about marijuana being a gateway drug was just that, a bunch of crap. *I'm not going to be, like, a druggie*, Marisol asserted, letting the stinky burning smoke escape her mouth like a cartoon bubble. The smoke wisped over Marisol's long, unruly blond hair, so many different shades of blond, of gold, and the smoke slid over it in a way that I thought was very Stevie Nicks. It was nice to smoke anything because it made life more like a video, framed in grey wisps. Marisol's blue eyes, which always looked stoned anyway, getting her into trouble even when she was sober, well, now that they *were* stoned they looked lovely—natural, bluer, wetter. Smoke and water. I'm Not Gonna Be A Druggie Either, I agreed, and took the fragile, smouldering paper from her fingers. There were Fuck Up Your Life drugs, like heroin, and there were No Big Deal drugs, like pot, which made you giggle. In the hilly, wooded expanse of land that tangled behind the VA hospital where Ma

and Will worked, me and Marisol smoked our secret joint and
lay in the weedy dirt, not even caring about the bugs and broken
glass and probably dried boy-pee getting in our long hair. We lay
back and we let the marijuana open our minds. We considered
LSD. Maybe it was okay, it seemed creative, a lot of artists did
it, right, so that could be cool, though hallucinations seemed
scary—didn't it make people think they were birds, make them
leap from buildings and die twisted on the concrete? Pills
seemed really unpredictable, and PCP was out of the question,
definitely, because it turned people into maniacs. Like Hector,
who hung out around Chelsea and was generally nice, not such a
big asshole, but then he'd do PCP and go crazy and start beating
up cars. Heroin was an absolute No, not ever ever ever, unless,
we conceded, we were doing it with Billy Idol. We agreed on a
general Billy Idol drug clause: any drug, no matter how dangerous, heinous or scary, could be done if you were doing it with
Billy Idol, who did lots of drugs, we knew. On David Letterman he talked about how East Village druggies honored him
by taking his song titles as code names for their drug of choice.
Quaaludes were "Rebel Yell"; cocaine "White Wedding." He
looked so fucked up, talking to Letterman. A big sloppy stoned
smile, pinned eyes. *You must be a very proud young man,* the
host said dryly. Billy was fascinating. I read in *Rolling Stone* that
he put his entire fist up a girl's vagina once. It hurt his hand,
made it red and swollen. Maybe there were teeth up there after
all. What About David Lee Roth? I asked Marisol, there in the
woods. We mulled it over. That area behind the VA hospital was
the only part of Chelsea, besides the cemetery, that had any trees
at all. Lying there like that, all high with the clouds skimming

the treetops above your head, you could pretend you were some-place better than Chelsea. I tried to imagine where else I could be, someplace cool with trees. Hmmm. New Hampshire had lots of trees, but who cared, it was boring. Plus it had *too many* trees. Too many trees was scary, you could get killed and there'd be no one around to help you. Even animals got killed in places with too many trees. *David Lee Roth . . .* , Marisol was musing. She had the butt of the joint, the tiny part, the roach. I couldn't smoke it when it got so small and burned my lip, but Marisol sucked it right up. Nah, Not Heroin, I decided for us. Just With Billy Idol I'd Do It. *I'd do anything,* Marisol sighed. We thought about Billy tying a bandanna around our thin muscles and slip-ping a needle into the most delicate skin. We'd be in New York City, wearing excellent clothing with rips all over, we'd be high on drugs and Billy would kiss us. I closed my eyes and felt dizzy. I wished some cute boys would walk out of the trees with more pot and share it with us and think we were pretty. Cute boys who didn't think Billy Idol was a fag, who weren't mean. How sucky it was to be twelve, or thirteen, and really understand that huge excellent things were happening all over the place, in all the places you weren't. I felt tugged, a real torture, like life was strung up inside me, bucking at the reins. It drove me to tears. There was nothing to do but grow up, and it took so long. In *Rolling Stone,* Billy Idol called the residents of New York City *my people,* and it haunted me, fired me with an anxious ache. Where were my people? I knew that I had them and maybe my people were the same as Billy's. Could they tell that someone was coming, growing up slow as winter in a bleak town, my heart churning toward them?

On Washington Ave in Chelsea, Massachusetts, where I was unfortunate enough to have been born, I passed one dollar and change to my best friend Marisol, and she bought the marijuana from an older teenager we called Jelly Crackers. Jelly Crackers was always stoned, and it seemed to keep him friendly. One of those extremely red-faced Irish boys, red as a lobster in the pot, translucent hair. It seemed like his eyebrows and hair had been singed by a flaming Bic, but they were just so light you couldn't catch them, only the tomato face, the bloodshot eyes. Sylvia Patti's big sister had gone to grammar school with Jelly Crackers, whose real name was Kevin, and she told Sylvia about the Saltine and Welch's sandwiches he would bring in his lunch box, falling out of a baggie, hence the nickname. Sylvia had a crush on him, and it gave her material to flirt with. Sylvia was an expert on nicknames, since she was unlucky enough to have a last name that leant itself easily to juvenile degradation—she was Beef Patti when we were just kidding around, Chicken Patti when she was being chicken-shit, Fish Patti when we really hated her.

Sylvia was my on-again off-again enemy, for no particular reason. It just seemed like you needed to have your own personal enemy, a mortal foe, a girl to hate, like a favorite color or rockstar on your wall, or a real boy to claim as your own with a crush. And Sylvia hated me first. She went to St. Rose with Marisol, and told her, my best friend, that I was a bitch, and that she was going to kick my ass. Oh Yeah? I said, excited. I was pinning a friendship pin on my sneaker laces, a shining safety pin Marisol had piled up with beads because we were each other's. I'll Kick Her Ass, I crowed. I was so glad to finally be threatened by a girl I thought I could take. As opposed to Lillian, my most recent problem girl. Lillian who gave blowjobs to boys in her hallway, who had called my house and told my *mother* that she was on her way over to kick my ass. We were coloring Easter eggs in the kitchen. Ma was holding her egg in its delicate copper wire, blue vinegar dripping into the little cup. *Someone named Lillian is coming over to kick your ass?* On the plastic stereo, Quiet Riot jeered its promise to get wild. *Turn that down,* Ma said, irritated. I was terrified. Let's Turn The Lights Out, I said in a panic. *We are not turning the lights out,* she snapped. *Who is Lillian?* A girl with no father, with a mean mother slowly dying on a bed in the middle of their lousy house. Parents had ceased to be a deterrent of any kind to Lillian. She was going to come and beat me up in front of my mother. Of course she never showed up, but I was so scared. She could have wrecked me. It was always girls like that coming after me, girls that made me want to make my whole family duck behind dark curtains. But a girl like Sylvia I could maybe beat up. We were drawn to each other the way people of similar levels of physical attraction are drawn to each other for breeding purposes. I read that one in *Cosmo*. Me and Sylvia were on the same plain of toughness, or lack thereof. So we got in a big fistfight in the big park behind the VA hospital, our wilderness. The big grassy park that sloped down into the tangle of trees and dirt where we liked to smoke our pot.

The day of the fight I had all my friends with me, but they all went to St. Rose with Sylvia and were being impartial, which pissed me off. I had a row of friendship pins jiggling on my sneakers from those bitches, like little implements of voodoo. Where were they when I needed them? Cheryl, who went to Assumption and was all mine, started heckling Sylvia right off the bat, very cool. Cheryl with her long brown tangles and a gust of freckles blown onto her face. Cheryl was Canadian, which was sort of exotic since nobody else was. Her mom was divorced, and recently she had gone out dancing and come home with a reddish-purple blotch of hickey on her neck. Cheryl cried about it in the schoolyard at recess, then asked her mother about it that night. Her mom had just been trying on punk-rock outfits at a store in Boston, and got her neck caught in the zipper! We thought it was so cool that her mom had gone to a punk-rock store in the city, and dreamed about what the violent shirt had looked like.

Cheryl was my opening act with her heckles at Sylvia. *Douche bag!* Cheryl huffed. God bless her. *Whore!* sneered Sylvia. Don't Call Her A Whore, Bitch! I jumped in. We were reading each other's cues. *What's she, your lover?* Sylvia taunted, which was my cue to punch. The suggestion of gayness was as low as you could go, there simply was no comeback for such a sick insult. I swung at Sylvia. My fist shot up and maybe thudded against her lamely before spinning up to the bright Chelsea sky. It was a nice day. We all had parkas on, light jackets. I never knew if the word was really "parka," or "parker," but the accent fucked it up. Sylvia slugged me pathetically, and we gave up trying to fight with any skill or dignity and grabbed fistfuls of each other's hair and spun around in the grass. Let Go *No you let go* No You Let Go! I had more hair than Sylvia, thick and wiry like a horse's tail, a mass of fat snarls you could sink your hand into and never come back. We were attached. I bit her face. Sylvia gasped. It was as if I'd kissed her, so intimate, my mouth on her face. That was gross. That was too much. A pink blotch bloomed in the place I'd just held between my teeth, a little pinch, the plump of her cheeks. We kicked each other in the shins, while shuffling awkwardly to avoid oncoming shin-kicks. It was slapstick, a dance of goons, while our friends cheered us on. Sylvia let go first, releasing a clump of my hair, which meant I won. Right? *Yeah, you won,* I was assured. Sylvia had let go first, and I had bitten her in the face, proving my intense dedication to causing her pain. Me and Sylvia were friends after that, but it was always shaky, and plus, her mother wouldn't let her hang out with me.

But it was Sylvia who introduced us to Jelly Crackers, and therefore to the giggly bliss of marijuana, my favorite gateway drug. Three for five, three joints for five dollars, skunky shake bundled up in fragile wrappers, you bit one end off, creating a hole to suck the smoke through. The other end caught fire and you blew it out, then sucked deep to keep the heat there, managing the burning tip by blowing on it, don't let it canoe—burn at an inefficient slant and waste the pot. My mouth would fill with water, water poured from my eyes and my whole body rattled with coughing. After my body settled I'd relax into the dirt and scraggle in the woods behind the Soldier's Home. I'd lean back against the big boulder where countless girls had spotted naked men sitting, perverts waiting for a girl to stumble down the gritty path and scream. My back against the rock, I let the pot open my mind. Thoughts were whirling in there, too complicated to talk about, but they felt good inside my brain. A certain understanding was entering me, and it made me feel peaceful and giggly. Soon I wasn't being chomped with longing from the inside, so impatient. I was alive and on drugs. Marisol, I breathed, We're On Drugs. That was funny, we laughed and returned to our fantastic thoughts. I had already accepted that I was being lied to by the world on a regular basis, that the things everyone told me to stay away from were in fact the funnest things, and my insides were marked from my craving. Why, I asked, Is Pot Not Okay, But Beer Is Okay? *Beer's not okay,* Marisol reminded me. Not For Us, But For Grownups, I sighed, the weight of hypocrisy squishing air from my wheezing, adolescent lungs. If you smoked Newports after pot it made you higher. It had glass in it that made your lungs bleed, but not if you only smoked them sometimes, like when you were getting high.

The places that were bad were always the places I most wanted to go. My mother pulled me out of my bed right around that time, to see the movie version of *Go Ask Alice*. She did it to make me scared of drugs, but it just made me want to pop Bennies and run away from home. It was exciting. Smoking Marlboros with Marisol, we planned our escape to New York City. We would wait till we were sixteen and had tits and were pretty, because the only way we could think to make money was to pose for *Playboy*. It was such a dirty thing, we figured not many girls would do it. *Playboy* would be desperate for models, and happy to have us. Me and Marisol would shave our heads into perfect Mohawks that stretched to the sky like the tall New York buildings. We would befriend Billy Idol. We had this plan, we would find out where he lived, ring his bell and pass out on his doorstep. He couldn't leave two unconscious girls on his doorstep. He would have to carry us inside, touch us, lay us on his furniture, and when we came to, he would see what wild young things we were, and he would want to be our boyfriend. We would extend our skinny arms and let him sink the needle in the tender crook. We wanted New York City because it was filthy, a city filled with dark streets, clogged with garbage and huge buildings to blot out the sun, to make it nighttime always. A place with sneaky subways rumbling under the ground, where all the men were murderers and all the women were hookers who got to wear sexy clothes, and there would be tons of punk rockers with Mohawks. God, we wanted to leave right then, lying around stoned in the dirty dirt. We wanted to rush onto a bus and let the crimped door swoosh shut behind us. If only our parents beat us we would have a reason to run away. As it was, things weren't abusive, just dismal. When we were sixteen we would be braver.

When Marisol was sixteen her hair was long thick gold and she had "Voivod" painted red like blood on the back of her motorcycle jacket. She borrowed my witchcraft book and did the spell where you sewed all your anger into a pillow and slept with it beneath your head. Next she read *Dianetics,* a fat little book she said explained everything. Then she started going to TWIG meetings—Teens With Interest in God. I went to one with her. I had such faith in Marisol, I thought maybe she had found something. On a couch in the den of somebody's house, Marisol spoke in tongues, a thick, rolling gibberish that was the language of the angels. Her eyes were closed and trembling as all the sounds tumbled out. This really hyper boy handed me a fake check and told me it was for eternal life but only Jesus could cash it. At the bank that was church. Something lousy was happening to Marisol. I called her house and her mom said she was at a Jesus meeting. *Why can't she be into sex and drugs like all the other kids?* she lamented. Eventually, Marisol would meet a strange, quiet God boy, and together they would hitch out into the country to go to a rural Amy Grant concert. I didn't get why she had to totally change her taste in music and stop liking Metallica and Voivod just because she started liking Jesus. Amy Grant was terrible. Marisol was looking for God.

She moved to the Midwest with that vacant, dark-eyed boy, she cut off all her blond hair and had babies. It was a terrible fate, not the one we dreamed foggy, marijuana dreams about, lying in the woods.

Sometimes Tiffany, who went to St. Rose with Marisol, would join us in our quiet forest. The two of them hallucinated on pot, or claimed to. I was skeptical. I had read it was possible, but never came close to such a lapse of control. They said they saw the Wizard of Marijuana traipsing through our urban campground. *There he is!* Marisol would gasp. *Like a little leprechaun!* Tiffany gushed. I didn't see anything. Tiffany and Marisol just wanted to bond, and it left me out, but that was okay. I was high and felt content and it didn't matter if I didn't see the Wizard. I knew that I was Marisol's best friend, I was the one most like her.

When the pot wore off and the doomed feeling, the restlessness, the idea of life passing us by returned, we'd start lighting things on fire. The cellophane that wrapped our cigarettes went up quick, a hot liquid collapse. Plastic bags bubbled like cheese and smelled awful. The smoke was thin and black. Styrofoam crinkled and melted beneath the attack of our lighters, and paper was perfect. You could hold it, twirl it daringly in your hands, a bouquet of flame. Dry leaves and grass. We nearly lit the whole forest on fire once, burned our little sanctuary down. When it rose up, we jumped into it like splashing in a puddle, stomping and stomping, a bunch of little witches, laughing.

Once, there was a guy at our rock. He had clothes on, and a little bottle of rush that he shared with us. *Sniff,* he said. He was older, not a kid, a real guy. I inhaled from the brown bottle. It started a whooshing in my head, a tiny storm. It buzzed away quickly, leaving a steady throb in my skull. Now I'd done two drugs, I thought proudly. Three if you counted the Vivarin. We'd bought a box once and scarfed a handful each, and by the time I got home I was freaked out nervous, just all twitchy and panicked and sick to my stomach. At home *Animal House* was on TV, and I sat in the armchair and fidgeted, nauseated, until I burst into tears. I told my mother what I'd done. *Those are drugs!* she'd yelled at me, her face crunched with concern. She put me to bed, the worst thing for someone who's overdosed on Vivarin. I rocked beneath my sheets, wishing I could just tear the skin from my bones and finally be free. I felt crawly, and remembered Uncle Markie's coke bugs. Was this what it felt like? *Those are drugs!* my mother had gasped, so there you go. I guess I'd done three: pot, Vivarin and the invisible fumes from the quiet man's bottle.

I was thirteen, at the mall down the tracks, the Mystic Mall, down at the edge of town. Chelsea was such a piece-of-shit city, it was horrifying that someone had put a mall in it. What would they sell? It was an act of desperation, something had to save our city. They built the mall on this patch of land that had been burnt to the ground during the big Chelsea fire, when half the city went up in flames and the sun was choked in soot for a week. It must have looked like Armageddon. I was an infant, and my grandfather was out of work with a heart attack, so he got stuck baby-sitting me. It was coming up on Christmas, and he'd been home making these ornaments for the tree, Styrofoam balls covered with velvet and gold and beads, fastened with glinting pins and ribbon. They really were beautiful, and the most fun ones to hang on our plastic tree, because of course we'd hear the story every year as we hung them. How he was making the Christmas balls and the town started burning down, so he went out to watch. Fire trucks came blaring in from all over Massachusetts, all their different colors and uniforms, people screaming, watching everything they had turn black and collapse into ash that blew up at the sun. It must have seemed like the end of the world. My grandfather took me out onto the steps in my diaper, and locked himself out of the house. There was no one there to let him in and I started crying in all the smoke and shitting in my diaper. He had just gotten out of the hospital, was in his undershirt, and we were both trapped outside in the cold and burning city.

I love fires. In first grade, Jenny's house across the street blazed all night, until it was pretty much gone, while we all watched out the window, the curtains pulled back from our faces. Watching out on the sidewalk would have been rude. No one at school liked Jenny, and I thought that would change once her house burned down but kids have no sympathy. Once, I saw a fire just getting started in the house next door, right on the porch, an orange rail of it, and I got to run down the street and pull the lever on the box. I'd always wanted to pull the fire alarm and never thought I'd get the chance to do it, so that was exciting.

They'd put the mall in the middle of the burnt lot that stopped smelling like fire a while ago and was filled now with brittle weeds, just daring someone to make it all happen again. The Mystic Mall. There was a Burger King in the parking lot, and the headlining stores were KMart and a giant Osco Drug. I got caught stealing lip-gloss in the KMart and afterward went and shoplifted more lip-gloss from Osco's just to make sure I could still do it, but I guess I didn't want to anymore. All the fun had gone out of it and now I was scared of getting caught. In KMart I had slipped the lip-gloss—Maybelline Kissing Potion, watermelon—up the sleeve of the bright red corduroy cheer-leading jacket Jenn Capoletti had let me borrow. Jenn was pissed that I'd done something illegal while wearing her precious jacket with her name stitched in cursive on the front. What if the KMart security guys didn't let her in the store now because they'd see that jacket and think she was the girl who clipped the lip-gloss? Jenn wanted all the angst of being an outlaw, but she didn't want to do any of the work. She was a cheerleader, after all. The worst was that I had screwed up, really screwed up: I'd made it out of the KMart with the smooth glass lip-gloss nestled against my arm, but then Vivian—a St. Rose friend of Marisol—who had been too scared inside the store to swipe anything, decided she wanted the lip-shaped eraser that had come free inside the package. I should have taken the makeup out of my coat, but I didn't, so high on the excitement of getting things for free. I walked back into the store with Vivian, brought her to the shelf of boy's underwear where I'd buried the ripped-open package, and coached her through slipping the lip-shaped eraser into her jeans. Then we walked out. We were stopped at the entrance by a guy in plainclothes who demanded to see the lip-gloss package I'd been walking around with. My heart was thudding up by my ears like a Sony Walkman. One pounding heart for each ear. I was dizzy. Vivian looked about to cry. I took the guy on a fruitless tour of the places I thought I'd "left" the makeup, until finally he asked to see my jacket. Okay I Took It, I confessed, and slid the tube from my wrist and handed it to him. *You, too,* he motioned to Vivian, and I burst out, She Didn't Know I Was Stealing, Let Her Go. Vivian looked bewildered enough, and was released from the KMart while I was brought back to a white room and interrogated by the smug security guard. *I got a sister your age,* he said. *I bet she doesn't shoplift.* I snorted. The guy reached into a desk and pulled out a pair of handcuffs, the serrated loops clanging on the chain. *I could put these on you, you know.* He was trying to be good cop and bad cop all rolled into one rent-a-cop. I almost wished he'd say something perverted so I could get him into trouble, and me out. But he just lectured. *First it's lip-gloss,* he said, *then maybe it's a shirt, then it's Mother's Day and you want to get some perfume for your mother. Next thing you know, you're stealing TVs.*

I got in a lot of trouble, and my life of crime went down the drain. I'd been sneaking into Boston a lot then, ripping off trinkets from the carts at Faneuil Hall. I'd wear a pair of tight and stretchy fingerless lace gloves, and craftily slide things into my palm, where they stayed strapped down by the lace. The gloves were stolen, too. Sometimes I'd keep the stuff, and sometimes I'd sell it to kids at Assumption who never got to go into Boston and were dazzled by the heart-shaped plastic key chains, the dangling earring, the purple shoelaces dotted with stars that I brought back on the bus, stoned off the adrenaline rush, elated. I kept my illegal earnings in a little cedar box my grandmother had given me, along with the stolen goods waiting to be sold. Sometimes I even took orders. But getting caught had put the fear in me, I could feel eyes on me whenever I entered a store. The hat was on the bed—I had bad vibes, I was jinxed.

There was a slush store at the mall, Ritchie's King of Slush, the best slush: watermelon, lemon, piña colada, and cherry if they were out of the rest. They had blobs of fried dough floating in a vat of spitting oil and special fried-dough sandwiches with ham and cheese stuffed inside the greasy bread. That was a great place. The T-shirt store next to it let me work there for a minute, searing glitter decals onto T-shirts or, the worst, fuzzy letters for entire Little League teams, letters that had to be arranged with a precision I had no patience for. They didn't fire me, they just cut down my hours until there was no point to me going in at all. My boss would come in and the place would be in shambles and I'd be engrossed in some trashy novel I'd found behind the register, *Mistral's Daughter*, *Portnoy's Complaint*. I fucked up so many shirts, I smuggled them into the bathroom at the back of the mall and stuffed them in the trash. I didn't know about inventory.

Suit Yourself sold designer jeans, Sergio Valente, Jordache—they had a booming business for a while in the eighties. For an eye blink there was Record Man, stocked with rocker salesboys for us all to get crushes on. There I bought Def Leppard posters, concert photos of Billy Idol, a sleeveless union jack T-shirt, Van Halen's *1984*. That was the year. For a minute it seemed like my city was almost a cool place to be, but then Record Man shut down. Marianne's sold good trampy-girl clothes. I would walk through the blindingly fluorescent store talking either in a fake English accent or like a Valley Girl, planning what I would look like when I grew up. I was pretty on target. I stole the fingerless lace gloves from Marianne's, and the communal dressing room was always an adventure. Deb's was a slightly toned-down version of Marianne's, like for the moms of the trashy girls. A Papa Gino's with jukeboxes at the tables. Waldenbooks, where we got kicked out for reading sex books, and I lectured the saleslady about how sex was okay and not bad and it was better for kids to learn about it from books and not on the street.

Me and my friends would roam the Mystic Mall, moving

through the wide corridors, cruising past all the shops, and then we would need to smoke. There were boxes of cigarettes tucked into the curving pleather of the Jordache purses that hung horizontal across our torsos, swinging on our hips. We smoked our cigarettes in the mall bathroom, deep in the bowels of the mall by the security and business offices, at the end of a long, fluorescent-lit hallway that looked so employees-only and foreboding that hardly anybody but us went back there. We would push open the wooden door and settle into our clubhouse. It was me, Marisol, Tiffany, who was funny, and Vivian, caked in Duran Duran merchandise, who was generally kept around for Marisol to be mean to. Marisol would steal Vivian's pin, I (Heart) Nick, and hold it just above the flushing toilet while Vivian howled and hit the tiled wall. We were smoking a communal pack of Marlboros we'd pool our change to buy. We'd sit on the floor, tiny square tiles with dust in the cracks, or try to get a perch on the little metal ledge that ran beneath the long mirror. Me, with my skinniest ass, would wedge into the long porcelain sink that didn't work, my butt cupped in the strong porcelain saucer. I loved sitting there, smoking, flicking my ashes in the wet sink beside me like a big white ashtray. I can't tell you how special the smoking was. It was our secret sacrament and I loved the motion of every drag, lifting my hand, sealing my lips around it, the tug of my whole body pulling, and the grand finale of the sexy tough exhale smoke leaving my lips like a train pulling out of the station of the most boring city in the world, leaving exhaust like a scar on the sky. Smoking does look cool.

We made up lists of the boys we liked, one to ten in order of the seriousness of the crush. Going over with desperate rakes the pathetically small snippets of conversation we'd had with the boy while buying our poster or slush. The bands we were all going to be in. We all wanted to be the singer, though if necessary I'd play drums. We'd be called the Scabs, Black Lace, JailBait. We would not sound anything like Duran Duran, Marisol said with a glare at Vivian. No fag music. Judas Priest and Mötley Crüe. I carved awkward, angular pentagrams into the bathroom door with my house key, digging and digging, making the side of my knuckle deep red and shiny and cramped, and sometimes took a lighter to the painted white ceiling and wrote my initials with dark streaks of heat, scorching my thumb on the hot metal tip.

We found Runaway Lydia in the mall bathroom. It was like finding ET pitching Reese's Pieces against the back of your house, a runaway. Like a gypsy, something mythical from television, which you are not supposed to think is for real unless it's telling you not to use drugs. Girls really ran away. They walked around without parents or school, and they washed their hair in the sink of the bathroom at the back of the mall, contorting their hungry bodies to fit their heads beneath the stream, pumping pearly pink soap from the dispenser to use as shampoo. That's where we found Lydia. It was like we'd walked into the wrong place, we all jumped back when the door swung open and she was there, hunched over, blotting the back of her neck with paper towels. It was like walking into her house, or catching her taking a pee. We all stood stiff and didn't talk, pulled cigarettes from the red box, not touching the lucky cigarette turned upside down in the box, to be smoked last while making a wish. Lydia shifted and looked sore, wringing the mall water from her hair, which was bleached to a deep nicotine yellow and fried from the effort. Still, it was bleached and that was good. We would have all been happy with a head of hair like that, but you couldn't bleach your hair with parents around. You had to be a runaway, and Lydia was. Like a girl in a book. Her jeans were so tight and her legs so skinny you wouldn't think you could find jeans small enough to look like that. Little white T-shirt, dirty like her white sneakers. I wondered briefly if she would beat us up. I always wondered that when I met a girl I didn't know. Sometimes one would want to, but Lydia smiled and bummed a cigarette, asked us our names. She told us right away she was a runaway, she was pretty proud of it and she should have been. It was an amazing feat, shucking off your parents. She lived in an abandoned store in Bellingham Square that was a real pit, she stayed there with her boyfriend who was older, and his friends would come over and they all drank beer together and hung out and it was really fun. I couldn't believe this. It was like a paperback teen novel had opened its pages and sucked me in like little Carolann's closet in *Poltergeist*. I had to be Lydia's friend. If I couldn't be a runaway, then at least I could know one. I could help her. It had to be hard, it had to be so hard. She was so brave and alone, washing her hair in the sink at the mall, she knew how to do all the things you had to do if you ran away. How to take care of herself, at once a grownup and a kid, like any other impossible combination of creatures, a unicorn, or a horse with wings.

I wanted to give Lydia everything I had. Stuff I loved lost all value in the face of having nothing at all like Lydia. Lydia needed things. Shoes, I gave her my cracked leather ones with the run-down heels and bows at my toes. She loved them. I gave her some shirts and she wanted more, wanted blankets and jackets but I couldn't give her those. What about food? How did runaways eat? Well, her boyfriend fed her, he sold drugs. I smuggled cans of stuff from my pantry shelves. I told her where I lived and she came to my door. *Do you have a can opener?* she asked. I gave her the can opener from the drawer in the kitchen. Lydia was such a secret. My mother would kill me. She was like a pet I knew I couldn't have, I had to feed and take care of her in this sneaky way, and like the stray animal I dreamed of someday finding and keeping, I never lost the fear that Lydia might bite. A girl who ran away from home was certainly capable of anything. I never asked her why she left. It was pointless, we all wanted to go. To be gone, to climb aboard our lives like a bus and leave. I wouldn't have picked Chelsea, I would have gone to New York or at least Boston, but Chelsea is where Lydia went. It was hard to imagine a place that made Chelsea look like a good place to run to.

Once, Lydia came to my door when my family was home. She had her boyfriend with her, and he was a man and that was a shock. He was much older than Lydia, who was a little older than me but not so much that she wasn't still a kid. I panicked at my mother finding this man at the door for me, hickey-necked runaway Lydia in tow. He nodded at me and smiled, seemed nervous or at least uncomfortable. Lydia did the talking. *Can we have some food? We're pretty hungry.* I Can't, I whispered, My Parents Are Here. *Really?* she asked. *Not even nothing?* Hold On. I shut the door and went into the kitchen. There was my mom smoking endless cigarettes with whoever, Will, grandparents, my aunt next door, cousins upstairs—there were always a million people in my house, filling it up with smoke, getting the shakes on milky cups of Tetley tea, talking shit about everybody. I really liked it. I'm pretty social, I liked sitting at the table doing my homework, soaking up the smoke and the gossip, offering my own jibe here and there, my grandmother biting her lower lip and shaking her head, saying, *Listen to you. Is she a hot ticket? Aren't you a hot shit. Do your homework.* I went into the pantry and gathered some snacks. *Whatcha doin' Shell?* Nothing. I grabbed Popsicles from the freezer, took it all back into the living room, where the front door was. The television blared. Out in the hallway were Lydia and the boyfriend. Here, I said quickly, Take These. The junkiest food. They were happy to have it. Eat The Popsicles, They'll Melt, I said. I wanted to give them instructions, like I had done something very complicated for them, because I really had, and it didn't show in the stale, half-empty bags of Doritos and Wise potato chips with the owl on the package. *Thanks, Michelle,* Lydia said, gathering the stuff in her arms. *Bye,* the guy nodded. They left my house and I went back to the television.

I went into Boston with Lydia and her boyfriend, whose name was something like Mike. Lydia never went into Boston, which I thought was incredible because she was a runaway and could go anywhere she wanted, but she just hung around Chelsea. I was taking them on a field trip. Boston Is So Cool, I promised them. I still wasn't allowed to go into the city, I had to sneak on and off the bus and tell my mother I was at the mall. I had a pin on my Jordache bag that said "My Mother Thinks I'm at the Movies." My mother didn't think it was funny. *You're a pip, Shell.* Lydia lit up a cigarette and smoked it right there on the sidewalk and I broke out in a sweat. Someone's Going To See You, I hissed. *Who?* Lydia laughed. There was no one to yell at Lydia for smoking. I couldn't imagine a freedom like that. It was almost too much. I knew I would get in trouble just for standing next to the smoking runaway Lydia, not to mention her grown-up boyfriend. We rode the bus into Boston and I took them to this great funky shop at Faneuil Hall that I went to so much I started to know the people who worked there, really cool older people who lived in Boston and were maybe punk-rock. I thought they were punk-rock. They had weird hair. I wanted to be their friend so bad, I wanted to show them all to Lydia but she didn't really care. She stole a bunch of stuff, pencils with shimmery stars, erasers shaped like frogs, scratch 'n' sniff stickers that smelled like pickles and chocolate. I was so mad at her for it. This wasn't the mall, it was Boston, the real world, where there were people who I wanted to like me, and if they caught Lydia stealing stuff, they'd never let me in again and I'd be trapped in Chelsea forever, smoking at the back of the mall. Lydia, Don't Steal From There, I said. I felt like she'd stolen from me. *Just a couple pencils,* she shrugged. Her boyfriend didn't say anything. He was a pretty quiet guy. Lydia gave him a sticker that smelled like pizza. The way I thought, it was like all the things I knew were great were one, not separate. Punk rock and runaways, if you were a runaway you were punk and all the realest punks would be runaways. But Lydia was just this fucked-up girl.

I saw her years later, at a party this kid Kenneth had at his parents' house while they were gone. I went to vocational high school with Kenneth. All these metal boys, with long hair static from the hair-dryer, were at the party, Metallica loud on the stereo. Lots of pot and beer and Kenneth's favorite, cream soda with Captain Morgan's spiced rum, delicious like candy, overwhelmingly sweet. There were hardly any girls there, just me and a couple of my friends, death-rock kids who lived outside Chelsea. I'd convinced them it would be weird and fun to go to a metal party in my town, I promised no one would beat us up. Was it fun? I got drunk, that was always fun. I smoked some heavy-metal pot that made my vision go weird, my head sick and spinny, and I walked out into the hallway to get some air. There was runaway Lydia, crying. She didn't look much different, better bleach in her hair, and those little Stevie Nicks boots with laces and a tiny heel. Same tight skinny jeans, blue eyeliner making trails down her cheeks. Hey! I told her who I was, she remembered me, stopped crying for a minute. *Do you got a cigarette?* We sat down on the stairs to smoke. Are You Okay? *Those fucking assholes,* she said, wiping the runny blue from her face, pulling furiously on her cigarette. *I passed out at a party here last week and they all ate me out. I just found out, I didn't even know, they just told me.* Who? I said, incredulous. *Chris,* she spat. *Andrew, Matt, Kenneth. Kenneth's okay, because we're going out, but . . .* He Let Them Do That? This was unbelievable to me. I had thought they were nice guys, they'd been nice to me, stuck up for me at school when jocks called me "freak" and threw food in my gigantic goth hairdo. I felt like an idiot for having trusted them. *Kenneth was fucked up,* Lydia said. *They were all fucked up. Fucking assholes!* She smoked more, pulling hard on her skinny white cigarette, her hands chapped pink and shaking as she held it to her lips. That's Awful, I said to her. That's Wrong, That's Really Wrong. She nodded, tears fell off her face and turned into dark spots on her jeans. Chris came to the top of the stairs. This pudgy kid with long, orange flyaway hair, freckles. *Lydia, I'm sorry,* he started. His voice was too large for the words, he was drunk, swaying at the top of the stairs. *Fucking asshole!* Lydia yelled, *Fuck you!* I just looked at him. I really hadn't thought they would do something like that. They were just kids like me, outsiders, only they listened to heavy metal and not the Smiths. If everything I believed in was one, then outsiders—metalheads and punks and skaters and goths—stuck up for girls, and boys who stuck up for girls were outsiders, metalheads and punkers, gothboys and skateboarders. It just made sense to me. My fragile philosophy dissolved beneath Lydia's weeping, and I felt a stab of despair—was there any way to figure out which boys were good, which ones bad? All my little experiments were failing. If rockers and punkers, goths and skaters, could be rapists, then they might as well be jocks, preppies, redneck normals. What made them different, made them outsiders, what did their fashions stand for? Nothing. Costumes. A different way to look intimidating and do the same things frat boys did. They did that to runaway Lydia. Was she still a runaway? If you never go home, are you a runaway forever, even when you're all grown up? Do you grow up and get a home and stop washing your hair at the bathroom at the mall? Lydia continued to cry, and my brain kept spinning, with marijuana and awful revelation. Chris stood like an idiot at the top of the stairs, and then he turned around and went back to the party.

THE HEADMASTER RITUAL

I went to St. Rose because I had no place else to go. There was Chelsea High, but my mother had bent herself into a fiscal pretzel scooting me through eight years of Catholic school, insurance that I would not end up beaten up, pregnant and ignorant at Chelsea High, killing the dream of being the first of my kin to go to college. Standing there, fourteen years old, tipping on the sweet edge of summer, creaking on the hinge of a future too vast and complicated to imagine, I submitted to St. Rose. It was July, and my mother still owed back tuition to Our Lady of the Assumption, the jail I'd just escaped. Most of the nuns there liked me okay, but the new principal, Sister Gertrude, hated my guts. Because I looked like a tramp. Every morning we would stand and salute the flag, poised straight beside our desks, and then we would recite the Lord's Prayer in a stiffly halting rhythm, like sounding out the syllables of a foreign language, the words meaningless. The whole time, Sister Gertrude stood outside the classroom door, the window displaying her from the waist up, glaring straight at me. As soon as I folded my plaid body into my wooden chair, Sister Gertrude would fling open the door and ask the teacher if she could please see Michelle Tomacheski. As if he or anyone could say no. We would walk just a little ways down the hall, past the water fountain and into the vaguely pink bathroom where Sister Gertrude would lean against the wall and look tough as I scrubbed the smudgy blue eyeliner from around my eyes. Every morning we would do this. I would be escorted back to my classroom red-eyed from the scrubbing, and I hated thinking that it looked like she'd made me cry. I hated Sister Gertrude.

Before Sister Gertrude was Sister Rita and she was just as bad, had yanked me out of sixth grade two years earlier for passing around an invitation to a boy-girl Spin the Bottle party I was throwing in the woods behind the VA hospital. The note had been addressed to Jack Amazza, the class asshole, and it said, Don't Come If You're Going To Be A Baby. Sister Rita acted like I was peer-pressuring poor Jack into coming to this nasty party that I had also invited forbidden public school kids to, but the reason I wrote Don't Be A Baby is that Jack was such a jerk and made fun of girls for being ugly, and I didn't want him showing up and spinning and landing on some girl and making barfing noises into his hand. Jack was the worst, would turn his eyelids inside out so you had to look at the slimy pink insides, but he was kind of cute too, and if I could just get him to behave I thought it would maybe be worth it to have him at my party. I was asking everyone to bring chips and tonic. I loved playing Spin the Bottle so much, I didn't want to have to wait for somebody to have a birthday party before I got to do it again. Then Sister Rita popped up and effectively ruined

The Chelsea Whistle

everything, and I got punished. My mother was pissed. After the divorce, Sister Rita sat with my mother in our car before school let out, and told her that she could never be with a man again, now that she was divorced. It would be a sin. When Will came around, Ma had tried to annul her first marriage, have it erased by God. It didn't work because Dennis refused to meet with the priest, so as far as God and everyone at Assumption were concerned, my mother was walking around with a scarlet iron-on seared to her chest. She was a divorced, remarried, excommunicated Catholic mother busting her ass to keep me in Catholic school, and I was still turning out like a public school kid.

Sister Rita got transferred out to another school, but Sister Gertrude proved even worse. And she didn't even wear a habit. Just short, sort of curly brown hair streaked with grey. It was the only leverage I could get on her, no habit. Both of us with our hairdos naked before God, my own crunchy with hairspray and sprouting up in a way that prompted Sister Gertrude to write "No Punk Hairstyles" in the school handbook, accompanied by illustrations to clarify exactly what a Punk Hairstyle was.

We had a graduation rehearsal in May, right as we neared the impossible cliff of forever leaving the place. Because it was a special day so close to our release into a uniformless world, we got to wear our regular clothes, no plaid skirts. The rehearsal was in the church where the actual ceremony would be held, a big red place full of different holy stinks, chipped statues, rows of dull pews where we waited for Sister Gertrude's instructions. The red leather kneelers you kicked down for the kneeling parts of Mass, the little metal clips nailed to the back of the pew before you, to hang a hat or purse on I guess. Bored at church, we'd fiddle with them and they would snap against the wood loud as God's bullet cracking through the dour stillness, and we would get in trouble. Sister Gertrude stood at the lectern on the altar, and one by one she called us up to practice receiving different awards that maybe some of us would receive. *And the award for the shortest skirt goes to . . . Michelle Tomacheski.* I wiggled down the red carpet in my denim miniskirt. What a bitch. She just smirked, up there without her habit. Can I tell you her sweaters were so tight and she wore those pointy bullet bras like some fifties pinup girl. She could fuck off. I was just about gone from the place and feeling emboldened by my impending escape. I accepted my facetious award. I didn't tell my mother, who would have been further shamed by the incident. She would soon have one last look at what Our Lady of the Assumption thought of her daughter.

My mother and I had already started fighting about my wardrobe. All the Catholic high schools were hosting open houses for prospective freshmen, and I of course could not go with a neon pink-and-black zebra-striped bandanna wound into a perfect, tight knot around the ankle of my jeans. She hadn't even noticed it until we climbed out of the car, nearly home free. *Take that off,* she ordered, all done up in her way, thin gold chains weighted with an impressive collection of charms, the big status thing in Chelsea. Fourteen-karat-gold teddy bears, "#1 Mom," Italian horns though we weren't Italian. It was lucky. A Nefertiti head. I Don't Want To Take It Off, I whined. Why, What's The Big Deal? *It looks cheap.* The big fear, aimed and fired at me so many times that I knew I *must* be cheap. Well, who cared then? They'd find out soon enough, why not let them know right off with a flag, so the ones who cared could stay away. I took the bandanna off, I was crying.

Broadway Avenue, Chelsea, where the wooden bridge stretched out over the railroad tracks. Across the street was St. Rose. That bandanna had Joan Jett's autograph on it. I'd met her at a record store, Strawberries, and had her sign my forearm with black marker, and then my bandanna, and when I asked if I could kiss her, she mumbled about how she was sick with the flu, but then she let me kiss her anyway. A quick dry one on the mouth. I kept waiting and hoping to get sick with Joan Jett's flu. An internal autograph, I could stay home from school and lounge on the sour wool couch watching MTV and telling friends who called, I Caught The Flu From Joan Jett. It was so cool but it never happened. I was healthy. I kept the autographed bandanna in my coat pocket as I moved through the eerie hallways of St. Rose, which smelled of old books, dry rot. Joan Jett's signature like a charm on the cheap fabric, to bring me something better, to please let me grow up soon. I was trapped in my age like I was trapped in my town. I told my mother, I'm Going To Chelsea High. I missed all the application deadlines for the Catholic high schools, I couldn't get it together. Pope John, which was co-ed and pricey, and their plaid was a nice grey; Matignon, also expensive—what were the other ones? Don Bosco and Dom Savio, but they were for boys. The Savio boys were cute, Italian toughies.

But wait. Before high school was graduation. Me and my mother had managed to agree on a graduation dress. It was white with black polka dots, ankle-length, strapless but sweet. My body was slight, I wasn't pouring out of it, it bound me into myself like an innocent waif. Cyndi Lauper, I thought, and my mom just thought it was cute. Compared with the other, cheaper outfits I'd dragged into the communal dressing room of Marianne's, it was okay. More than one friend on a similar graduation pursuit had caught me crying real tears at my mother in that dressing room. So the polka-dot dress couldn't have been all that bad. I looked pretty at my graduation, flouncing into that same pink bathroom where all my female classmates pressed pale pink makeup onto their faces. They all wore variations of the same dress I had successfully resisted—a minidress with a straight body not giving in to any tits that might have been born that year, bursting into a little-girl ruffle right above the knee. Maybe a couple of bows. They looked so stupid done up like little dolls, one last parental effort at an expired childhood. I knew which of them smoked, and who'd tried pot and even mescaline, and who let a boy do what things to their bodies. They all looked so pink and froofy, it was a big scam. I felt like a queen in my dress, grown up and more real than all these little princesses. Not that it even mattered, we all had to walk through the church in the same gold graduation gown, goofy square hats on our heads as if we were graduating from somewhere important.

Sister Gertrude burst into the bathroom like she knew I was in there. She looked right at me. *You are not walking down the aisle in that,* she snapped like a strong branch breaking. What? She put her hand on me, spun me into the mirror to look at myself, which I'd already been doing before she'd interrupted. *Look at yourself,* she ordered. *Look at that dress. You look immoral. You do not look like the product of a Catholic education. Do you?* All the girls were still as Easter baskets, staring at me in their ugly pastel dresses. *You have to change out of that dress.* But I Don't Have Anything Else. I hated myself for crying. It was like the awful spinning fights I had with my mother, only it was inside my school where everyone could see. I looked at her straight on, glaring, and the trying not to cry made my whole face twitch like an idiot. *I'll find your mother,* she said and burst back out. The Easter baskets moved around me slow and cautious, murmuring soft hesitant words, but I knew they thought the same of me and they could go die with Sister Gertrude. I yanked rough paper towels from the dispenser and pressed them gently to my eyes, trying to catch my crying before it left dirty blue eyeliner trails down my cheeks. The only good part of this incident came from my teacher, Mr. Buzzle, who had already been fired for taking us out of class and down to the auditorium to direct us in a production of *A Midsummer Night's Dream,* with choreography lifted from *Cats.* Mr. Buzzle, who directed us with a flamboyant scarf flung around his neck and a long Benson & Hedges dangling from his suspiciously limp hand—Mr. Buzzle caught Sister Gertrude by the arm on her way out of the toilet and said, *Why do you have to be such a bitch, it's her graduation day.* My mom simply told Sister Gertrude that she had approved the controversial dress, and she would not go home to get me a different outfit. My mom really did think it was a nice dress. It was.

I covered it up with the robe and walked down the aisle to receive my diploma. If I had decided right then to go to stupid St. Rose, I would have received the creative writing scholarship, but as I was all geared up for public school the award went to Erica McGinn, the bitch who had pulled my skirt up in front of the drugstore where everyone stopped before school for Jolly Rancher sticks and those two-toned chalky lollipops with the hollow plastic sticks. Then St. Rose, being on the verge of bankruptcy, decided to accept all late applications, and at the last moment I was admitted. My mother sent me to the Our Lady of the Assumption convent with a check paying for the remainder of my pathetic education, and she told me to make sure I told the nuns that I would be attending a Catholic high school. *You tell them you're going to St. Rose.* My family hated Sister Gertrude now. Even my grandmother gossiped about her wearing such tight sweaters with those big boobs of hers. *She was just jealous,* said my Nana, like we were discussing a classmate and not the principal.

I walked into the convent with pink color sprayed into my hair, which I had tried to get to stand up stiff and crinkly like that chick from 'Til Tuesday, but I couldn't figure out how she did it. I had big black question-mark earrings hanging like fruit from my ears, and a necklace of tiny purple chains around my neck. Sister Terese came to the convent door, the quiet secretary who was nice and liked me. You went to Sister Terese when you forgot your lunch, she would give you saltine crackers with jelly and peanut butter. She was the librarian of the pathetic Assumption school "library," a few shelves outside the principal's office stacked with Laura Ingalls Wilder books. My mother loved to tell me that in real life Laura's pa was not like Michael Landon on *Little House on the Prairie,* he was a real bastard who hit Laura and the sisters. I never read the books because of that. My grandmother gave Sister Terese all the messed-up clothes from the department store where she worked—otherwise, they would get thrown away. My grandmother was a self-loathing Protestant who had married a Catholic, raised her children Catholic and believed she was going to hell for not being Catholic herself. She would do all these nice things for the nuns, and take me and my sister to church, sit in the pew with us and not get up for Communion. Sister Terese was glad to hear I was going to St. Rose. I think I caved in just to spite those nuns and everyone else who thought I was cheap.

Truthfully, St. Rose was the bottom of the Catholic-school barrel, just a couple pinches of respectability away from the public schools. Girls who couldn't afford or didn't get into Pope John or Matignon went there, girls who had no intention of going to college, girls whose marriages were announced as they received their diplomas at graduation. Italian girls from East Boston, huge hairdos that swooped out around the face and lay flat in the back parts they couldn't see in the mirror. Terrible accents. The LaRocco triplets—Moradana, Flarinella and Lola. Shirley Lombardi. East Boston was just one town over from Chelsea, but these girls were from a different zone.

Genelle was a girl who had a locker right by mine. She was a Chelsea girl, we were kind of set up to be friends because our moms were nurses together at the Soldier's Home. Genelle was the biggest dyke I'd ever seen. She had that short-long hairdo, blond, a big red Polish face, and she carried herself like all her older brothers who were in jail. Big metal rings on her fingers, eagles and skulls and grim reapers. Genelle was another last-minute addition to Saint Rose, and her uniform was late in arriving so she got to wear her sweats for the first week of school. They should have designed special Catholic-plaid sweatpants for Genelle, because when her uniform did show up it was so wrong to see her wearing it. Her big legs and butch strut moving through the halls in those dumb pleats. I mean, all the girls tried to butch it up a little, tough is always the aesthetic in a poor town, but Genelle couldn't butch up the skirt enough to make it look right on her body. She sat next to me in homeroom and we would talk before the nun called for silence and prayer. Sister Marie Esther, a dry, humorless woman with an expressionless face and a blinking disorder that prompted us to name her Sister Blinky. Her eyes just blink blink blinked, she couldn't stop, and we were all happy to have an obvious defect to latch on to. We also called her Sister Marie Easter, Easter not being much of an insult but we just had to rename her so we could own her, so she could be ours, smaller than we were, Sister Blinky Easter, dark habit, old clothes. She would shuffle at her desk and big Genelle would reach over and poke me, pass me sheets from her notebook, heavy-metal song lyrics. Genelle wasn't in a band but she would be someday, and these would be their songs. One about partying in a cemetery called "Rockin' the Dead." Everyone knew Genelle was queer and nobody made a big deal about it, not like some horror stories you hear. Everyone was pretty polite. Genelle was just rabid in PE. She flung her red, muscly body into the game viciously, and was so competitive you just stayed away from her or you would end up tossed onto the floor of the subterranean gym that doubled as our cafeteria, and consequently smelled like armpits and lunch meat. At our lockers one morning Genelle turned to me and said, *I know people think I'm gay but I'm not.* I just looked at her. It was so necessarily unspoken, I couldn't believe she would say anything out loud, even a denial. *I mean,* she continued, *I think about sleeping with girls, but I would never do it.* Right, I said. I didn't feel close enough to Genelle to be hearing this. Polish, like me, same type of complicated last name, long with a lot of hard sounds banging into your teeth, ugly syllables.

And what about Carla Donnallo? A tower of a girl, so tall, legs like a highway running straight up her body and a topping of hairdo to make her even taller. Smoky swoops of purple eye shadow glittering grittily above her green eyes, sharp as an animal's. Every-

The Chelsea Whistle

188

thing about Carla was large and joyously disruptive. Her presence in the classroom was so big the nuns had to hate her. Carla was loud with her mouth closed, edging out their lessons, driving the presence of God out of the room as she entered. She threw her giant frame into the shuddering desk and I knew I had to make her my friend. We passed thrilling little notes, the tiny sabotage of tossing the folded lump of paper to the floor and watching Carla's foot in its big flat shoe come down on it and drag it close, then she picked it up like a dropped pencil. In the bathroom Carla put the purple on her eyelids, an impressive palette of color in her hand. She would groan about the many choices but always she went to purple, digging the packed powder with the spongy brush. Swoop, swoop.

At a glance Carla looked like the rest of the Italian girls from East Boston with her mammoth hair and fourteen-karat-gold initial ring, the boxy Louis Vuitton purse carried at the bend of the wrist. But Carla was different. She was loud as traffic, and she had opinions. We both did, we would share them in the alley of the public library that stood across the street from St. Rose, passing our thoughts between us like cigarettes. 8:00 A.M. cold Chelsea morning, smoke and frozen breath in white puffs around our heads. Marlboro Lights, pronounced *Mahlbahroh* in that East Boston accent, and we'd cover the nicotine stink with Bubblicious and Primo— Giorgio for girls who couldn't afford Giorgio. You were allowed to wear makeup at Saint Rose, but since I smoked cigarettes I still had something good to hide from the nuns. Carla wore these pins on her puffy purple winter jacket, they said: "Prince Makes Me Cum in My Pants." They said: "Leave Me Alone, I'm Having a Sexual Fantasy." The nuns of course made her remove them. Sister Blinky nabbed her in the cafeteria. *There is nothing wrong with sexual fantasies,* Carla said loudly at the table, all the girls in their skirts sitting with their cold brown sacks of food. Sister Blinky blinked sternly. *They're normal, everyone has them. Everyone,* Carla repeated the word meaningfully. Blink blink. Carla's braying voice ricocheted across the dim, depressing cafeteria. It was like being underwater.

As the year wore on, our shared inner weirdness sharpened into a visible point that cut a line between us and the rest of the girls at St. Rose. We penned messages of protest on the plaid of our skirts, on the expensive face of Carla's Louis Vuitton bag. At St. Rose the thing to do during classes was pick all the yellow thread from your uniform with a safety pin. It took all year to do it, this painstaking anti-weaving, and it was proof that you paid no attention to the stupid nuns, a skirt of resistance. Girls were always checking out each other's skirts to see how far along you were in your yellow-removal, and the girls would look at mine and Carla's and they would read the lyrics gashed into the plaid, the anarchy signs and FTWs, which meant Fuck The World. *Ya gonna kill yaself listenin ta music like that.* No Suh, we snapped. They'd end up killing themselves, we said, living in the world the way they were, blind. The world was fucked up. It was hard to say how exactly, but we could feel it. There was injustice, lots of it, we saw it as a dull shape coming slowly into focus. We fucked up our hair. We shaved away the sides, I shaved little stripes above my ear—it was dangerous then. They said we had Mohawks. Who could know, as our classmates began to persecute us, that in a mere year or two all their jock boyfriends would have that very same hairdo. I bought black hair dye and darkened all my tips like Teri Nunri from Berlin, and Carla dumped the rest of the inky bottle onto her whole head of hair and together we walked the lightless halls of St. Rose, stinking like Aqua Net, Marlboro Lights, sugary gum and cheap perfume. It was sealed: our classmates hated us.

At the onset it was only snickering, though it gave way to more open, unbridled displays of hostility. By the time we were preparing for finals, girls were threatening to kill us, and Yaz, an older boy with a car and a crush on Carla, would leave his own high school early and be parked outside St. Rose with the motor running. At 2:30 we would fly down the stairs, clutching the banister so as not to slide in our shoes, push through the doors, hop into Yaz's car like it was the General Lee and screech away from the curb. St. Rose was really such a reformatory, these girls would be saying all kinds of awful things to us right in the actual classroom, in front of teachers and nuns who would bow their heads at their desk and pretend not to hear any of it. Miss Landers I had thought was maybe cool, because she was young and dressed a little funny herself, baggy pants instead of skirts, short hair, beads like a hippie. Really she looked like a lesbian, but I didn't know so much what lesbians looked like then, save more obvious examples like Genelle. Miss Landers told us that the reason she wore pants and not skirts was so that men wouldn't rape her, men being more likely to rape girls who wore tight clothes and dressed like tramps. This information was directed at Shirley Lombardi in particular, whose hair was just incredibly enormous, a big blond radioactive desert. Supposedly Shirley had gotten some very expensive, high-tech perm at a salon in Boston. A spiral perm. Even I wanted one. Shirley's hair was like a natural force. On no-uniform days she wore the tightest black-and-red leopard-print jeans with a curving zipper that bisected her ass into neighboring countries, her right and left labia split into plump little leopard-print pillows. Ankle socks like miniature tutus, and shoes with ridiculous heels.

Shirley Lombardi was inevitably called into the principal's office on no-uniform days. I was actually ready to have Shirley on my team, considering my recent history as the Slut of Assumption, but Shirley also thought me and Carla should be killed, so as far as I was concerned she was a whore and I hoped her outfit got her pregnant. Miss Landers had us all write an essay either for or against abortion, our choice. I supported it, and Miss Landers brought me to the front of the class and ordered me to explain how it could be okay to murder sweet and blameless babies just because you made the mistake of acting cheap with a boy.

Another teacher who was not a nun was Miss Gabrial. Miss Gabrial was kind of a hippie, she was really flaky and you wondered how she had gotten a job at a Catholic school, especially as the theology teacher. She would make us play instruments like tambourines and wooden clackers while she read stories about caterpillars and butterflies—the moral was everyone is different and that is a beautiful thing. Miss Gabrial would go on these rages about teen alcoholism and teen pregnancy and teen suicide, and to be honest I think she would have loved for one of the girls to slit her wrists so she could unite us in our adolescent pain and really process it and sing some songs and have a meaningful moment with us. All the girls hated Miss Gabrial, so me and Carla loved her. Because she was so weird, and we were down with her "be yourself" message. Miss Gabrial would get so intense and rile the class into a frenzy, trying to get everyone to admit that they were depressed and drank too much on the weekends. *Why don't you just talk about it?* she pushed. *Why don't you just fuckin' shut up!* yelled Alyssa Gildea, who actually hopped out of her little desk and shoved Miss Gabrial back against the wall. Me and Carla just stared at each other, knowing we should stand up and shove Alyssa, but not wanting to bring any more violence upon ourselves. These girls were crazy. If they would shove a teacher, what would they do to us? We phoned Miss Gabrial at her home, she had given the class her number and was always urging us to call if we needed to talk. She answered the phone with a big slur, completely shit-faced. *Betty's Maid Service,* her voice rolled out of the phone. We hung up.

Was there anyone who could really help us? The next day in Sister Blinky's class Sharon Estrada, the most graceless of our tormentors, was calling Carla a freak bitch or whatever it was they called us—Sickos, satanists, homos, sluts—and Blinky was just up there at her desk blink blink like nothing was happening. Sharon Estrada was so stocky and unfeminine we knew she had nothing to lose by just pounding the shit out of us. Carla rose from her desk to her full stunning height, with her long legs ending in blocky heels and all the extra inches her tall snarl of spidery black hair lent her, and Carla yelled *Fahck You!* in her loud East Boston accent. Blinky looked up, eyes round and tearing mid-blink, and Carla turned and left, she just walked out the door as if she were an adult, someone with freedom. Without a thought, I freed myself from my own desk and stomped out behind her, passing through the door as if I had the right to leave a place I didn't want to be. Together, me and Carla pounded down the windowless halls and Carla began to scream, she began to yell, a holler that filled the hall like bubbles, and then she laughed, and I laughed, and we shrieked together out the front door and into the streets of Chelsea. Carla. She wrote a poem about it, it was called "The Rebels" and it was about the rebels—us—and how they were the only ones who were real and true and how they would prevail. Carla was so brave, rearing up like an animal in that classroom, cursing them all and breaking free. It is because I knew love that I knew to leave with her. Out on the street—well, now where do we go? Carla had some money so we went to Dick's, a pizza place with an adjoining bar where Will drank. We got pizza and waxy cups of Coke and we smoked brazenly at the table. We were giddy with the leaving. What would happen to us? You can't just walk out of school. We would get suspended. *I don't fahking care,* Carla said, *I'm quitting.* Me Too, I lied. For a second we cried, then we smoked some more cigarettes.

At school the next day we were called immediately into the principal's office. Sister Jane Michael. We called her Mike the Dyke. Slick black hair pointing out from her habit in a V, like a vampire. Me and Carla had already been in her office once together, for passing around a slambook of our own creation. A whole notebook packed with questions like, *What boy do you like?* and *How far have you gone?* and *What's your favorite drink?* I liked to slip in questions like, *Would you ever go out with a boy who wore eyeliner?* or *If you had to kiss a girl, who would you kiss?* That was back before everyone wanted to kill us so bad. Mike the Dyke's office was filled with Smurf figurines. This was long enough after the Smurf heyday to be a really absurd backdrop for any kind of discussion. The nun kept talking sternly to us and I kept staring at the little toys, Vanity Smurf and his rubbery mirror, wise old Papa Smurf, Brainy Smurf and his stack of books, Smurfette with her yellow curve of hair and short white dress. Smurfs in cars, Smurfs with bouquets of flowers, Smurfs turning cartwheels.

Sister Jane Michael said, *You cannot just walk out of this school whenever you feel like it.*

The Girls Were Threatening To Beat Us Up, I said.

You do not just walk out of school because you have an argument with another girl.

It wasn't an argument, Carla said. *They always want to beat us up.*

Your hairstyle is a distraction to the students, said the nun, and Carla repeated, *They said they were going to beat us up!*

If you want to continue attending St. Rose, you are going to have to bring your hair back to normal, the nun said finally. *This is not a public school.* She thought we asked for it with our hair, the way Miss Landers thought Shirley Lombardi was begging for rape with her leopard-print cameltoe. Me and Carla were suspended. We were suspended, and we never went back. Carla quit, just like she'd declared at Dick's, she flung up her hands with the big gold initial ring, the glinting swirly C for "Carla," and she was done with school. My mother owed back tuition, on top of all the problems with my violent hair, and if she didn't come up with it they weren't going to let me take my finals anyway so we just decided to forget it. I wasn't going to change my hair.

AT HOME WITH SAM AND KEVIN

Kevin worked at Faneuil Hall, in my favorite little shop that sold funny clocks—Elvises with rocking legs, rhinestoned cats with swirling comic-book eyes. It sold cigarette lighters that were fire-breathing monsters or tiny pistols. Scratch-and-sniff stickers and miniature plastic babies and rubber bugs and postcards of punk rockers with colored Mohawks and pins in their faces. I would walk into the store with the loud British music playing, and I'd see Kevin at the glass counter. Very self-consciously I would saunter over and lean against it, my elbows propped on top, above a row of silver skull jewelry. My book bag full of ninth-grade books spilling onto the floor by my feet, I would gaze at Kevin and his very long, curly hair, hair so long you could count each inch like the rings of a tree to find out how long he'd been cool. Gaze at his sad, droopy eyes, rimmed in black kohl, and wait for his smile to span out for me, stretch across his face like bird wings. Kevin would tell me I was amazing, and it would carry me through the next however many days of lousy education and girls who wanted to kill me. It would float me through boredom and crying, tense mothers and suddenly sick grandmothers. Kevin worked on Thursdays. Sometimes when I'd visit he'd be sad, for no reason, and I found it so touching. And hopeful—a boy so sensitive, so prone to sadness, would not be quick to make another person sad. I would ask him, Kevin, Why Are You So Sad Today? tilting my face up at him like a cup to catch a bit of it, his melancholy, his depth. *Oh, I just woke up sad this morning,* he'd shrug with a smile-grimace, sort of apologetic or embarrassed. Kevin woke up in the morning, looked in the mirror, and started crying. I was thrilled that a boy could be so emotional. When the space shuttle blew up with that lady teacher inside, Kevin just cried the whole day, at work behind the counter of Goods. He sold toys from Japan and rhinestone earrings, his muddy eyeliner rivulets trailing down his cheeks. My plaid and pleated pelvis bumped up against the glass case full of spy watches and telephones shaped like ladies' high-heeled shoes. *I like your pony tail,* said Kevin, wiping his watery eyes. *What record did you buy?* I opened my Newbury Comics bag and pulled out the green-and-orange square of *God Save The Queen*. It's About Time I Got It, I said, ashamed that I hadn't been born with it.

Kevin shared a house with Sammy, his co-worker, the one with the long thin sideburns that slid far down his cheeks, a shag of dyed black hair, tight, tight pants and shiny Chelsea boots. I was thrilled when I discovered Chelsea boots. I couldn't believe my shitty town shared a name with these mainstays of rock 'n' roll footwear. Short-heeled ankle boots with no zippers or buckles, just that stretchy insert that helped you pull them onto your feet. Never mind that they were named for Chelsea, England—

I knew that. Still, it gave me hope. Lots of cool things were named Chelsea, and I thought they were all for me, all omens. The famous Chelsea Hotel in New York where Nancy Spungen died, where Sid Vicious killed her. Probably the punkest place in the world, or in America anyway, filled with musicians and drug addicts. Chelsea, New York, was where lots of gay people lived, that was cool. Gay people were cool, they were against the law, or the law was against them, that was punk. Andy Warhol made a movie with Chelsea in the title, and then there were the boots, and the original Chelsea, in England, that the British settlers had named my town after. It was strange to think that my town had been created by people from England, a land I viewed as a real Mount Olympus, birthplace of a legion of dark gods and goddesses—Siouxsie Sioux, Robert Smith, Peter Murphy. My city was hatched by settlers from that magical land—who I knew were real assholes, uptight pilgrims who did a serious flimflam on the natives nice enough to stuff them with corn and turkey so they wouldn't starve to death in the New England freeze and end up eating each other. Imagine if that had been the outcome of the *Mayflower* excursion—another Donner Party. History would be really different if the Indians hadn't nicely shared their squash before being massacred. Stuff like this got me really riled up, Carla too, which was great because we could talk about it forever, chain-smoking, feeling more outraged and hopeless as our pack dwindled.

What was great about Kevin and Sammy was that *they* got it too, how fucked everything was. Sammy, who wore the famous boots and had been in a very popular rock band in the seventies, locally popular, they'd opened for David Bowie, for the Pretenders and all sorts of other fantastic bands. Sammy and Kevin lived together in a little apartment on Mass Ave in Cambridge, and after Sammy showed Carla the Lifesaver trick, we began visiting them on our trips into the city. Sammy had a roll of wintergreen Lifesavers, chalky candies, and he called Carla into the supply closet at Goods, the closet dark without the pull-chain light tugged on, and he tossed one of the candies onto his tongue and chewed it open-mouthed, creating a tiny pyrotechnic show for Carla, there in the dark space between his lips. The candy sparked fluorescent off his teeth as he crumbled it, tiny greenish bursts. It looked like electricity, Carla'd said. He gave one to her, and she put it in her mouth and made fireworks back at him, and then they kissed. I couldn't believe it. Carla pulled me, gasping, out of the little shop, back into the tourist hell of Faneuil Hall, where out-of-towners gaped at us—at Carla in her tall, spidery hair, and me in my black-lipsticked mouth. She told me how Sammy had kissed her. Oh My God! I shrieked girlish excitement. The story hit my face in minty puffs, Carla's breath. We swiftly lit cigarettes and plopped onto a bench to smoke them. It was great that Carla kind of had a crush on Sammy, because he was best friends with my crush, Kevin, and me and Carla were best friends, so it was a perfect circle. I doubted that I'd have gotten to spend as much alone time with Kevin, time outside the whir and buzz of kitschy Goods, if Sammy hadn't become somehow involved. Now my visits, accompanied by the loud wildness of Carla, seemed more like a real event, and less like the minor stalking of a lovesick teenage Catholic schoolgirl. It never really mattered that Sammy was thirty and Carla, like myself, now fifteen. It mattered only for that first moment, when I began to tease her—You Have A Father Fixation!—but Carla's angered and grossed-out reaction swiftly shut me down. *Don't you ever say that,* she scolded darkly. Okay, I touched her shoulder. I was just kidding. Sammy being thirty mattered only in that we knew it would matter to others. They wouldn't understand how Sammy was just like us, how rock n' roll was timeless, and it replaced regular age, how me and Carla were practically thirty anyway, in our souls. We had to keep it secret, first from parents, the obvious, the ones who would have him locked up in a heartbeat for molestation or worse, and also from Yaz, who still had an obsessive crush on Carla. We loved riding around in Yaz's car, smoking, flicking ashes out the windows, getting to go places we'd never have the time or energy to go to if we were left to our own resources. Beaches in Nahant, parking lots in Revere, more places to drink, further away from people we knew who could bust us. Yaz played the Outfield, that was the only thing about him that was hard to endure. They were a sports-theme-band, I couldn't imagine a more terrible idea. We tolerated his music selection, and ignored him when he got intense about Carla. Usually it was just sulking, but once he put his hand through his own windshield. If he'd known about Sammy, he'd have flipped out for sure. It was our secret.

Me and Carla would ring the bell and Sammy or Kevin would buzz us in. Their apartment was so tiny, the kitchen little more than a pantry, it was hard for two people to stand in it at once. Unless you were making out. In the squat foyer stood a mannequin dressed in fishnets and flash. I thought that having a mannequin in your house was about the coolest decoration you could have. It sealed Sammy and Kevin's status in my mind, not that I'd had any doubts. They were the coolest boys we'd ever met. It felt weird to refer to Sammy as a "boy"—even Kevin was pushing it, being eighteen years old, technically breaking the law with me just as Sammy was with Carla, but it seemed less serious. But calling Sammy a "man" felt even weirder, it gave what was happening a disturbing ring. I didn't want Sammy to be a man. We called them "guys." Sammy had Kiss dolls in his room, lots of real Kiss memorabilia from the seventies. *Worth some money,* he said. Kevin didn't have much, he'd only just moved in, and aside from his bass guitar leaning in a corner and his bed on the floor, the room was bare. The mirror in their bathroom was plastered with backstage passes from Sammy's rock n' roll heyday. It was still awe-inspiring to touch the shiny fabric stickers, inked up with marking pen. U2, Patti Smith. Sammy had been a star.

Carla wasn't having sex with Sammy. Like, fucking him. I'm Not Having Sex With Kevin, Either, I told her. He didn't even pressure her to, she said. Kevin Doesn't Pressure Me, Either, I said. We thought it was so great that we weren't being, like, date raped. That it wasn't a struggle to keep paws or cock away. Older guys were cooler. Not rabid to lose their own virginity, they left yours alone. It was dreamy play. Me and Carla didn't really ask each other for, or share, any additional information. When we walked into Kevin and Sammy's apartment, Carla went into Sammy's room, and I went into Kevin's. I don't know what went on with Carla and her guy, except once Sammy made a joke about pearls, a pearl necklace, and Carla swatted him. I wondered what sex thing could be done with a strand of pearls. Did he put them up her? I doubted it. Maybe he just liked her to wear them. Nothing esoteric involving jewelry went on with me and Kevin. We'd make out for an hour straight, and he'd grind his crotch into me, the rough zipper making me sore later, on the bus back to Chelsea, though at the time I didn't feel it. Every time we took it a step further, Kevin would ask, *Is this okay? Just let me know if it's not okay, okay? We can stop.* I nodded, my Catholic-school skirt crushed between our hips. Kevin's big, mournful eyes. Sometimes I'd hear Carla's shrieking laugh from behind Sammy's door. Sammy's room had a door, a luxury. Kevin's didn't, so our sessions would end when we heard Carla creak out from Sammy's dark room and pad into the bathroom on her big, bare feet. That's when me and Kevin would pull away from each other, and lie back on his mattress, reddened and breathing funny. I'd pull down my wrinkled uniform. Kevin would pat my hair, a mess. His radio played Depeche Mode, INXS.

Once, I had a slumber party with Carla and Marisol—not the best idea. Marisol was feeling increasingly left out as my connection to Carla deepened. As me and Carla became gother and gother and explored the many English bands that excited us, Marisol sunk into ever more obscure speedmetal and, showily, classical music, like Vivaldi. The shots she took at Carla were cheap, calling her a nigger-lover for dating a Puerto Rican boy named Danny who looked just—I swear—like Prince. I was shocked when Marisol lobbed such a predictably Chelsea insult at Carla. I'd expected more of her. This sleepover was my final effort to have my best friends like each other, but it was hopeless. I put on my new Smiths album, which Marisol insisted was country music. *That's not "death" rock,* she scoffed, and put on something screamy. *Shut that off, it's making me tense,* Carla waved her hands around in irritation. We stayed up all night, and as the sun began to lighten the dark sky, me and Carla hatched the terrific idea to take breakfast to Sammy and Kevin in our pajamas. We were frenzied with it. I dashed into the bathroom

and swiftly shaved my legs. Carla went through my pajama drawer
looking for something to borrow, but settled on her own nightshirt,
gifted to her from Sammy—a purple thing that ended just above
her knees, with a black lace negligee silk-screened over it. I picked a
fluffy baby-doll pajama set that I was almost grown out of. We had
enough money for bus and train fare, and some Dunkin' Donuts.
But Marisol wouldn't come. *What am I supposed to do while you're
off getting fucked?* she spat. We were aghast. *We don't fuck them!* we
cried. We thought we'd been being so sly about our affairs, me and
Carla, but any idiot could see that something was going on, and our
secrecy only encouraged them to think the worst. Marisol was a big
dark cloud. There was no boy there for her, she wasn't going to be
the third wheel. She left my house and went home, at five o'clock in
the morning. Walked all the way across Chelsea, to Library Street.
Me and Carla shrugged. It was exciting to be on the bus in our
pajamas. We'd tossed coats over them of course but we knew what
lay underneath and it made us delirious with giggles. Sleep kept
approaching, little waves of exhaustion, and we'd bat them away,
get a second wind, a third, a fourth. We got a cardboard box filled
with Dunkin' Donuts donuts, lots of apple crumb and apple cinna-
mon, my favorite. We rang Sammy and Kevin's buzzer. *Who's that?*
grumbled a sleep-rasped voice over the intercom. Girl Scouts! we
chirped. They buzzed us in.

In Kevin's bed I grew bizarre. It was the sleep, the no-sleep, it
kept filling my head with dreams even as I was awake, awake and
aware of Kevin on me, of my hand stroking his cock up and down,
up and down, the rhythm lulled me. I saw dreams in my head, Marisol walking onto a white balcony, wearing a giant white T-shirt with
a big black question mark. I shook my head, it was creepy to think

of Marisol while I was messing around like that. Kevin was asking me something. What? I murmured. He was asking me if I'd ever given a blowjob. No, I said, shaking my head against the pillow. Then he didn't want one. Kevin didn't want the responsibility of being my first in any category, in case it was horrible and later I held it against him, as Carla would hold it all against Sammy many years later, when she was finally the age that Sammy was then. When she looked and saw how small fifteen-year-old girls are, how small and young, how curious and precious. She would give him all the names we guarded him from so ferociously. Molester, pedophile, statutory rapist. Sicko. Sammy, who wanted us to dress up in negligees and let him take pictures. *It'd be tasteful,* he promised, and it's amazing that we never did it, ready as we were to do almost anything, anything but fuck for real.

Me and Kevin were pressed together closely, my hand wrapped around his dick, his hand burrowing in my baby-doll underwear. I was drifting in and out, watching my weird dream-visions. Carla's suitor Yaz appeared in one, just an image of him facing me. Yaz, I said out loud, softly. Kevin stiffened. He knew Yaz, had met him once, had heard me and Carla talk about him. He bristled, his hand stilled above my crotch. I flushed with shame and panic, thought fast. I started chanting Yes, like a cheesy, breathy porn star, a "yes" that started out sounding suspiciously like "Yaz," but slowly morphed into an undeniable affirmative. I was cringing at the thought of Kevin thinking I liked Yaz, thinking that I envisioned Yaz while he touched me. Kevin rolled onto his side, facing away from me, and I curled around him like nothing had happened, kissing his neck and winding his long, streaked curls between my fingers, falling in and out of surreal sleep. We lay like that until Carla filled up the doorway in her purple negligee nightshirt, a jelly donut crusting her mouth with sugar. *Time to go, kids,* she clapped her hands together. I lifted myself from Kevin's bed, covered myself in my coat, kissed him goodbye. A tiny peck on his sad, sad face, sadder now, staring at me with hurt eyes that I ignored.

RADIOACTIVE

Nana got sick during that first year of high school, during my time at St. Rose. On Thursdays I would go to her. A day that would normally have me hopping a late-afternoon 111 Woodlawn-via-Tobin bus into Boston, book bag on my shoulder, my unintentionally pornographic Catholic-school skirt swishing above my knees, rolled up at the waist to raise it higher, a mini not a midi. Pale yellow button-down shirt unbuttoned a bit at the neck, hair in a ponytail, a girlish ribbon tied in a loopy bow around the elastic. I almost got my ass kicked for that bow—the Italian girls found it infuriatingly hilarious. Sitting in my teenage costume, I'd let the bus rumble me toward Kevin. I was fourteen, and Kevin was eighteen, and he worked at Goods on Thursdays, the day my grandmother had to go into Boston for radiation once she started to die.

For a little while we weren't supposed to know—Nana had forbidden my mother to tell us. When she came over for meat loaf, me and Madeline had to pretend that everything was normal, that Ma hadn't been crying all week, angrier than usual about what a mess the house always was. We had to pretend we hadn't seen the flimsy plastic x-rays of her ghostly lungs, haunted by the dark masses, tumors that looked like black holes, voids on the plastic pictures. At some point it became okay that we knew the truth, but still we couldn't talk about it, not even when I lugged my book bag out of St. Rose at the end of my day and traipsed up to the worst part of Chelsea, Chester Ave, where Nana and Papa had lived since back when it was a good neighborhood. When the cemetery across the street was a sacred ground for the dead and their mourners, not a place where hoodlums got drunk and knocked over tombstones and spray painted their names on the mottled mausoleums. A white and yellow van-bus would idle in front of Nana's house, the house tiered in rough, green shingles, the house with the bush of tiny, thorny roses and the bitchy landlady who lived alone on the first floor, Ellen. When the van-bus slid open its doors, me and my grandmother would climb inside and arrange ourselves on the pleather seats, sliding around as the driver took corner after maniacal corner. *Watch how he drives,* she'd cluck tensely, gripping the seat or her purse, gripping me with hard, varnished fingernails that pushed the blood from my skin, leaving moonish, white indentations. The van-bus would stop for other sick people, and the door would slide open with a clack to admit them. Old men stumbled in, gnarled tree-branch hands clutching canes. Old women with suspicious skin and wet coughs. A school bus for the dying, a cruise down Route Styx. Nana didn't look as ill as the other old people. She was thin but not sickly, thin how she'd always been, the way I was too, bony arms and legs and a round, jutting belly. I knew that my own body would eventually age into the frame of my ancestors, the hereditary bulging torso, limbs like toothpicks stuck into a potato. I was aware, at that moment, of being as pretty as I would ever be, an understanding that made me anxious. I didn't want to waste a minute, wanted to lean over the glass counter of Kevin's store and watch my bobbing, multicolored ponytail bring a smile to his face.

Nana's hair was brown dyed over grey, and every night she would roll bits of it around pink plastic curlers, or wrestle locks into twirls against her scalp and lance them with bobby pins. She slept all night like that, her head bumpy against the pillow. In the morning she'd unwind her hair from the painful gizmos, and the freed locks would unspool gratefully into the air, to be tamed and shaped and sprayed by Nana, creating a smooth helmet head of old-lady curls. Later her hair would simply come out with the curlers, the entire pinned lock lifted from her scalp, snagged between the thin metal rods. Brittle clumps of Nana's hair clogged her hairbrush, they lay wetly in the porcelain bowl of her sink, to be nudged gently down the drain. She bought a curly greyish wig. She bought an aqua turban that fit tightly over her scalp. When she slid it from her dome, everyone would breath a sharp breath of heartache, and she'd cackle, *Humpty Dumpty. Give it a rub for good luck.* Perfectly smooth and tender as scar tissue, the giant wound of her head. She'd tug the turban back on. Nana had plucked her eyebrows to death in her youth, and for years had been drawing them on with thick brown pencil like Joan Crawford, painted arches above her wide eyeglasses. She knew that the cancer would eventually chew up her brain, and reminded my mother daily, *Don't let them bury me without my eyebrows.*

I won't, Ma.

The van-bus careened over the Tobin Bridge, and I could see the glinting rooster weather vane spinning on the roof of Faneuil

Hall, where Kevin and Sammy would be working along with Sean, who played keyboards and looked so much like keyboard genius Howard Jones that he wore a T-shirt that read "No HoJo" when his band made a video for the Boston cable-access video show. And Van, who was gay, and wildly funny in that way that only gay people, gay men specifically, can be. Van was madly in love with the singer from Ministry and would talk about cocks and blow-jobs until tears carried mascara down my face and my belly hurt from the clench of laughter. Greta worked there, too. She used to be Kevin's girlfriend, so she hated me and now hated Kevin more than at the time of their breakup. At work she would call Kevin a pedophile, to which Sammy would quip, *That's an awfully big word for an eight-year-old.* All of this activity, this banter, was happening right at that moment, somewhere beneath the bridge that I rolled over. I felt guilty for wishing I were there, for wishing I were any-where other than there with Nana, who was dying. Every moment with her should be special, heightened, branded into my memory with a deeper heat. I stared out the van-bus window, my forehead bumping against the smudgy glass, and Nana swatted my shoulder. *Cut it out, you're gonna get a bump on your head.*

The radiation treatment center was a round brick building that immediately made me think of a nuclear power plant. The way the brick rose tubelike from the ground like those infamous silos. An elevator brought us deep beneath the sidewalk, deeper than sub-ways. Signs on the walls said WARNING, with the black and yellow triangles that meant radioactive. My grandmother would go into a room and then come back out in a paper nightgown, her stick legs pale like a little girl's, vulnerable without their polyester slacks. When I slept at my grandmother's, she wore nightgowns to bed that shimmered, that were embroidered with flowers and stuck with bits of lace, and didn't make her legs look so frightened. I kept my eyes away from them, like they were her boobs or some other part of her body I wasn't supposed to see. Nana would leave for a different room, where she was stretched out on a table and pummeled by invisible rays. I felt the radiation all around me and it made me nervous. On summer drives to Florida my grandfather used to point out the car window to a cluster of curving silos and say, *Look, Three Mile Island,* and I'd think of Jane Fonda and frightening, white hallways, and hold my breath so nothing poisonous would get into my body. I sat in the radioactive waiting room, and aides brought me paper cups of ginger ale like I was sick, too. I leafed through old copies of *National Geographic,* hunting for photos of half-naked tribal people with feathers and bones jammed through their skin, rings stacked onto necks, plates pulling lips out into tiny shelves. I would look down, down, down and not up into the anxious faces who sipped their ginger ale alongside me, the friendly nurses. Nana's female doctor with the smile and the shiny dark hair, the wheelchairs carrying bodies dying, bodies burning from the inside with this terrible medicine.

When my grandmother was through getting radiated, we left the sunken, toxic building and headed down antiseptic hallways to the Mass General cafeteria. I got a hotdog and French fries and a Coke: Nana got coffee in a Styrofoam cup, always too hot for her tongue. She'd stir her cream and sugar around, and then scoop some ice cubes from my Coke and plop them into her cup. The small drip of coffee from her spoon grossed me out as it slid into my Coke. It ruined it every time. Once, after I finished my dog, Nana told me to have a cigarette, and I twitched. I didn't know that Nana knew I smoked. I knew that Ma knew, she snooped around my room, she'd found the ground-out butts in an empty Swiss Miss pudding container I kept hidden beneath my bureau. Ever since, she'd rap on the bathroom door when I was in there forever, smoking on the toilet and reading the *TV Guide*. Spreading my legs to flick the ash into the bowl. As the smoke wafted up through my pubic hair, I wondered briefly if I could get cancer down there, if I was giving it to myself right then. I'd stand and toss the butt into the water, where it expired with an electric fizz and sank disgustingly to the bottom, its papers unraveling, a trail of filthy brown water in its wake. When I opened the bathroom door, a cloud would rush out into the greater smoke of the house. It was hard for Ma to prove I'd been smoking when the evidence, the smoke, was everywhere, pluming from the fingertips of every adult in the house.

I was embarrassed to smoke in front of Nana, who was currently dying from the man-eating blob that cigarettes had created in her lungs. *We'll have one together,* she declared, *and after this one, we'll quit.* I knew that I was not going to quit, and neither was Nana. Even the doctor had told her not to bother. It was far too late for that. I had always pledged that if someone I knew got cancer, I'd quit—a gruesome, fucked-up resolution. Ma had her own pledges to quit, too, just not now, not with someone, her own mother, dying right in front of her eyes. Now was the time to smoke copiously. She had been planning to quit before, but then she got divorced, and before that was the stress of nursing school—students smoke, especially while cramming for a test. They chain-smoke. What Ma needed was for life to stop lobbing tragedies at her, a pause between calamities so she could stop smoking. I pulled my gold and white box of cigarettes from my book bag, and me and Nana lit up in the late-afternoon sun that brightened the hospital cafeteria in a drowsy way. Heavy, golden light, the sun's last gasp. I thought of Kevin, and a wash of melancholy cascaded. Nana watched as I breathed my smoke in and out in a deep sigh. *You inhale?!* she exclaimed. She shook her head and clucked, scolded me. *Don't inhale. I never inhale.* Cigarette smoke left her mouth in fat puffs, ethereal cotton balls, the empty word balloons of comic-book characters with nothing to say. Smoke left my mouth in thin streams, in a *whoosh.* To make Nana happy I tried not to inhale, but I couldn't help it, it was my habit. I had trained myself to inhale, to inhale elegantly or fiercely, without choking, without tears pooling in the corners of my eyes and trickling babyish down my face. The uninhaled smoke felt so odd in my mouth—thick, oddly solid, a strange food I couldn't swallow. Nana smoked Benson & Hedges, Papa smoked L & M's and Pall Malls. Ma smoked Vantages and Will smoked Newports, with the minuscule shards of fiberglass that tear up your lungs and leave you feeling fresh and minty. I started with Parliaments, moved on to Marlboros, and by then had settled into the more feminine Marlboro Lights. The smell of Nana's smoke mingled with her perfume and the scent of all her makeup—the compact of hard-pressed powder, the pot of rouge, the thick, cloying smell of her lipstick. I always knew which cigarette butts had been Nana's from the greasy red filters. When I was very small, I had thought the red spots on the tips of candy cigarettes were not the burning cherries, but the lipstick marks from the glamorous female mouths that had smoked them. I ate them backwards.

The white and yellow van-bus picked us up out front of Mass General, where we waited in the front hallway clotted with sick people and the people who dealt with them. On the way to the exit, we would stop at a bathroom and Nana would warn me not to sit on the toilet seat. I'd take a drink from the water fountain outside, and she'd hiss at me when my lips bumped the metal spout. People are deadly, splashing inside with all sorts of liquid disease. Nana had never placed her ass upon a public toilet, she always squatted above it with shaking thighs, or festooned the seat in layers of safe, cushy toilet paper. She never wrapped her mouth around a drinking fountain and sucked the metallic water. She never gulped cigarette smoke deep into her lungs, but that's where her cancer had birthed itself, that's where it nestled and grew till she had to be shot up with nuclear rays, no more hair on her head. The van-bus pulled away from the hospital, back across the tall, green bridge and into Chelsea, arcing past Faneuil Hall as I daydreamed of Kevin's curls, blond mostly but streaked with black and orange, and brown at the roots. I went back to my house for meat loaf and homework, then lay in my bed, playing "People Are People," then "Blasphemous Rumours" on my stereo. Madeline, who hated all the music that I enjoyed, who found the music ugly and sometimes frightening thought Depeche Mode was okay, and "Blasphemous Rumours" an anthem. She came into my room and listened to the scratchy vinyl with me, lay on my bed and cried.

CREAKS

It was pretty squishy, me and Madeline, Ma and Will, all crammed inside that little house on Heard Street, a house without doors. When the apartment upstairs from Lisa, Ma's best friend since they were both twelve years old, opened up, we got it. A real house, with doors, a room for me and a room for Madeline, and a room for Ma and Will to sleep together. Plus the regular rooms—a bathroom and a parlor, a kitchen with not one but two pantries, one for food, and one for the refrigerator. That last pantry was where the back door was, a back door that led to a back hallway and ultimately down to our backyard. My room was off the kitchen, right by the fridge pantry. Madeline's was off the parlor, and Ma and Will shared the big room that overlooked the dead-end street below, Lash Street.

It happened sometimes, when I was shut inside my room, when Ma wasn't home because she was working nights—the three-to-eleven, or the more horrible eleven-to-seven shift. Maybe she was just at bingo, or downstairs with Lisa, or upstairs with Tracy, or next door with Meg, or maybe asleep in her bedroom. It happened sometimes, when I was shut inside my room, when Madeline wasn't home because she was with her friends, sleeping over at someone's house, or at a dance thing or a cheerleading thing or a studying thing, or was maybe just asleep in her girlish, pastel bedroom. Madeline had one of those bedroom sets, the kind you bought in one shot for some kind of deal at a cheapo furniture store in Bellingham Square. Headboard, dresser, nightstand. I thought Madeline's bedroom set was stupid—cheap and frilly, trying to look fancy, but it was all particleboard beneath the paint. A kind of creamy paint on the wood, and a thick, curved indent that ran like a little road along the edge of the furniture, like someone drawing their finger through the whipped icing of a cake. The curve was a scratchy gold color inside. Madeline's perfect girl-room was always clean, with the palest lavender wallpaper and wall-to-wall carpet of the lightest rose. Her dresser rose up into an arching mirror, and its surface was sparse and deliberate—a couple of perfume bottles, some glinting tubes of lipstick. The tiara that had been plopped on her head when she won Junior Miss. I loved that tiara. I loved it more than she did, but in a different way. I would beg Madeline to let me wear it out to my wild drunken nights in teenage Boston. I would beg and beg, and when it was clear she was not going to allow it, I would just take Madeline's modest but deeply glamorous tiara, and stick it into the chemical snarl of my hair, wedging the teeth of the comb snugly into my tangles. Madeline would wail. *Don't ruin it!* When I returned, she would count the missing rhinestones, the dull spots in the gleam. She'd scream at me. There were always rhinestones missing after I'd worn the tiara. Madeline kept her tiara like Ma kept her rosary beads. They looked like jewelry, but they weren't. They were to be worshipped, not worn—artifacts, holy things.

Madeline's dresser held trophies—dance, cheerleading and that pageant. The satin sash that said Junior Miss hung from the edge of her mirror. She had curtains. A poster of a pair of battered toe shoes collapsed beside a rose. Her own soiled dance shoes looped around her closet doorknob. I could have had all those things too, but I didn't want them. More than that, I was mad at Madeline for wanting them. I was mad at her for not being okay with being poor, for the way she cried, demanding things that Ma would then provide, to shut Madeline up and assuage her own fears that she was depriving her daughters—being a bad mother. Once, Madeline watched an episode of *Oprah* that claimed that *anyone* could own a house. If you thought you couldn't, you were mismanaging your money. Madeline laid into Ma about her mismanagement of money, how we should be homeowners. *What money?!* Ma shouted. What if I were like that, too—wanting things? We couldn't both be. The family would collapse. There was only so much money, and because Madeline knew what the world could provide, and because she knew she should have it, she got it.

My bed had been Ma's bed before she and Will upgraded. A brass headboard. Brass was gross, but the design was simple and I needed a bed. Not only did I still have my childhood dresser, I got Madeline's when her chintzy new baroque crap arrived. Plain wood, the handles dangling by single loose screws. I carved into the finish with keys, painted it with nail polish like I was an artist. My comforter had hideous bright stripes of color, orange and green and yellow, but it kept me warm when the tiny metallic heater was broken, its rusty knob stuck, the silver metal cold. An ugly little stereo, lousy, with a cubby for records beneath it from which my records spilled out and grew in rickety columns up my walls. No curtains in my room, just yellowed blinds with confusing strings that raised and lowered them, that looped and tangled around the bent aluminum slats. Cracked linoleum on the floor peeled off in chunks to reveal the ancient floor beneath. I could have had stuff. Ma offered, a tiny guilty sound in her voice. I could have asked for anything, but it felt so greedy. Really I just wanted more records, and clothing—piles of black lace that smelled like old homes.

That was my room, a real mess. Inside my room was where it happened, where I started to think that something was wrong, that maybe Will was peeking through my door at me. Once I thought about it, I couldn't stop. Sometimes I'd be alone in my room listening to music, and in the rest of the house was no one but Will. Maybe I'd hear a creak, or maybe nothing, just a giant silence when the needle lifted from the record. A creepy, suspicious silence. *Creak.* Someone was right outside my door. If it were true, it was Will. Sometimes, inside my room, getting dressed and undressed, pouting in the mirror as I applied my new, goth-style makeup—the thick white, the smeared black—I would imagine someone, a boy, a rocker boy, a boy with hair like creeping death climbing up from his skull, watching me. I'd imagine him outside my window, in our neighbor Meg's yard, crouching beside a tree and dreaming up at me, in love with me. I'd twirl and act nonchalant. Every movement was for this spying dream-boy. Someone loving me in secret, biding his time. But the feeling I had about Will was different, and it leached into my normal voyeur fantasies. Was the dream-boy Will? In the midst of my exhibitionist fantasy, I would freeze, the quiet suddenly too much. *Creak.* Something flooded me, I think it was Crazy—if Crazy is a hormone secreted by a hidden, defensive gland like a syringe into the blood. No, He Isn't. *Creak*. I'd be sitting on my bed, reading. My body would freeze, I was all bone then, hard, aware of my skeleton. The creak of my joints. The soft creak of bedsprings as I shifted. It made me dizzy and ashamed. What was wrong with me, imagining my father outside my door? Too many talk shows, too many advice columns, too many bad eighties movies—the made-for-TV ones, the after-school specials about creepy stepdads. Too many vain daydreams about lovestruck vampire-boys.

Facing the door, my blank white door where years of messy paint created a tactile landscape of bubbles and drips and made the door sticky in its jamb, staring at the door from which the creaks issued, I'd make a mean face. Frozen in that pose, in the thundering silence, I'd move my hands around, contorting my face more, and I'd let the Crazies flow. Twisting the flesh of my face—every muscle flexed, teeth bared, eyes bulging, staring at the door—I'd begin to finger my crotch. Unlatch my jaw so that my chin swung out and drooled and my tongue hung out, the fat, canine meat of it. I'd rub my crotch and smoosh and grab at my tits, gurgling at the door. I'd growl. This insanity was absolute, logical proof that nothing was happening, that I was Crazy. Because if Will was really out there watching, if I really believed that to be true, then I could not do that, touch myself and act insane. I would not do that if I really thought he was looking. I'd relax. Giggle at the mania I'd just indulged in. *Creak*. Maybe it's how people become schizophrenic, become obsessive-compulsive, become really sick, the kind of sick only other people can make you. Paranoid. I think that when you doubt what you know so deeply, so importantly, when you take an ax to the delicate neck of intuition, you go Crazy. Obsessive-compulsive. Sitting on my bed when the house's silence and the house's creaks roared, I would rub my crotch, rub rub, squeeze my tits like bundles of cloth, the skin clutched in my bony fingers. I'd make a lewd face. It only lasted a minute, my ritual, and it meant Will was not watching. It meant he was not there—a charm. Dizzy and relieved, I'd slide a disk of vinyl from a battered cardboard sleeve. The crackling scratch of the needle engulfed my room again, and the house was gone. It was just me. I'd lip-synch.

In the mirror, to Siouxsie, making enigmatic faces, my fingers around my eyes like a witch sprinkling potion into a pot. I liked to watch my mouth move around the words, the wet dart of my tongue. I still loved to lip-synch. Sometimes I'd get an attack in the middle of a song. That was bad, when the silence of the house invaded the music, made it sound tinny and canned, mechanical. Suddenly the music was just furniture, the stereo no different than my bed or the linoleum. I'd freeze in the mirror, mouth half-formed around the croon of a word. I'd freeze and rub my crotch. It was so gross I'd try to make it pretty. Sexy, or something like that. The mirror reflected the reality of my gargoyle facial expressions, the rude grope of my hands. I tried to be smooth and pornographic. Lick my lips so that Will wouldn't be there. But he was always there, even when he was stoned in front of the TV, watching *Cheers.* Thinking that he was sometimes there meant I could never be alone with my body. I would respond to him to make him not be there, because it was just too terrible that I was having this relationship with him, my father. The yellowy light from my ceiling, and my body in the mirror like roadkill. Rub grab rub grimace, anytime I approached myself in the mirror and attempted to enjoy what I saw. I froze and waited for the *creak.* I hurried into my pajamas. Into my bed, into the comforter, face pressed into the pillow. Lights out. *Creak.*

DONKEYBOY

Beau Manson was really not my type. He and his friends were known as the "donkeys," a nickname hurled at them by an angry father in the process of kicking them all out of his daughter's room. Like Pinocchio's pals, gone bad and braying on Pleasure Island. They were straight, skaters—not quite punk, not quite jock. Certainly more punk than jock, but Beau and his buddies had such *guy* energy it made me think of jocks. His big, steely shoulders. With the exception of his bleached hair, tugged up into wormy spikes with a clumpy gel, he looked like he could have gone to my new vocational high school out in Wakefield. I'd never thought about going after any of the Donkeys. Mostly I pursued death-rock boy-nymphs, which was perhaps why I was seventeen and still a virgin. All the death-rock girls were. The boys did not want to fuck us. It was fine by me, I liked being drunk and settling into lush, endless make-out sessions with them—to take it further would have introduced a hardness to the softness, something awkward and unromantic. Still, I wondered how old I could get before I just gave it up. I read *The Bell Jar*, the part about Esther's day pass from the nut house to hunt down a guy to lay her. I wanted to lose my virginity before I lost my mind, and official adulthood was around the corner, lugging its knapsack of anxiety. I brought Beau with me to Vinnie's basement, to hang out and drink beer. We snuck over to the wooden stairs that led up to Vinnie's house and made out, Beau's hand wedged beneath the elastic of my underwear. I've tried to remember any kind of meaningful conversation, or moments of connection, or anything eventful that preceded us having sex, but there is nothing. I didn't know how to talk to Beau Manson—I never hung out with boys like him. I think the reason I decided to like him was that he was who he was, and yet he didn't fuck with me. I had only ever seen Macho on jocks and assholes— Beau was totally boy. A Donkey.

I told Beau about my plans to cut school, and invited him to come view my shabby house in Chelsea. I barely went to school senior year, to the point that I had trouble graduating. It seemed so pointless—I could sleep at school, or I could sleep in my bed. Bed was more comfortable, bed won. But I couldn't sleep in that morning, knowing that Beau was on his way, hopping train-train-bus from Jamaica Plain over the hulky green Tobin. I cleaned up my house, folded the knitted afghan over the back of the couch, moved ashtrays around, the years of ashes a thick grime against the glass. I washed teacups, untangling teabag strings from their moorings beneath the handles. I stood in the doorway of my bedroom and tried to imagine what it would look like to Beau. Christian Death posters, Skinny Puppy lyrics painted on my blinds, more goth lyrics blobbed on the linoleum in black nail polish, dismembered Barbies and Catholic knickknacks. My bedspread, that bright orange and limey green and yellow, it ruined everything. I sighed. I went into the shower and smeared Nair all over my legs, a pink paste with a toxic stink. It was the color of Pepto-Bismol and I could not get the terrible smell of it off my skin. Beau showed up with some bags from the McDonald's on the corner. We ate cheeseburgers on the couch. The possibility of my parents coming home and finding me not at school, at home in an empty house with a boy who was not a fag—this was a real possibility. They had caught me before, when I had cut school just to sleep, and they were furious. I knew that for them to find me today would be the worst, possibly run-away material. I prayed they had taken their lunches to work at the hospital, or were eating in the cafeteria or wherever nurses ate.

Me and Beau went into my room. It was so mechanical—we both knew what was going to happen so there was little pretense of foreplay, or even affection, though he wasn't cold. We were just two different species, and we both wanted something and had met here, in a Chelsea bedroom that smelled of cheeseburgers and Nair, to get it. Maybe Beau went down on me for a minute. A mixed tape was playing on my stereo and I lost my virginity to the Sisters of Mercy. "Anaconda." Or Kommunity FK, "Something Inside Me Has Died." Beau fiddled around with his dick and then shifted above me to move it inside. Do You Have A Condom On? I felt kind of stupid asking. *What do you think I was just doing?* That made me feel worse. Maybe Beau *was* an asshole. I mean, of course he was, but I was also so weird, it made me want to cut him some slack. As he pushed into me, I said, Be Careful. *What?* He sounded annoyed. I Never Did This Before. I wanted him to know that. That this did have some kind of meaning for me, because I really had no connection to Beau, this boy. I could feel it there on my bed, the profound lack of connection, and I could feel his no-connection to me. But I wanted him to know I had a real connection to the moment. Beau looked at me like he didn't believe me. We had sex. I was really glad that I was in my room. I looked up at the Christian Death poster above my bed, the one that came with that live boxed set. Beau was moving all around on top of my body, and I thought that he shouldn't be doing all of the work so I started thrusting up at him, a sort of spazzy bucking which he soon asked me to stop. I was supposed to simply lie there, how weird. I couldn't believe that the girl end of this whole thing was just to lie there. It was embarrassing. Don't ask how it felt physically, it was somehow not a physical experience. It was mental, and aural, Peter Murphy's quivering howl, something inevitable was happening. Beau was sweating an amazing sweat, he was dripping. I'd never seen anyone sweat so hard. When he was done, he took off the condom and he threw it on my floor. I knew my room looked like a dumpster, but that I couldn't believe. Are You Going To Leave That There? I gasped. There's A Trash Bucket Right There. He got up and threw it away properly, put his underwear on. It was over. I'm Going To Take A Shower, I announced with fake cheer, and left the room. The bathroom was still a fumy cloud of Nair. We had to get out of there before my parents got home, and I had to go to my job at the Copy Cop in Boston. Leaving the house was a serious challenge—Lisa lived downstairs, and Will's brother and his family had just moved in upstairs. But we did it. We walked blocks to catch the bus because the regular bus stop was too close to my house. I felt under siege. I was no longer a virgin, big deal. At the bus stop I petted a leashed bulldog, and it sneezed on my face. Beau laughed.

Beau's favorite book was *The Little Prince*. We were killing time at a bookstore before my shift started at the Copy Cop, me in fiction and Beau in the children's section. He brought me the book, small with a white cover, a little boy on it. *Have you read this? This is my favorite book.* I bought it. I thought it was nice that Beau had a favorite book. I read it and thought it was a strange book for kids. It was about death. I thought it was very sad and beautiful, and it made me think about Beau. We hung out a few times during the school week. I met him in Boston, at night, on the library steps where everyone hung out on the weekends. It was weird to be alone with Beau in the city, none of the other kids around, not drunk. I think I actually suggested we get some vodka. I bought it with my new fake ID—Cossack, the cheapest vodka. I thought maybe if we got drunk we'd have fun. I didn't know what to do with Beau. He was applying to colleges. I was doing that too, but in such a scatterbrained way—applying to the School of Visual Arts in New York City to study filmmaking, to UCLA for English literature. The applications, and their attendant essays, were piled into an anxious architecture on my kitchen table. They'd get shifted about as the day moved from breakfast to dinner, and I'd find little twigs of cereal crusted on the pages, a smear of Ragu, a dark stain of chicken grease. It's Such A Bunch Of Bullshit, I raged to Beau as we sat on the library steps, passing the bottle of Cossack. College, I continued. The drink was hitting me and I felt very passionate. It's Just Bullshit, All Of It. I wanted Beau to chime in, *Yeah,* talk to me about life, about feeling lost, feeling like you wanted to eat a giant world that was not edible. *Bullshit,* he said with a little laugh. Beau would go to college. His world was easy.

Me and Beau had sex one more time. Behind a park where kids were drinking 40s. We hopped a construction fence and climbed inside half-finished buildings. It was all raw lumber, beams and shavings. A good smell. Some stairs took us to the roof where the sky was closer and all of Boston rolled darkly beneath us. We had sex there and it didn't hurt as much. I didn't move this time. My writhing that first time had left my thighs bruised and sore for days, so Beau must have been right about my keeping still. I lay on the rough, papered roof and looked up, past Beau. I was going to have to find a way to enjoy this, if I was going to keep having boyfriends. More than anything, it was boring. Beau finished and got up, peeled the condom off and flung it on the floor again. Not my floor. I got up and pulled my skirts down, arranged them, found that my favorite silver angel, a little cherub, a cupid with a bow, had fallen off my neck. The thin silver chain had snapped. That had to mean something. I was fallen. I put the charm in my pocket, and took the smoking Camel Beau had lit for me. We didn't talk, we walked back down the stairs that smelled like freshly killed trees, and we could hear our drunk friends screaming in the park.

Beau took me to one of his friends' houses, one of the Donkeyboys. We were in the basement, a carpeted rec room where Beau's hardcore band, Lost Children, practiced. There were amps, and ratty flyers from their shows on the walls, a few all-ages gigs on Sunday afternoons in Allston. We drank beer and watched TV. It was dark, and I felt drowsy from my bottle. I draped myself across Beau's back, hugged into him. He shrugged me off. Gently. I knew it was going to stop soon. It would stop before I could figure out what it had meant. If it meant anything. It was close to Xmas, and I'd already bought Beau the *Alice in Wonderland* video, the Disney one. He loved *Alice In Wonderland*. And *The Little Prince*. They were like codes from his boyhood, beaming out at me. I was sure they meant something but Beau was like a block, a hunk of chiseled silence. He played me the Pixies for the first time, and I still love them, so there's that.

I had lent him a Christian Death tape, and the night he showed up at Vinnie's house to go sledding he had it in the pocket of his bulky plaid coat. *Here.* We went sledding down this hill in East Boston. At the top of the hill was a giant illuminated cross, which we found hilarious. There was a sign that said, "Come See the Forty-Foot Madonna!" with a sign pointing to Orient Heights, where there stood a towering shrine of the Virgin Mary. We would often go to the shrine and steal glass candles, lie beneath Mary's giant feet so that she looked scary, a Catholic King Kong about to swoop down and grab you. The legend was that when they shipped the thing over from Italy, there had been no tear on the Virgin's face, but when they unwrapped her here in America—a tear! Deeply etched upon her moldy green cheek. But her face was too far up in the sky to see for sure—a mottled, patina face.

Up on the holy hill with the glowing cross, it was snowing some light flakes, and we were trying to sled down a weedy path that led to the highway. You couldn't really let yourself slide with abandon, or else you'd zoom all the way down and get flattened by a car. Beau broke up with me there, by the cross. The other kids were careening carefully down the windy trail, hollering, loud, and me and Beau were alone together in our quiet. Okay, I said. I wasn't going to cry in front of him, though I felt a swelling in my throat, a slow squeeze. We walked back to Vinnie's house, lingering behind our friends, dragging the plastic sled on the ground like it was Christ's cross. It made an awful scraping sound, and our friends trotted ahead of us, escaping our bad breakup vibes. *Well, do you want to talk?* Beau asked, exasperated with my quiet. *Do you even care?* My not-caring seemed to irritate him, which irritated me. Why did he care if I cared? Did he want me to cry and flip out, beg him to stay with me, threaten to kill myself? I Care, I said defensively. I Just . . . I Don't Know, I Don't Want To Get All Upset In Front Of You. We crunched through the thin coat of snow. Mostly I felt like I'd failed, hadn't had sex right or talked about the right things or anything, I was boring. I wanted Beau to go home to Jamaica Plain so I could tell Vinnie I got dumped and really have a cry. What would I do with the *Alice in Wonderland* video? Beau went home, and I did cry. I cried for about four or five days, maybe a whole week. After Beau broke up with me, I realized that I loved him, that love had come my way and I hadn't fought to keep it. I was broken. In my bed I read and reread *The Little Prince*—the rose that had loved the Prince, the rose the Prince had abandoned, that was me. Thorny on my lonely planet. I wouldn't go to school. My mother was at my bedroom door yelling at me, but I was righteous in my refusal. I'm Not Going To School, I sobbed. I had a crown of lead on my skull, weighting my head to my pillow.

Beau Manson. One night he'd gotten arrested, as we were walking down Comm Ave on the way to a party. I had just dropped my empty wine cooler into a trash can, but Beau still had his beer when the cops roared up and *bam,* arrested him for drinking in public. I had escaped it by a quick blink of time, I had a beautiful split-second knack for avoiding the drinking arrests that snared most of my friends. The cops were such assholes about Beau's name being Manson, *We got a Manson,* they said, passing his ID around, laughing. *Any relation to Charles?* Beau rolled his eyes. As his girlfriend, I got to be the one who hysterically ran around the party, organizing the ride to the station to rescue my imprisoned boyfriend. When the cops had Beau empty his pockets, they found a chocolate lollipop shaped like a penis, and a pot pipe, which they sent to the lab. It only cost twenty-five dollars to get your friends out of jail for drinking—it happened all the time. You had to find a kid with an ATM card, which was rare in the eighties, they were new. I set Beau free and then he dumped me, and I stayed out of school for a little while.

I Need A Mental Health Day, I wailed at my seriously irritated mother. It's not like she didn't call in sick to her job all the time. *I need a mental health day,* she'd say, not to her boss but to me, and settle down in front of the TV or take a nap. I just lay in bed and read that book, *The Little Prince.* Beau was such a hypocrite for loving it, he had no right to it. I didn't share any of this misery with Beau—he probably never knew I cared at all. I'd nod and say hi when I saw him on the library steps, drinking beer with the skaters. *Hey,* he'd say, and I'd go sit with the death rockers, and drink vodka, not beer.

DIVINATION

I went to the psychic tearoom to find out if I was being sexually abused. By Will, my rock n' roll father, who picked me up from high school on my detention days in his big black car, blaring Black Sabbath, wearing mirrored asshole sunglasses, scaring all the boys from the shop classes, boys who called me "Cunt" in the hallways but froze now, because this big hesher dude seemed like my boyfriend.

You'd think a girl would know if she was being sexually abused, but what if it were something so secret it was almost psychic, a certain witchcraft or a magician's trick, then how would you know? And what if it were nothing more than the creaks of an old, settling house, anyway? I knew about a place in Boston where desperate people went to glean bits of their own information from the gobs of cosmic knowledge that roost around our bodies, invisible. Certain gifted people—psychics—have the ability to fetch yourself for you when you are lost. The place was a tearoom, I'd discovered it years ago on a preteen sneak into the city, right upstairs from the black-light abyss of Stairway to Heaven, the coolest place in Boston. It sat on one of those side streets that existed mainly to funnel bargain hunters from the Park Street T station down to Filene's Basement and Jordan Marsh. Inside Stairway to Heaven longhaired rockers and girls with unfriendly tattoos sold you concert T-shirts, plucking them from the ceiling, where they swung like bats on their hangers. A long glass case held concert photos—glossy David Lee Roth in midair, a spandex boomerang hurling toward the crowd; Billy Idol's stoned sneer and knuckly fist; Angus Young with his head dipped over his guitar, sweat-wet curls hiding his mouthy pout. There were cases of buttons and patches, and a little nook of necessary accessories like studded bracelets, fingerless gloves, miniature chain-link jewelry, blue lipstick, green hairspray. Another cave-ish corner, where the black-light posters glowed that creepy burnout glow under purple light bulbs. I would buy pins for my jacket, and posters to hang in my paneled bedroom, and I would look for punk rockers. I didn't buy concert T-shirts, because it seemed phony to buy something like that in a store.

But upstairs from Stairway to Heaven—which was simply called "Stairway"—was the psychic tearoom. Once you knew about it, it was hard not to go a lot. It was a kind of stark, cafeteria-looking place, discolored white everything, white that's been stewing in nicotine and old ladies. Formica tables arranged in a little room that looked like a normal coffee shop, except there were framed illustrations of the Book of Revelations hung on the walls, and some of the customers were falling into trances. I would convince my grandmother, who had a resentful fascination with psychic things, to take me there. Nana was Aquarian, thus hopelessly drawn to such stuff, but she was so worried about being flung into hell for it, she could never go all the way. Horoscopes in the paper were okay, and she had these ancient, coverless paperbacks on her dresser, pages so discolored and brittle they seemed fire-damaged, falling apart at the spine. They listed every possible thing you could ever dream about, and translated it into a lottery number for you to bet on. If Nana dreamt of a turtle, she'd wake up, hit the book and put her money on the turtle number. She hardly ever won, but she never stopped playing. She believed in the system, she had a trust in fate and destiny and the will of God, and if it wasn't her time to win, she knew she wouldn't, but that turtle number was still a good number, and it was hers. Occasionally, Nana would have psychic dreams. If she'd still been alive, maybe she could have told me if Will was fucked up and sick, doing something slick and scary, abusing me not with his hands but, like a sorcerer, with his eyes. Casting tricky holes in the walls of our house, little magic hats to pull his new daughters through. Like Athena, we'd come full grown. No fatty baby flesh like molding putty, no soft minds that could grow around secrets. Will had to be a master sneak. Either he was, either there were holes in our doors, keyhole monocles, either Will was a sick witch or I was simply crazy, fed on hysteria and TV talk shows and trashy teen paperbacks about heroically abused girls. I thought I might be turning, like a carton of milk kept past its date. Every day I woke up feeling a pinch more dislodged, like sanity was a job that was slowly letting me off the hook. Every morning I woke into stillness, my ears grasping at the floorboard creaks that were perhaps my stepfather doing a perverted ballet outside my bedroom door. Or maybe it was just my spiky black cat on an innocent prowl.

If Nana hadn't gotten a rotten glob of cancer in her lungs, if all her determination not to inhale, if that little health plan had paid off and allowed her to live, not die an incoherent, jaundiced alien-Nana with toasted chicken skin stretched taut across her bones like a starving child, if she hadn't wasted away, lost her mind and finally died in a crappy little room at General, maybe Nana could have helped. I like to imagine that her scorn of the sexual impulse, coupled with her dim view of men, would have made her an ally. That, and the fact that she loved me, even when she stopped loving my hair once I stripped away its shine, stopped loving my clothes once they descended into thrift-store morbidity, black upon black upon black, ancient lacy things last worn by dead Italian widows. She still loved me. When Dennis had kicked us out and we had nowhere to go but her house in arguably the worst part of Chelsea, Nana had cornered me at her dresser, where I was playing dress-up with her stuff. Probably the best part of having to cram our cracked little family into her place was the twenty-four-seven availability of Nana's shimmering polyester nightgowns, her thin gold neck-laces that I liked best not clasped around my neck, but lying on my forehead like a modest crown. Big, dusty squirts of Emeraude, which smelled green and made me sneeze. Nana's wooden jewelry box was a stack of blue velvet-lined drawers, where chunks and strands slinked and sparkled. The grape hunk of amethyst I'd get when she died because it was February's stone, and we were both born then, in the month of virgin martyrs, a cursed and evil month that infused its babies with a bad magic. Another of Nana's rings, a cluster of tiny round stones, polished to a pastel gleam like a bunch of Easter eggs—if you flipped the stones up, underneath was the tiniest ticking clock. After Dennis left, when Nana caught me in her swishy nightgown over my Catholic-school uniform, I was lowering a third layer of gold chain onto my exotically glinting brow. Nana asked, *Does your father hit your mother? Did you ever see him do that?* No, I said, shaking my head. The chains slid away and were caught in the severe nest of tangles at the back of my head.

If Nana were alive, and not stuck in a cement case under the ground at Woodlawn Cemetery, in a grave I'd only seen twice, a flat plaque flush with the ground—if she were alive and not dead, maybe she could have helped me, with her Aquarian dream magic, with her protective suspicion and with her love.

Me and Nana used to ride up the elevator three stories to the psychic tearoom, and Nana would grumble and arm herself with skepticism, because she was doing something weird and disreputable and perhaps sinful. Each time we would visit the same psychic, and each time she would tell us both the same things. *You will live to be one hundred and fifty, you will take a trip on a plane,* she'd say to Nana. Nana kicked it at fifty-five, and never once flew in the sky. The psychic was old and fat with wiry brown hair where she pinned huge bows and plastic flowers. She always wore red, and kept bright dots of red rouge on each cheek, like a doll. She was the craziest looking psychic, so we went to her. On the walls, beneath the comic-book illustration of the Whore of Babylon astride the great beast, were clippings from the *Herald* and the *Boston Globe* about the lady's psychic accomplishments, how she helped the police find children, and children find their pets. That crazy old woman was gone by now, and I wouldn't have gone to her anyway. I needed real information. Was my father the very worst man ever, worse than the widely hated first dad, Dennis, worse than the packs of boys who called me a dog in the street, who grabbed at my tits and then laughed that there was nothing to grab. *A carpenter's dream—flat as a board and easy to screw.* I wasn't easy to screw. I was such a challenge to get a kiss from you had to steal it, with a shove against the wall as I walked back from school. So difficult to even glimpse that secret holes had to be chinked and chiseled, clandestine mining operations, acts of art and mathematics.

I'd gone to another psychic a few years back, and she had cracked a great mystery for me and Marisol, concerning the spider-haired rock god who worked the elevator at the record store in Boston. We didn't know his name, so, like the stray dog, we called our crush Nikki, after Nikki Sixx. This Nikki wore leather pants. God! we gasped, fluttering out the creaky elevator door—those *pants*, fucking *leather,* where did you even get pants like that? Me and Marisol went together to the psychic cafeteria and traded a scrunched-up fiver for a steaming styro-foam cup of tea. No tea bag, this wasn't Tetley, it was loose, psychic flecks of brown that swirled in the cup like mucky lake water. All the people who worked at the place were odd—queer, punky in an awkward way, old and lost and, it seemed, suspicious of *me.* They squinted at me like actors in a Western, like I'd come to unload a crate of snake oil on them. It made me weave through the tables carefully, on tiptoe. You could feel the psychic buzz in the room like a slight caffeine in the air. Can You Feel It? I whispered to Marisol, who nodded solemnly. Marisol's hair was golden-blond fluff, too thick to hold the Aqua Net flip of bangs cresting stiff above her face. It all flopped about heavily and irritated her. Marisol's eyes were blue like the sky, and like the sky they showed their weather—clear and sunny at times, sparkling crystal, and then icy, flat as cloud cover. At those times she was hard to peer into, like her eyes had their blinds down.

I knew I was inside a sort of temple as I ripped open my small packets of sugar and sent a fall of the stuff into my tea, whipped the brackish water around with my stir stick. It was too hot to drink, but the psychic people were all watching, sort of psychically hovering, twitchy as call girls to see who we would choose for divination. It was competitive. I slurped the hot sweetness and strained the leaves with my teeth, spit them back into the cup. It was hard not to swallow some, but I didn't want to eat my future. *Slurp, slurp,* stir; *slurp, slurp,* stir. I was supposed to be concentrating on my life's grand questions, so I meditated on Nikki. His stark ghost-face, an anemic mask, black cords of hair sluicing across his cheek. I sighed into the steam. I had worn my coolest outfit that day, for our earlier trip into the record store—white stirrup stretch pants and a white half-shirt featuring a big cartoon koala bear wearing a pair of hot punk sunglasses. "Why B Normal?" Leftover pink Halloween hairspray on my shapeless mop, and gigantic plastic question-mark earrings, the punctuating dots fuchsia balls that looked like Crunch Berries. Me and Marisol both held our breath when we entered the cramped space of the ancient Boston elevator it was Nikki's job to operate. I so desperately wanted his face to crack into a human expression at the sight of us, if not a smile then at least a sniff, an eyebrow shifting his forehead, anything to know he was alive under all that coolness. Nothing. Just a rigor-mortis stare at the floor. His ass a tiny leather package.

I sucked the last swampy puddle of tea from the bottom of my cup. I'm Ready, I announced timidly to a bleach-blond girl with an asymmetrical do. *Who do you want to read you?* Whoever, I shrugged. She sent me to a big woman with long hair, brown and greasy. Her face seemed blank, sort of vacant, but maybe she kept it that way so she could fill it all up with cosmic vibes. *Stir three times, counterclockwise,* she instructed. I scraped the plastic stick through the muck, and then turned the cup on its head. *Cover it with your right hand, and make a wish.* I thought about Nikki. I could wish for him to fall in love with me, but I knew that wouldn't happen and was reluctant to waste a wish. What about wishing for infinite wishes? What a trick. But she wasn't guaranteeing the wish would come true. And didn't I already have a churning stew of infinite wishes that I ate from daily? I could wish to be as cool as Nikki. Was that shallow? Nikki. I Wish, I recited clearly, inside my brain, To Know Who Nikki Is. His Name, At Least. I sat with the thought, palm on Styrofoam. The woman flipped the cup over and laid her own soft palm on it. She breathed. Her eyelids lowered and twitched, and her eyeballs rolled right back into her head. They were spinning backward to some deep place where the answers to everything lived. It was like she'd been struck by something, a current, epilepsy. She was either totally for real psychic, or the biggest faker ever. Her eyes came back and she told me some stuff, who knows what. It's hard to tell the fortune of someone with no life. She said, *Your wish will come true very soon, this week, maybe even today.* She lingered for a tip and scowled away.

Me and Marisol took the claustrophobic tearoom elevator back out into bustling Boston. *What did you wish?* Marisol asked. I hedged. I Don't Think I Can Tell You, Right? It Won't Come True. *Was it about Nikki?* I nodded. Maybe We Should Go To Strawberries Again? Downtown Crossing was a slow sludge of humanity, we entered the throng like gum wrappers into a gutter current and let the people shove us toward the record store. I hadn't noticed the flyer in the window on our earlier visit. A band called Twenty-One with a new album entitled *Dress Dangerous.* A xerox of the band, nothing special save for the guy clutching his guitar with a skeleton claw, the gaunt spider boy, Nikki. Oh My God, Marisol! I jabbed the glass. Oh My God, Oh My God! We zoomed inside and ransacked the Local Bands bin until we found a shrink-wrapped copy of *Dress Dangerous.* I flipped it over—Guitar: Antoine Maybe. *Antoine!* we gasped. The bag-check girl rolled her eyes and shot us a painful faux smile. Antoine! Oh, it was so much more romantic than Nikki. Less street, more eloquent, French, a gentle name, not mean. Suddenly the facade of his fashion seemed not sinister—*Dress Dangerous*—but sad and alienated, eternally misunderstood. I changed my spiky black cat's name from Nikki to Antoine. Then to Antoinette, when she had kittens. We hadn't known. Marisol and I memorized the exotic spelling to properly carve it into our arms later. I was thrilled by the psychic capabilities of my tea leaf reader. Psychics were real! What else was real, then? Astral projection? UFOs? What a fantastic day, to learn the true identity of the mysterious rock hero, and prove the existence of supernatural phenomena.

Marisol and I languished at the back of the bus as it hauled us over the Tobin Bridge into Chelsea. The Boston Harbor buckled beneath us like Antoine's leather knees as he bent to unlatch the elevator doors. Knowing Antoine's name made him real, made anything possible. Certainly he knew many people—maybe someone I

237   Divination

knew knew Antoine. But I didn't know anyone but nuns and losers. I thought about Will, my rock n' roll father with the India ink tattoos on his fingers. Could Will know Antoine Maybe? Will knew lots of people, everyone in Chelsea it seemed, all the rough-looking guys in the streets. I lapsed into a grand delusion—I'd swing open the wooden door to my home, and there, beyond the worn, carpeted living room where the television lived and breathed all day, in the kitchen at the table like neighborhood gossips would be Will and Antoine, drinking beers. A couple of cans on the table, and cigarettes burning in the green glass ashtray. *This is my daughter, Michelle,* Will would introduce proudly. Antoine's face would shift, he'd actually speak. Maybe he was even British, and his voice would chime the most delicate accent. You could believe that he was too cool to be American. Antoine would recognize me from earlier, in the elevator, he'd remember the wacky koala bear on my half-shirt. *Nice shirt,* he'd smile. *Nice shirt,* whined a voice, cutting into my little dream-snack. That horrid accent, not British. Some rotten woman across from me on the Chelsea bus. *A koala bear with sunglasses.* She shook her head like a grand shame had occurred. I tried to sneer, but probably looked like I had to sneeze. Marisol rolled her eyes. I trudged a slightly broken but still dreamy trudge from the bus down the deadend street where my house sat. The last house on the left. Was that a horror movie, or a porn movie? The apartment was empty, I walked into Ma and Will's bedroom and snatched a Led Zeppelin tape from my father's dresser. I took it into my room and popped it in my stereo, set about listening to it like learning something. It was huge, psychic music, foggy. Didn't they sell their souls to the devil and live together in a big satanic castle, doing drugs? I spread out on my bed. It could still happen. Will could come home with a friend—not Ricky, the gay nurse, or the spooky guy with the bifocal glasses who smoked Old Golds and studied the occult. He could come home with Antoine, blazing into our tired apartment like everything that wasn't Chelsea, like everything else in the world there was.

Five years later and that psychic still worked at the tearoom, the eerie, correct psychic with the sociopathic blankness in the face and the Linda Blair eyeballs. I wondered if she was a lesbian. Sometimes I thought everyone in the tearoom was gay or bisexual, like everyone at *Rocky Horror*. In a corner of the room I daintily scalded my mouth with tea. I dwelled heavily on Will. I could not simply ask him if he was watching me in my bedroom and bathroom. When? As we sat watching television together in the dark living room, smoky as a bar, Will's zoned-out face staring through the dumb TV? He was barely there sometimes, you'd have to say his name three or four times before he'd pick up the signal and respond. Will, Will, Will? Was he stoned? He smoked pot in the back hallway, behind my bedroom. Maybe Will was blankly psychic, like the woman at the tearoom, picking up vibrations. Were they mine, did I have a sexual leak like an animal stink that drew him to my keyhole? I believed in all psychic phenomena, in vibes and auras and energy. And I suspected that I not only thought about sex too much, I thought about the wrong kind of sex, sick and not healthy. Girls being kidnapped and mating with dogs and pimped out by gangs. Daddies. Was I transmitting some kind of signal? Will in his armchair, like a big satellite dish waiting for waves from outer space.

To confront Will with my suspicions, I would first have to catch his elusive attention, then the equally elusive courage would have to be fetched from inside myself, then I'd have to fend off the vertigo that hit me like a hallucinogen whenever I thought about it at all. And then I'd have to somehow work it all into a sentence, speak. Dad, Are You Spying On Me? Do You Watch Me In My Room? It only illuminated my own dirty mind. Paranoia of the worst kind. Just hearing the question unfurl in the privacy of my brain made me feel gross. Maybe I was a Sicko. They looked just like everyone else. But the real bitch was, even if I succeeded in spitting the awful question out into the room, Will would say no. He'd say no whether it was true or not, because he had been a criminal, and criminals know to deny everything. He'd given me that exact advice, if I ever got caught doing something—not by him or my mother of course, but by other people I guess, the cops. Will always tried to be down by making cryptic allusions to the stuff he knew I must be doing out there in the world with my freaky friends. It often seemed like he thought I was more of an outlaw than I really was, and I worried about letting him down with how not-bad I was. But sometimes he was right on, like when he brought me home a Duncan yo-yo that lit up with crazy flashing lights as you spun it, saying, *That's for when you're tripping out in Harvard Square.* If I asked Will my question and he followed his criminal credo, Deny Everything, a sting of shame would shut me right back up forever. I'd turn back to the TV for the rest of my life and I'd never know anything. I just wanted someone, a stranger, to walk up to me in the street, grab my arm and whisper, *Your father is doing terrible things,* and scurry away. Something certain falling down from the sky, like a grand piano. Either I had to catch him, or someone, a psychic, had to say something uncanny.

In the tearoom I dumped the Styrofoam cup onto the saucer and placed my hand on it like I was making a promise. Make a wish. Wish for a million wishes, keep wishing till you make the right one. Wish for Will to be good and Michelle to be crazy. Wish for there to be help for Michelle's particular mode of crazy, wish that she was born into a different family, one with the money to tuck her into McLean, like Sylvia Plath, like the dozen self-mutilating, well-off goth kids she knew from Newton. I'd visited them there, and it's a real nice place. I could be institutionalized and assigned a woman psychologist. I would write a stunning book about it all before I stuck my head into the oven. I tried to observe it all objectively. It was Will's potential for detachment, evil and pathological sexuality vs. Michelle's potential for delusions, paranoia and a preoccupation with sex that was also, certainly, pathological. I loved psychology—like most mentally ill people, I wanted to be a psychologist.

The psychic flickered her eyes around, I watched the void blue irises float away beneath her twitching lashes, a strobe. They were scraping information from the back of her brain. She told me about . . . who cares, a bunch of crap, useless. Nothing about any fathers, about my family, about me being sick in the head. *Is that all?* My fifteen minutes were up. The empty-vessel expression was about to get filled up with the tip-me expression. Do You See Anything About My Father? She halted, looked into the cup, the clumps of tea clinging to the Styrofoam curve. Is He Doing Anything . . . Bad? She paused, flicked her eyes around, came back. *He hit on one of your friends, he did something inappropriate to her.* I sat and stared. Wondered at the urge to hit her that had inflated in my chest. I felt feverish. Tried to sigh it away. I did not need a whole new after-school special to investigate. I was not the Girl Wonder Sex-Crime Sleuth. Her eyeball act was a sham. Okay, Thanks, I said, and split the scene. I could try a different psychic. I could try psychic after psychic until I was truly broke, until I heard the divination I liked best. I flipped cards from my own tarot pack onto my bedroom's cracked linoleum, song lyrics nail-polished around the fissures like New Age affirmations on Post-its. I flipped the cards into the dust and they didn't say anything. There is no Sneaky Secret Molesting Dad card in the tarot. There's the Devil, but I wanted him to be good, all about drinking and sex. Even if he was bad, how did I know the card didn't refer to me, the filthy-minded girl so preoccupied with sex she thinks her own dad wants her? My mind warmed into some Freudian calisthenics. Paranoia as warped desire—I really *wanted* Will to be spying on me. Wished for him to. Maybe my brain thought things it kept even from me. Wasn't that the essence of psychology? So, if my body operated on its own, doing things without my knowledge, like you know, converting sugars and secreting hormones, and my *brain* was churning out thoughts and desires and witholding *them* from me, who was Me? If I wasn't my body, or my brain, what was thinking? I felt on the verge of a terrible fracture. I shut it down. I loaded my brain's pockets with rocks and swam into my house. It was fogged with the excellent meaty stink of Spam, sizzling on the stove. Spam and eggs. Breakfast for dinner, fun-house eating, everything inside out. Will fixed me a plate of morning and I brought it into the living room, affixed myself to the television and ate.

CLIVE

My boyfriend Clive drove an old Continental, a long steel boat of a car. Clive had spotted it nudged up against the curb of some random street in Beverly, Massachusetts, the sweet, sleepy seaside town where he lived with his parents. Clive first seduced me after we went on a date to the Children's Museum, where he'd stolen a lamb vertebra from a skeletal exhibit and impressed me with his aesthetic and his daring. I, too, had been coveting the lamb vertebra, imagining it looped onto leather cord, making a really cool necklace. Clive had seized the moment, and I was interested in what he would do with the pilfered treasure. Afterward we went back to the house where he'd been living in Dorchester, and we drank some beer and I let him suck on my tits. My experiments with Kevin and Beau had left me with a growing understanding of my body in a sexual context. The shocking newness of those past encounters had felt like stealing cars or something, like vandalism. I could feel the vapor of sex becoming solid, becoming something that lived inside my body, a new hormone suddenly leached into the stream. A few weeks back I'd made out with a minor rock star at a Landsowne Street club, and he'd done his best to try to bring me back to his hotel. So many years jockeying for this position in life—the desired sex object of a rock star—and now that the man was in front of me, bragging about all the wine he had uncorked back at his very fancy rock-star hotel room, aiming his droopy, Sicilian eyes at me over his enormous Sicilian nose, begging, and all I was filled with was a sense of absurdity. He Doesn't Want Me. I Couldn't Do That. *Michelle, I'm trying to seduce you,* he finally spat, exasperated, and I murmured, I'm Only Eighteen, I'm Not Even Legally Allowed Inside This Club. As if that would be a deterrent. As a young nymph, I was oddly oblivious to the powers my youth held over the men I was fascinated with. I thought I was a kid, bumbling, and that they could see it, too. The following morning I awoke alone in my bed with a new ache sunk deep in my body. Later, in the living room, watching made-for-TV movies, hungover, the sight of the cheesy male hunks made it swell and crash harder. Oh My God, I thought, I Need To Get Fucked. I Think I'm Horny. I felt like a girl in a magazine, one of those ladies' rags. A deep, cellular hunger. I was embarrassed. I thought I was above such cravings, that my desires were intellectual, artistic, but this felt like *Wild Kingdom.* I thought of the rock star I'd sent away. Was I a fucking moron? I called his hotel, but the band was gone, flying over my head in the atmosphere, on the way back to England.

A short time later, Clive's wet mouth concentrated on my nipple, and he was my boyfriend. He was then living in a giant, heatless house in Savin Hill. Tiny, fire-hazard space heaters with intense orange coils radiated a sparse, dangerous warmth throughout the place. Occasionally Clive would get together with his roommate

Alvin—a beautiful sylph of a boy, willowy and effeminate though he kept girlfriends who wore their hair long and stringy in a hippie fashion, twins of the fair Alvin. Alvin's mother was an alcoholic, and it is because of the stories he told about her that I knew to drink gin when feeling bloated. That's what she did. His sister was a pregnant schizophrenic girl who ran away from home a lot. Alvin made his living by busking with his acoustic guitar in Harvard Square. He'd take his can of change and dollars back home on the T each night. Occasionally Clive and Alvin would shiver through the house, scavenging piles of old Sunday papers and ratty copies of the *Phoenix*, the odd slab of wood from a broken chair, and we'd build a roaring fire in the fireplace that arced in the otherwise empty main room. It was us, a pile of newspaper rolled into crunched puffs like snowballs, and the flickering, mysterious orange, the wild fire we tossed the paper into. We were medieval peasants, trembling into the wall of heat it gave off, drinking beer and worrying about burning the house down. The place was owned by a couple of Irish guys who lived upstairs, Irish from Ireland with thick, tangled accents. They kept dogs, big barking ones. They didn't masturbate, and urged Clive and Alvin to also abstain, because it wasted an important, nebulous energy called Chi. A psychic power reserve. Clive and Alvin would mock their Irish brogues, *Bad for the Chi!*

When Clive quit his education at Mass Art it was goodbye to his extravagant poverty and back into his boyhood room, a creatively shelved place his father had built. His father had built the entire house in fact, a cute, cottagey home, and his artwork hung all over it, paintings and sculptures of rusting cars and bicycles. Wow, I said the first time I entered the place, through the sliding glass doors and into the sun-washed wood. I was awed by the father's work. I thought perhaps I loved art, but I hadn't been around a lot of it. It felt like being in a church, that small, respectful feeling. Wow, I said to Clive. I Can't Believe Your Dad's An Artist. It Must Have Been So Great And Creative . . . Clive cut me off with a laugh, a bitter snort. Apparently the guy was a tyrant. He was a cold man, wolfish, with unruly curls of hair and icy blue eyes. Fathers always made me unbearably uncomfortable. I liked Clive's mother much better. She wore her hair in a blond bowl cut, and had the same turned-up nose as her son, the same wire-rimmed glasses perched on the sloping bridge. I could spot Clive clearly inside his mother's face, and so I loved her. They had had Clive young, a hippie mistake. An early photo showed little Clive falling into a pile of rusty autumn leaves, his mom behind him with a remarkable length of hair gleaming golden down her back, a long gingham skirt and those same eyeglasses.

Clive's parents went flyfishing. Often I'd come over and the kitchen table would be strewn with real dead bugs, the models for the intricate lures of thread and feather that Clive's dad made, hunched in a chair with a clutter of tiny tools. They were beautiful, miniature pieces of art, designed to trick and dazzle the fish. Curiosities from the natural world littered Clive's house: mouse skeletons, the delicate skull of a fox, beetles with shiny shells, moth wings decaying like old, torn lace. I was delighted, but the spread embarrassed Clive. Clive's Parents Keep Dead Bugs All Over Their House, I told my mother proudly. I was happy to have discovered normal people—parents—who liked things such as dead bugs, found them fascinating and even beautiful. I wanted my own mother to know that I was not a gross anomaly, other people liked the things that I liked, the things I liked that bothered her. Clive, a reddish boy to start, reddened deeper when I talked about his parents' insects. *They don't just have dead bugs all over the place,* he defended, imagining cockroaches and flies, termites, the yucky mundane pests we *try* to drive from our homes. No, Fancy Dead Bugs From The Woods, I explained. Clive looked pained. It's Art, I finished. If that didn't explain it, then I didn't know what else to say. *Oh, yeah?* my mother chirped. She loved Clive. I would sit on his lap in the dim living room, arms wound round his neck, watching TV. I felt like I had added a tiny family of my own to the larger familial entity. I guess that's how families do it, the normal expansion of the normal family—kids reaching out and snaring mates, bringing them home, breeding, producing new kids to snag mates to breed with. Outward it grows like a fractal, family. In the kitchen my mother clattered about, fixing supper, while me and Clive watched *The Simpsons.* It felt so comfortable and normal. Probably I would marry Clive. We would have children. I would bring them to visit my mother, their Nana.

Clive's parents, his father, really hated him moving back home. He wanted Clive to be more like himself—independent, out building houses, making babies, working working working, bringing home money if he wasn't getting an education, no idle time, no wishy-washy confusion. Dad wanted Action, he didn't understand how his great and hardy seed had spawned this boy who liked to spend his Saturday nights huddled on the futon, eating nubs of Velveeta stuck onto triangles of Doritos, watching *Saturday Night Live* and then *American Gladiators.* It took Clive forever to find a job, and meanwhile he infuriated his father by taking the money his parents had meticulously saved for his college fund and getting an inky tattoo on his shoulder, then buying the enormous Continental. I remember peering through the window at its insides before Clive bought it. It Looks Like A Diner, I breathed. So much chrome on the dash, the broad shine of the steering wheel. I wanted to have a boyfriend who drove such a grand automobile. I swooned and turned girlier, fingering the twin swords of windshield wipers. Prior to the Continental, Clive only had a moped. It was great to clutch him as we sped through quaint New England landscapes, dizzy with the fear of death, but this new mode of transport was so much more sophisticated. I could do my hair, tie a scarf around it, look nice and not like an alien, wearing the bowling-ball safety helmet required in order to ride on the back of Clive's puny moped. It felt so ridiculous to buckle your skull into the globe of headgear, and then straddle the sputtering toy that was the moped. Whenever we puttered by the white-trash house down the street, rednecks would push aside the Confederate flag hanging in the window like a curtain, and yell *Get a Harley!* We were amateurs.

I was thrilled when Clive squandered the rest of his education money on the car. Now we had someplace real to drink, as opposed to sitting with our asses on the pavement behind his old high school. We weren't teenagers, for chrissakes. I mean we were, but we weren't *high schoolers*. We should no longer have been forced into that undignified, juvenile way of getting drunk. Once Clive had a car we could drive to the convenience store and leisurely pore over the pornography rack, selecting the mag with the punkiest-looking pornlette, purchase it fearlessly from the embarrassed teenage clerk and bring it back into the car like civilized adults. No more getting busted by cops for drinking in public. No more getting flashlights shone into our faces by the smug, piggish men. No more feeling furious and creepy as they snagged the glossy smut and flipped the pages, looking at me with greasy, insinuating faces, pouring our Jack Daniels onto the ground. Now we mixed the Jack into our Cokes privately, and scanned our pornography with greater care. I felt fabulously grown up. I wasn't scared of anything, not the amber liquid that seared a smoking trail from gullet to groin, not the air-brushed pink pussies glistening from the magazine. I wasn't scared of blowjobs, or drunk driving, or doing both at the same time.

Clive was the first person to whom I let slip my fears about Will. I told him about Madeline in my bedroom, years ago. How she'd come inside and wedged the door shut behind her, sticking it in the paint-swollen jamb. *I think that Will might be spying on us.* She was so little, little like a thirteen-year-old girl is, just small, you know? Her long black hair and thin, scared face, so pale. It made me mad. What Are You Talking About? I snapped, though of course I knew. Trying to shame her into being quiet, taking it back.

Madeline worried, you had to know this about her. She worried so much about nuclear war that she wasn't allowed to watch *The Day After* when it premiered on television. Her therapist said her enormous terror of nuclear bombs—a terror that woke her up in the night, or prevented her from sliding into sleep at all—was really a fear of abandonment that haunted her psyche after Dennis discarded us. Therapists always want to blame everything on fear of abandonment. Fear of nuclear annihilation seemed like a worthy fear in and of itself. Madeline worried that the bombs would fill the sky and drop the ultimate, fiery poison on us. She worried that we'd vaporize in a flash, or waste away slowly, scavenging for food as our hair left our blistered scalps in clumps. She worried she had cancer, throat cancer specifically, whenever she had a dry or scratchy throat. As she grew older and began to deal with her female parts, it became cervical cancer, and AIDS, though she hadn't had sex with anyone. That fact didn't stop her from obsessing over being pregnant, either. Get Tested Then, I would say to her, about her T-cell decimation, or the tiny, supposed embryo clinging wetly to her insides. *I don't want to know!* she'd wail. She'd rather just sit and worry over the millions of things that can go wrong inside the body, the dizzying production and direction of red and white blood cells, the industry within that exhausted and terrified her.

I didn't call Madeline crazy, but it had rung in my voice, a shield. Because I knew about the weird creaks outside the bathroom door when I was taking a piss. It froze me there on the bowl, made me shiver like a ghost had passed through the room, like something scary was happening, something scary that you couldn't quite see. It's The Cat, I told myself. The cat who would often wait for me outside the door while I lingered in the bathroom, taking a crap or reading a magazine, whatever. But the cat only weighed a few pounds. Not enough to make the deep, cracking creaks in the floorboards, the ones I heard while alone in the bathroom. When I'd exit, Will would be so close, changing the channel on the cable box atop the TV. Flipping through ancient magazines in the magazine rack by the bathroom door. And the creaks outside my bedroom. One time, snug under the covers, I realized I had to pee, I hopped from the bed, flung open my door, and in the dark of the kitchen there was a sudden flash of light—Will flinging open the refrigerator door, about a foot from my bedroom. I nearly screamed, it was so startling. *Hungry,* he murmured, and I wondered why he hadn't turned the kitchen light on to get his snack, why fumble across the kitchen in the pitch black, why had he been there, so quiet in the dark, dark room. I had been talking myself out of all these evil thoughts of Will, and Madeline in my room saying them out loud made me want to puke. She'd heard the creaks too, outside the bathroom and outside her room as well. She'd sit on her bed and face the door, flip her middle finger up at the noise she had decided was Will. No, I said. No, You're Mistaken. I started to cry when I told this story to Clive. I was drinking a can of Coke shot with liquor, and the vinyl seat of the Continental crunched against my leather jacket. *Wow,* he said. *Maybe you should talk to Madeline.* I was just getting an understanding of feminism, and realized that it had been wrong of me to shoo Madeline away, not to listen and consider, to simply be scared and scrunch my eyes shut. I'd made her feel bad, like a loony, and it ate at me now. I hated the thought of Madeline having a secret, a bad secret to take to bed each night like a stuffed animal. Even If It's Not True, I said, It Was Wrong Of Me To Blow Her Off Like That. I gulped some Coke.

Clive, too, was feeling creepy about his parents. They fought at night in prolonged whispers, fierce hisses stretched against the dark. When gathering old papers for a papier-mâché project, he'd discovered a single personal ad clipped from the Women Seeking Men section. A perfect hole, a scissored space in the long run of print. Maybe Your Mother Knows? I suggested. Maybe They're Swingers? We were thinking of finding a girl to get naked with, too. Parents Are Just People, I said. Clive was skeptical. My confession made Clive hate my father, even though I didn't know anything, nothing for sure. Clive was convinced. He didn't like to come to my house after that, and I cried harder. My tiny, fledgling family, wrecked. My house made Clive feel weird. My mother made him sad, the way she'd pick us up little gifts at Walgreens. She thought of us too much and it made us feel guilty. Clive, You've Got To Come To My House, I begged. I would never have told him about Will if I'd thought it would make him pull away from me, out of my life, my family.

For Will's birthday, Clive sketched him a picture. It was of me, asleep in the morning, asleep in Clive's bed. My hair was messy but pretty, my mouth slightly open in dream, I looked dewy, vaguely religious. A sick present for the father of the girl you're fucking. I felt like the busiest corner in a turf war. Once, I'd asked for a ride to Clive's house after a night out with my parents. My mother got tense. *You can't ask your father to drive you over there,* she said. I could take the endless series of trains and buses, just sneak away like going to a girlfriend's house, but I couldn't ask Will to deliver me to the door of the boy I was sleeping with. I felt suddenly creepy. Was I Will's? Was I cheating on him? They knew I was going to Clive's house, but Will couldn't sanction it by giving me a lift? Clive's delicate pencil sketch said, She's Mine, I Have Her Now. I hated looking at myself in that drawing, unconscious, not knowing I was being observed, to be delivered to another on a slab of cardboard. Clive was a good artist, it looked just like me. *Thank you, Clive,* my father said, looking at it. *That's beautiful.*

Before there was Clive, there was Mack, when I was still in high school. Mack had a hearse, and to be perfectly honest, that was why I went out with him. He gave me stuff, too—Cure albums, a necklace of silver bats linked wing to wing like paper dolls, a slew of Roman Catholic tchotchkes. Mack wasn't that cute, but he was older, and he was pretty authentically death rock. I mean, owning a hearse is a pretty big commitment to goth. It was long and black and somewhat round—kind of a cross between a limo and a station wagon. White lace granny curtains dangled in the windows, and if you concentrated your vision through the tiny weave, you could make out the plywood coffin lying on the floor in the back.

I was in a black lace dress with psychotic ruffles, dancing on the disco-smogged floor of Axis, flailing my floppy arms like a ghost in the dry ice. Axis used to be Spit, back when I was too young to go to such places, and it was better then: punk, grimy. I knew that when I got older I would go there and dance the way you danced to punk music, and it was a big rip-off that by the time I was old enough to start sneaking into clubs, they gave Spit an attitude-lift and named it Axis, and it wasn't tough and threatening anymore. It was snooty and arty and everyone wore black clothes and smoked cloves, but they didn't really mean it. The place was full of poseurs. *Axis—the pole stuck up the earth's ass,* quipped Carla, who'd been kicked out of the place so many times for smuggling in vodka that she had truly earned her bitterness. Still, we went. There was nowhere else to go. We smoked and drank our smuggled booze poured into Cokes in the bathroom, feeling superior to the fools who thought it was a cool place to be and were actually having *fun.* Mack asked me to dance. Actually he sent a friend over, in fifth-grade fashion though it didn't seem so much shy as arrogant, like Mack was some underworld boss, very important, and this boy was sent to deliver me to him. Me and Mack danced together in the choking dry-ice fog that sucked every bit of moisture from our bodies. We danced to a Eurythmics song—me kind of swaying and spinning in a way I hoped looked ethereal in my froofy lace dress, Mack doing a stiffer, male version in a high-necked, long-sleeved black pirate shirt. Vinnie rushed out and grabbed me as I spun and hissed, *I saw him shopping at the Salvation Army, he has a hearse!* Our fate was sealed.

Mack's hair was thin and curly, receding swiftly into baldness—a tragedy in a subculture whose chief aesthetic was a tangled thatch of endless hair. He used this terrible shampoo that stank like poison and was meant to bring the hair back, but it didn't. Ironically, the rest of Mack was thick with hair, another tragedy in a subculture whose beauty standard required skin pale and smooth as a sliver of bone. It's why he only wore those high-necked shirts, to hide the patch of chest hair that crept kudzu-like toward his collar bone. But Mack compensated for all of this with the hearse, and with the bat tattooed on the inside of his wrist. He kept it covered with a wide band of leather and that drove me crazy. I mean, hardly anyone had tattoos. They were illegal in Massachusetts, you had to go all the way up to New Hampshire and brave the bikers and go through all that pain, and I didn't understand why he didn't show it off. I wanted everyone to know that my boyfriend had a tattoo. And a hearse. I loved riding around in it like the queen of the underworld. Once Mack drove me to work, this dumpy grocery store in the slums of Bellingham Square. I worked in the deli, illegally operating the shining chrome meat sheer you needed to be eighteen to operate, slicing up liverwurst and head cheese for the sick people who ate such things, fielding questions about my hair, which was blue, scooping mouse turds out of the potato salad. When Mack dropped me off, it confirmed for my co-workers that I was hopelessly, satanically weird. *Who was that?* That Was My Boyfriend, I said proudly. Mack. Mack was pretty full of shit, but in a melodramatic goth way that I appreciated. He claimed to be a direct descendent of Vlad the Impaler, Dracula, and got really offended if you didn't believe him. It was such a cliché, such a predictable lie for a death rocker to attempt that you almost had to believe him. Mack *was* Romanian. Certainly Vlad had descendents somewhere, why not Mack? He said he could only fall asleep with his arms crossed over his chest like a dead person.

Me and Mack didn't go out long, but the repercussions stretched further into the future than I knew right then, at sixteen or seventeen, climbing coolly into the hearse, the interior smooth white leather like a coffin on wheels. Mack lived in Salem, of course he did, in a little grey room with a bed of black lace and curtains to match, a big rusty scythe hanging on the wall. Lots of antique crucifixes and candles and a shining brass candle snuffer. He had a photo album chock full of naked shots of his last girlfriend, who was disturbingly normal-looking, blond with hefty tits, and I wondered, looking at her: did Mack go goth with a vengeance only recently, or did he share that crappy predilection of punk boys who, even as they proclaim their alienation from and rejection of society, continue to chase cheerleaders? *When you go on the pill, your tits will look like that too*, he said in a voice that promised big plans for our relationship. I broke up with Mack. I couldn't have sex with him, I couldn't have sex with anyone yet. It was just too freaky. I slept at his house once, but by the time we hit the black lace bed I was pretty drunk and I couldn't really remember what happened. Probably I touched his dick and he touched my . . . god, I just didn't have any names for it then, but I probably let Mack touch it and I think he even had his mouth down there for a minute. The room was dark, lit only by a couple of Mack's candles. The craziest part is that a few years later, when I met Clive, he was playing bass in this band, and Mack was the singer. They were a good band. Walpurgisnacht. Dumb name, pretty unpronounceable, but the music was big crashing death rock and Mack commanded the stage in leather pants, crouching atop the monitors like a gargoyle, howling a low round howl every bit as good as Peter Murphy.

Mack and Clive had a really intense, competitive relationship, both being Aries and sort of vain. When Clive found out I had dated Mack, he had to know all the details. We were in his house, back when he was in art school, he was on his futon sulkily sculpting something out of a white glob of clay. Prince was playing. I was crying. It was a worst-case-scenario of heterosexuality. Clive wanted to know everything about our lost night together, me and Mack. Most importantly, was Mack's dick bigger or smaller than Clive's. Oh Smaller. Smaller, I assured him as he pouted, disbelieving, prodding his clay ball angrily. *Are you sure? Are you positive?* Oh, I didn't know. Mack's dick could have been mammoth, the devil's phallus, all I remembered was the subsequent hangover and ride home in the hearse. But I understood it was my job to pamper Clive's ego, an organ considerably larger than his dick, which was, in all honesty, a fine size, but it *had* to be bigger than Mack's. I have a thin scar, faint on my forearm, where I cut myself with an Exacto knife as a blood promise to Clive that he was the winner. Me and Clive really had a terrible relationship, and it went on forever. But somewhere between its start and finish came Juniper.

She was Mack's girlfriend, and she was beautiful. The whole point of Mack was that he led up to Juniper. We were at a warehouse party in the south end and there she was, high on Ecstasy, her eyes huge with it. A drug I had never done. A drug that makes you love people, that makes you want to touch them because it turns them so beautiful. A drug that siphons fluid from the tank of your spine. Juniper's eyes were black and swirly and her smile was something luxurious, slow—it spread across her face like water. Juniper's hair was a perfect shiny bob on her head, short and black like Louise Brooks, whom she loved. She smudged dark eye shadow around her eyes to accent how fucked up she was. She wore black slips stolen from Victoria's Secret, where she worked, and funny little sandals, ugly, really, but they looked exotic on her perfect feet. In the dark warehouse packed with smoke and people I decided that I would fall in love with Juniper. It would be real and it would be tragic. Because we both had boyfriends, the restraint of their presence would only make it more beautiful. Juniper Juniper Juniper. An artist, a painter. At the warehouse our eyes locked as the cops crashed through the door and flipped the lights on. *Oh shit oh shit*, the DJs scurried to collect their equipment before it got confiscated, and like cockroaches everyone scattered away from the keg, dropping their plastic beer cups. *Clear it out, time to go*, barked the cops in their humorless cop way, and Juniper was gone. Clive, Juniper! I said as we walked the late streets. Like a revelation. Juniper, I pulled on his arm like a kid asking for something. Me and Clive had been looking for a girl. Unsurprisingly, his debilitating jealousy did not extend to other women, even as I confessed to him that I was probably a lesbian, and certainly he would be my last boyfriend, and undoubtedly I would leave him for a girl. Clive, Juniper. *Juniper is Mack's girlfriend*, Clive said warily. So, I Don't Care. I Don't Owe Mack Any Loyalty. I had adopted a position of hostility toward Mack, to soothe Clive's ego, and it was serving me well. *Mack would kill me*, Clive said with simple drama. *I mean it. He's crazy, you know. And he loves Juniper. He'd, like, stab me or something.* Oh Clive, I scoffed. Mack Wouldn't Stab You. *You don't know him*, Clive said darkly. *He'd kill me.* Juniper, I repeated. Mack was a small obstacle. I knew, when Juniper's eyes snagged mine, that we were each other's destiny. I willed myself in love with Juniper in that young way that enables you to truly, deeply love a person you do not know at all. What did I know about Juniper? She loved taking Ecstasy, loved to look at herself in the mirror. Could you blame her? She was like the moon. An artist, she painted herself, again and again. She was bisexual, score. Had that Victoria's Secret job, lifting boxes in the warehouse, but still they made her wear heels.

It was a lush, wet summer like it gets in Boston, when the air fills with moisture that traps the pollution and drags it low in the sky like a sick sunset, and the newscaster tells you not to leave the house, not to breathe if you can help it. I kissed Juniper. I did. Clive had a party at his parents' house in Beverly. The parents were gone and the kids were blending daiquiris in the kitchen, using all the parents' appliances to get fucked up. Sometime after the sun rose, me and Juniper took a walk. What did we talk about? She had to buy her friend a birthday present and I suggested Contempo, and then felt really dumb and trendy. Actually, I thought her friend was kind of dumb and trendy and would probably really like a gift from Contempo, but Juniper was deep and mysterious, she'd melt like the wicked witch beneath the fluorescent lights of a mall. Really Juniper was more vain and elusive than she was deep and mysterious, but let's not shatter the dream so quickly. Right then she was pure possibility. We were in this little alley behind a bingo hall, and the morning air smelled like the stale cigarette smoke of a hundred senior citizens seeping slowly out from the building. Juniper leaned against a fence and looked at me. Her eyes were enormous, wide and black even when they weren't dilated. She looked at me and threw everything into my lap with the look. With her silence and her stares Juniper controlled the whole thing, but I would have to be the one to do the work. I kissed her. I asked first. I had to draw it out, this tension she had strung with her careful quiet, let the words hang in the stale air, make her answer me. Because I didn't want us to be some straight girls who drank too much at a party and, giggle giggle, smooched. I had bigger plans for Juniper. I wanted her to break my heart, to bring me to the dark and painful place that was love and drop me off its cliff. I knew that love was a great and terrible thing and all the best people nearly died of it, and I was anxious to be among them. I leaned into Juniper. I kissed her. She was really soft. I mean, compared to Clive. Clive was a big rectangle, angular, blocky. Juniper was a pillow, but a pillow I could break. I touched her softly, her little face, her hair all mussed up from the night, the shiny stuff she heaped on it worn away so it looked more like regular hair and less like a cap or a wig. She looked really tired. I finished my kiss and we walked back to Clive's, found our boyfriends, went to bed.

So I had an affair with Juniper, and like an annoying little brother, Clive came along. It was the law of the land. Juniper lived in this tiny apartment on Park Drive, across from the Fenway Victory Garden where fags stalk and fuck in the tall, dry grass. At the edge of the park was a rose garden and a wall of lilac bushes. I picked a messy tumbling bouquet of the purple flowers, my favorite. I tied the stems together with a hair ribbon and I sat on the curb with Greg, drinking those Jack Daniels cooler drinks, Lynchburg Lemonade in the little bottles, waiting for someone to leave Juniper's building so I could slip in, tie my floral package to her doorknob and run. In the orangey light of her window I could see her moving in her slip, leaning out for a smoke. There She Is, I grabbed Greg dramatically. Look! Greg cackled. He was incredibly amused by my recent lesbian activity. *You're going to do cun-ing-u-lus!* he'd shriek. Greg had that fag fascination/repulsion with female genitalia. Hanging out in a bookstore he'd grab a book, *The Joy of Lesbian Sex,* and he would run up and down the aisles, howling and chewing his fingers, the pages flapping. In Juniper's hallway I tied my gift to her door and a longing in my chest swelled with a new craving, sucking itself inside out; my heart imploded. I could hear the faint tinkles of whatever esoteric death rock she was playing, I wanted to knock on her door terribly, but I knew that my secret flowers were more beautiful than any interaction we would have in her hallway.

Later, me and Juniper had a date and we had sex. The night built up to it with slow jerks, like a cranky, overtired child, impatient. We drank vodka, ran around Boston, up Newbury Street, into doorways to kiss, the dark empty fountains of the public gardens, the benches beneath the trees, back up to her loft with the candles in their glass and the wind bringing to the windows the smell of all the flowers across the street. I wanted it to be romantic, and it was. At one point I had to stop to tie my hair back with a ribbon, and that was the part Juniper told Clive about later, when she went to visit him at the job he finally scored, a copy shop downtown. *It was beautiful*, she said. It Was Beautiful, I said. *That's what she said*, he said. It was perfect. It went on all summer—me and Juniper; Clive and Juniper—I didn't like that at all, but if I had time alone with Juniper, then Clive had to, too. Actually, I don't think they fucked. They made art, Fimo sculptures and papier-mâché. Me and Clive and Juniper together—well at least I was there, that was good, but not as good as me and Juniper alone, all tangled up in each other. It was the summer *Truth or Dare* came out and lesbian chic was upon us. I felt like I started it. Inspired, we played games of truth or dare that were big excuses for boys to kiss boys and girls to kiss girls—specifically for me and Juniper to kiss each other. *I don't want to play,* huffed Greg one night. *You want to kiss Juniper, just, go kiss Juniper.* Greg! I said. It was a secret. Mack couldn't know, he'd beat up and murder Clive. Mack and Juniper were still going out, and Mack had just gotten a tattoo on his shoulder of a bat and a moon, and the moon's face was Juniper. That was when Juniper decided she either had to stop seeing us, or stop seeing Mack. She took herself away for a week, to think and to choose, and all I had was Clive. Clive, I Love Her! I wailed. Clive was annoyed. *I love her too,* he said. You Do Not! *Yes I do!* he shouted. *What do you mean I do not?!* You Just . . . You Don't, Clive, You Don't Love Juniper! God, Clive was pathetic. Did he really think whatever little boy-girl feelings he had for Juniper were at all comparable to the immense and noble act of civil disobedience that was my affair with Juniper?

On the day of her decision I was at work, my stomach filled with nervous rodents. A fax came, from Clive. It said "We won." That's all, two words in magic marker, an alarm clock to jolt my sadly sleeping heart. Juniper! We went to her house, me and Clive, we all had sex. Clive would have me and Juniper kiss and he would cry because it was so beautiful. Clive was an idiot. His hands on my clit were gigantic and clumsy like baseball mitts. I moved them away. Juniper took her hand, small and cool, and cupped my annoyed pussy. She just kept it there. Clive went nuts. *How come she can touch you, but I can't?* Clive, It Just Feels Different. *Forget it.* We put our clothes on, left. Clive was furious. *No more sex with Juniper.* What? *That's it,* he stormed. Clive! I screamed. Clive, You Can't, You Can't Do That! Clive! I did what I always did when arguments with Clive moved out of the sphere of the rational, I collapsed on the sidewalk and sobbed hysterically. *Michelle get up.* I sobbed and sobbed. *Michelle get off the sidewalk.* I sobbed until my body jerked in weird spasms and my breathing turned scary. The last train came and went, people passed by, walking in huge arcs around my convulsing body. We had to sleep at Juniper's. We rang her bell shamefully. We Missed The Train. *But you left hours ago!* she said. I Couldn't Stop Crying, I said, and burst into tears again. I Don't Know What's Wrong With Me, I lied. *She does this all the time,* Clive said. *Maybe it's your birth control pills,* Juniper suggested. Oh, I wanted to tell her all about it. All about how awful Clive was, how stupid and jealous, how lousy it was to have sex with him, and how beautiful she was, how she glowed like the candles by her bedside, how I loved her and would never push her hand away. I lay on the futon with Clive and hiccupped all night. In the morning Clive said we could still see Juniper. He had never intended to make us stop. He was punishing me. He loved her too. Right? He made art about her, little papier-mâché heads with her flapper hair and her big made-up, fucked-up eyes. I wrote her poems.

Together, the three of us went to Lollapalooza. The first one, before Jane's Addiction got so tired, when you could still admit you liked them. We were going for Siouxsie, that's why we were there. Nine Inch Nails was iffy. We slept out for tickets and were first in line and then this crazy guy cut us. He just plopped a folding chair down in front of our blanket and said, *I'm first.* A big guy, obviously fucked up, thick Dorchester accent. You Are Not, I snapped, ready for a fight. His knuckles were all cuts and scabs like he'd just been in one. A scalping agency was paying him bucks to get all the good seats he could. *I'm first,* he repeated. I'm Getting The Cops, I said, and those were the magic words because this guy had just gotten out of jail, was on parole and had a gun in his bag. He didn't need the police. He moved behind us and we lived in fear for twelve hours. He was crazy. Wet-brain—how much alcohol do you have to drink for that to happen? That's what happened to him. One minute he was nice, talking about getting us stolen TVs, and we'd say Cool, and he'd say, *Are you fucking with me? Do you want to die?* No, Tony, No One's Fucking With You. No One Wants To Die. He walked in front of buses and collected the insurance money.

In the morning, the record store opened and we bought our tickets, third row, good seats. We ran through the streets sure that Tony was after us but he was not. We had these excellent seats to Lollapalooza and we figured we'd do Ecstasy at the show. All of us—Juniper and Greg, who did it a lot and loved it; me and Clive, virgins. Also this boy Greg was dating, Eric. Eric was beautiful to look at, but he had an evil gleam in his eye. There was something about him that was not kind, and it added to the type of good-looking he was. Eric knew where to get the Ecstasy. Somewhere in the south end, he took our money, twenty-five dollars each, and he ran into a brownstone, came back with drugs. I was only going to do half, with acid I only ever did half and it worked just fine, I tripped so hard I was scared to imagine what would happen if I ate the whole thing. But no one wanted to split one with me. Juniper and Greg and Eric already had their established dosage, and Clive the little thrill-seeker wanted a whole pill to himself. *Michelle, just do a whole one,* Juniper pushed. Would my eyes swell up like hers? I couldn't wait to be filled with love and watch everyone turn beautiful. I had the chalky round tablet in my pocket, waiting to be eaten.

Lollapalooza was at this big outdoor stadium in rural Massachusetts that was always kind of a strange place to see the bands I liked. A lot of locals would go to shows just for the fuck of it, or because their brother worked security or maybe they knew one song, so the crowd contained all these normal people, jocks, mom-and-dad-looking people, burnouts. I went to see the Smiths once and got made fun of for looking weird. At a Smiths concert. So Lollapalooza was even weirder, with Jane's Addiction so famous, and Ice-T was there, and Living Colour. There were lots of people who would maybe want to beat us up, but there were plenty of freaks too. Thousands of people, we pushed through them to our excellent seats, established our presence, left to do our drugs. Me and Juniper went into the girls' room and locked ourselves in the stall, swallowed our drugs, made out. I figured I should eat some food then, before the drug kicked in and killed my appetite. See, I try to be really responsible when I do drugs. I try to cover my bases before I lose touch with reality. The food at the concert was bad, of course, and cost too much. I got a hotdog and one of those big doughy pretzels. I was at the condiment stand squirting mustard on my food when, like a bottle at the back of my skull, the drug hit. Just this *whoomph* like my brain was being sucked out of my head, the sensation flooded down my body and I gripped the metal stand so I wouldn't fall over. It coursed through my blood like pure panic, that's what it felt like, and I thought, What Did I Just Take? Then, I've Got To Sit Down. All my friends were sitting on the ground a few feet away. Very carefully I navigated the sea of Lollapaloozers moving in all directions, very carefully I sat down with my hotdog and pretzel and leaned against a chain-link fence. Wow, You Guys. It Just Hit Me . . . Really Strong. Talking was hard. My body was swimming inside, rolling over and over. *Really?* asked Juniper. *We just took it, it shouldn't be starting so soon.* Well It Is. I stared at my food. It was too bright, it looked gross. *Is it nice?* Juniper asked, excited. Her face was so big. It's . . . Kind Of Overwhelming. I Don't Think I Can Stand Up. *Just relax.* She smiled. *You'll love it.* I tried to eat my food. I took a bite of my hotdog and chewed it forever.

Swallowing was difficult, I couldn't find whatever muscles you used to swallow. Come On, Michelle, You Swallow All The Time, Just Swallow It. The hotdog roll felt huge in my mouth. I got it down. I figured I would just eat the hotdog. I took it out of the bun, little bites, teeny bites, I chewed it, tried to swallow, gagged. I kept gagging, I spit it out. *It's okay,* cooed Juniper. Her eyes were going swirly. *You don't have to eat, it's okay.* The roar of all the people was deafening, they were a swarming mass, I couldn't look at them. I realized that this was not going to be fun. The panic was not subsiding, it was growing and I realized that it was only the beginning. I had just eaten the stuff, it hadn't even fully dissolved, more and more of it would be released into my bloodstream and I would lose my mind. That's what would happen. I was an idiot. I took this drug I knew nothing about, a drug that affects your brain, and like a fool I just ate it and now I would go mad. I was overcome with grief. I was going to go crazy. And I was so smart, I had such a good brain, I loved to think, and these were the last thoughts I would ever have. I looked at my friends. I couldn't let them know I was freaking out, I didn't want them to freak out too. I knew how bad trips were contagious. It's Just A Bad Trip, Michelle, I tried to talk to myself. I had never had one, but lots of my friends had had them and they were all fine and their brains were okay. But there was that one girl—what was her name—she did too much acid and saw demons with numbers for names crawling out of the sidewalk and had to go to the hospital and they gave her some drug to counteract it and she didn't see the demons anymore but she knew they were there and it was actually worse, since they could see her but she couldn't see them. What if I ended up like her? I looked around. I couldn't see any demons but the people hurt my eyes. I looked at

Clive. He looked pretty freaked out. Juniper and Greg and Eric were laughing and looking around and laughing at all the private jokes drugs let you in on. They wanted to walk around. Go On, I said, I'll Stay Here. If I stayed in one place I'd be safe. Everyone left but Clive. *I feel really weird,* he said. I Do Too, I said. I Don't Like It But It's Okay. It'll Wear Off. Just Take It Easy. *I'm kind of freaking out,* Clive said. I Know, Me Too. Let's Just Stay Together And Stay Calm. Taking care of Clive was a nice distraction, it made me feel like I hadn't totally lost my mind. See, I could still think. But who would take care of me? I thought about going to the first-aid station and telling them I did drugs and letting them do whatever with me. But the place was probably filled with tweakers, forget it. I didn't need that. I thought about going out into the parking lot and finding Clive's car and lying down. I wanted to be alone. Being at Lollapalooza was about as far from solitude as you could get. *Maybe we should go to our seats,* Clive suggested. The concert would distract us.

It was a terrible trip down to our excellent seats so close to the stage. We bumped into Juniper, high as a kite. *How are you guys?* We're Going To Sit Down. *Oh . . .* you could tell she wanted to get away from us. We were bummers. Juniper, How Long Does This Last? *Oh . . .* she rolled her giant eyes, *about twelve hours.* She was blissful. There is no fucking way I would stay in this state for twelve hours. I would kill myself. I would go to a hospital and get whatever drugs they gave the demon girl. Up on the stage Ice-T was yelling at the audience. *I say . . . what good is a beautiful girl if the bitch don't fuck?!* Oh no. He said it again. *What good is a beautiful girl . . . IF THE BITCH DON'T FUCK,* chanted frat row, the millions of white boys with baseball caps cheering Ice-T with their fists in the air, over and over. Oh god, I wanted to die. Ice-T was evil. I was on drugs and he was the devil. I looked at Clive. *That's not cool,* he said uncomfortably. Duh, Clive. Nine Inch Nails was next. Trent was really fucked up, throwing bottles into the audience, spitting at people. If I got hit with a bottle, I would lose it. Why was he doing that? What's His Problem? I asked Clive, who was nodding off in the seat next to me. Are You Sleeping? How Can You Sleep? *I don't know, I'm really tired.* Someone just told me that Ecstasy back then had heroin in it. If I'm going to do heroin, I want to know, I want to Do Heroin, have the experience, sure, fine, but I don't want a mickey slipped into my mickey at a giant rock show.

By the time the show ended, me and Clive felt a lot better. Things were still off, but the panic had subsided and I was pretty sure I wasn't going to emerge from the experience brain-dead. We met up with the druggies back at the parking lot, they'd had the greatest time. Greg had made out with all these boys, and who knew what Juniper'd been up too. She seemed weird, distant and kind of nervous. I got in an argument with her and Eric about Ice-T being an asshole. They thought he was okay. *Lots of women like that stuff,* Eric said. So? I said. It was all I could think to say. They got a ride back to Boston with someone else. I was full of closeness and affection for Clive now, like we had gone through battle together. We were okay. I Was Really Scared, I said. I Really Thought I Was Going Crazy. *Me too,* he said. We held hands. At some point it started to pour, and the Continental's windshield wipers were broken. They'd move to the center of the window and just stick there. I took off my bra, this tiny joke of a bra, cotton and elastic, and I tied it to one of the wipers. I tugged them back and forth on the glass, for miles I did this, rain pouring in the window, soaking me, but I didn't care. I had my brain back. I thought about all the most horrible things that could happen to a person—I could have no home, be locked up in a terrible prison, kidnapped, but as long as I had my mind I would be okay. I tugged the bra and the wiper snapped off and flew away, trailing my underwear behind it. *Oh shit,* said Clive. We drove home very carefully.

Juniper never called us again. Fuck Her, we unanimously decided. She was so stuck up anyway. She thought she was the coolest. She was shallow. I was tortured. She had cracked my heart like I prayed she would, and now I could be truly tragic. Why had she left me? Not even a call. All mine went unanswered. Was it because of Ice-T? Because I couldn't hold my drugs? I saw Juniper everywhere and nowhere. An art gallery I passed every day had taken some of her work, enormous self-portraits, life-sized and real. They sat in the windows and looked at me. She had gotten a job at a boutique on the same street, and she made up all the mannequins to look just like her, the big painted eyes, sleek little bob. I saw her once, at an abortion rights demonstration where everyone walked in a giant circle chanting and holding signs. We kept passing each other in the circle, it was so embarrassing. *Hi,* she said sheepishly, and that was it. I hated what I was wearing. If I'd known I was going to see her, I'd have dressed a lot better.

GHOSTBUSTER

I was at my new job at the publishing house when Madeline called, the job that was going to save me, that would somehow and finally propel me into a future that was normal and not rickety. After a year spent slopping in cafés, I'd come to realize that surely I could not work in such places forever. At some point they would simply stop hiring me. You had to be young and cute, and I was both the day I got hired on the spot at Avenue Café, to fling bowls of soup around, steam eggs. I was wearing Madeline's clothes, so I looked normal. I had even gotten my hair to lie straight on my head after so many years of ceaseless ratting, of stretching it sky-ward and blasting it with Aqua Net. I took my place behind the counter at Avenue with the other young, cute girls, students from Emerson who were study-ing to be newscasters. I don't know why they were there, their parents were paying for everything. Leona was the first person I ever heard use the word "flatware." She needed some for her apartment. Her mother was getting it for her. I didn't know what flatware was, but figured it was frivolous since my own home seemed to operate fine without it. Leona was from Georgia and her mom was getting a face-lift. It was time, and plus she deserved it after surviving her skin cancer scare. She had spent many dangerous afternoons in the southern sun, gardening and playing tennis. She loved to garden, and it was sad that she couldn't now. It was a health hazard, and so they paid somebody else to do it. Leona's mother was on her ass to get a haircut, she said it was too long and made her look like a whore. Leona's hair was a wild mane, wiry brown curls that spun out from her head like a carnival ride. Probably it had gotten her hired. Trevor, who owned the place, was nice enough, and not a lech, but I watched which girls he hired and which he turned away, and it was both flattering and insulting that he thought I was attractive enough to make ham sandwiches among his cadre of coeds. Natasha was another one, blond curls like Nellie from *Little House on the Prairie*, incredible hair, each lock a bobbing spring of gold. Blue eyes, and a face that seemed hostile at first, but as you observed it all day and noticed that her look never changed, you realized that it was just the expression her face settled into, perhaps from generations of bitchy rich people breeding with one another. Natasha would make a great newscaster, cold and pretty, detached from the litany of bombings, maimings and airplane crashes she'd report. Working at Avenue was all right. I got free food, hot chicken soup stung with pepper, congealed cheese soup I punctured with tufts of broccoli and ate when I was bored. My hands were always red and burned from the blast of steam that hit them when I opened the industrial metal steamer. Clouds of hot fog would rush out like a storm and drench the room, curling up against the front windows and raining down the glass. It was always warm and damp inside the café.

Mornings Will would drive me to work in his big black car. He'd pause at the Dunkin' Donuts by the on-ramp to the Tobin Bridge, getting an enormous Styrofoam tub of coffee at the drive-through window. *Regular,* he'd tell the girl, and she'd dump in the sugar and stir his milk around. He drank it as we crossed the harbor, and the caffeine would wake him and he'd get chatty. We'd talk. When I was still heartbroken about the fickle Juniper, when rumors of her heroin use and her new girlfriend and their yellow eyes were ripping me up with some new emotion, I asked Will about it. Will knew drugs, I didn't know how much or how intimately, exactly, but I knew that he knew. My . . . Friend, I Heard She Was On Heroin, And That Her Eyes Were Yellow. Does It Make Your Eyes Yellow? *Hepatitis makes your eyes yellow,* he informed me, *but you catch that from shit. People not wiping their hands after going to the toilet and then touching your food or something.* But he knew a little about heroin, how it ruined the girls so quickly, faster than boys. *This one girl,* he said, *within a month, two months, she was getting on her knees for the Puerto Ricans in the square.* I thought about Juniper, floppy and high, giving blowjobs. It was different than my usual fantasy of her new life without me and Clive: lounging on pillows in a dark, flickering room, sucking on her girlfriend's mouth like a hookah stuffed with fragrant tobacco, lush and spinning.

Will had quit drinking. I wouldn't even have noticed if he hadn't told me during one of these rides, the electric windows barely cracked against the cold outside, the inside swirling with cigarette smoke. Will had hardly ever drank in the house, he was a different breed of alcoholic. He explained it to me. *I'm not one of those guys who, you know, gets bombed every night. But once I do go drinking I can't stop, and I get into trouble.* I thought about how it was for me, how one gulp of wine begged for the next, the constant flow lighting up my body, my hand reaching for the glass neck until the bottle was empty and it was time for the lurching, giggling adventure of the liquor store, to purchase another and keep on going. Will was going to meetings, and he even had a therapist. He told me that talking about it made my mother uncomfortable, which was why he never mentioned it at home. But he was doing the work, and was on the step where you say you're sorry to all the people you fucked with while you were a drunk, and he wanted to apologize to me. I was frozen against the dense, plush seat of his luxury clunker as it rambled into Boston. Nothing uncomfortable got discussed for very long in our house. Only during intense bouts of trauma, when everyone yelled and cried and needed, and then the next day there was a brief check-in and the slate was wiped clean. Why dwell? Why dwell on Will's alcoholism, since it was gone now, and we could all settle into being the happy family we'd been straining to be for so long. I felt a rush of pain for Will, making such a huge and noble change and still having to bear the shame of it, not able to talk about it at supper and get a big sing-song of praise around the Hamburger Helper. It was too scary that he had been a drunk at all, that the drunk was presumably still in him. Acknowledgment might draw the beast back out, or at least make Will feel like a loser for having this weakness, and make my mother feel like a fuck-up for having married another, a second weak man, a drinker, and so quickly on the heels of the first. None of it was fair. I'm Proud Of You, I stammered awkwardly. That Must Be A Lot Of Work. I felt flushed and embarrassed. Will didn't seem to notice. *Yeah, it's all right.* He stared at the road. *I'm sorry for what it put you and your sister through. I couldn't have been much of a father.*

Will's vulnerability ballooned inside the car, suffocating, like the sickly sweet cherry thing that swung from the rearview mirror. Oh, Don't Worry, I swatted away his distress with my hand, smiling. It's Cool, You Were Fine, You Don't Have Anything To Apologize For. *Yeah . . .* He trailed off. We were at my café. *Okay sweetheart, have a good day.* He smiled, a big grin on his ruddy face, very rough, his pale blond mustache nearly invisible, surrounded by so much red skin. I gave him a kiss. Inside the café I fixed an egg sandwich quick, before we unlocked the doors. Leona was unwrapping the soups. *Chucky's been in there for thirty minutes,* she whispered, motioning to the bathroom door. Chucky was Trevor's nephew, a blocky, red-faced jock from Southie. *I think he's jerking off.* Soon a tiny roar of plumbing sounded from inside the bathroom, and Chucky exited into our curious stares, grunting hello. He strutted, hunched, back to the kitchen and began peeling the plasticky shells from the cold, translucent bodies of shrimp.

Mornings Will didn't drive me into Boston I'd buy a magazine at the Cumberland Farms on the corner and read it on the bus. I read *Cosmo,* and for the first time the concept of a career really occurred to me. With a slight shock I realized I was maybe supposed to have one. I slapped the slick cover shut on my lap and gazed out at that boat, the *Constitution,* in its home in the harbor beneath me, the dark polluted water banging its hull. The bus crawled over the bridge. *Cosmo* made me anxious, the imaginary women in tight Chanel suits managing their careers and their men, agonizing over how to ask for that promotion or get that guy to settle down. I hadn't thought I might be like one of those women until now. Who were they? *Cosmo* gushed about their careers and offices and meetings in the vaguest possible terms—I mean, what were these women actually doing? The bus hauled into the city, where office buildings rose and fell like a mouthful of broken teeth. Millions of offices, and I had no idea what was going on inside of any of them. The whole world was being run beneath my nose as I served soup, oblivious. I felt a swell of doom as something called me to take my place in it. Was it time to join the world? My mother suggested I might become a nurse. I actually considered it. It was an exhilarating thought, like suicide. I was out of high school, my life was in my hands and I was free to ruin it however I chose. I could go to the free nursing school at the VA hospital in Chelsea, like my mother and Will had done. I could study the body and all the things that go wrong with it, the medicines that manage and control it, mathematics and needles and test tubes filled with blood. It made me want to cry. *The young, single nurses have a great life,* my mother said knowingly. *They make good money, have no one to support, work three till eleven and go dancing all night.* The three-till-eleven bit did sound good. Instead, I applied at a publishing house, way out in Newton. *Newton,* my mother said. Rich people lived there. To get there I took the bus into Boston, then a subway train to Downtown Crossing, past the throng of Filene's Basement groupies—old ladies clustered in the peanut stink around the glass doors, waiting for their bargains. I walked a couple blocks and grabbed the Mass Pike bus into Newton. It took forever, it was heartbreaking how long it took, how early I had to wake each morning to get to my cubicle by eight. I could not stay awake on the bus and I was terrified of missing my stop. I'd nod off and wake in panicked, three-second spasms.

The office was a grey hive. Julie Doule was the supervisor, she had hired me to sit in a cubicle and slice up waxed articles about machines and stick them to big boards for further slicing and arranging by the more talented paste-up artists. It took me about a half hour to do this, and for the rest of the day I just sat there. The fabric walls of my cubicle were feathered with glossy photos of celebrities torn from magazines. I would read their tarot cards. Slap down the cardboard icons and imagine what I would say to Joan Jett, to Vince Neil, to Robert Smith and Billy Idol if they came to me to have their fortunes told. It was interesting how all my most loved stars seemed to be fading away at the same time I was. Joan Jett had vanished, the Cure's new album was dull, Billy Idol had exploded into a garish caricature of his former glory, and hadn't Vince Neil just killed someone? All my old goth friends had been inhaled into colleges, no one hung out anymore, and it seemed pathetic to still want to. I had been so happy back then, running around drunk, all dressed up with makeup smeared across my face, fighting with other goth girls over who loved which band the most, more than anyone else, whose fandom was most passionate and obsessive. With despair I realized I had allowed myself to become frighteningly attached to something that was, for everyone else, a phase. Everyone was making the transition to adulthood with grace and excitement, while I sagged and pouted, aimless, corraled into this lifeless cubicle where I read imaginary fortunes for has-been rock stars.

In the telephone cubicle a few boxes down the hall, a phone rang. The company didn't give us phones of our own, they knew we'd spend all day on them. There was rarely any work to do in my department, and we really had to keep up appearances and look occupied so we wouldn't get laid off. I could tell that Julie Doule was nervous about how little effort I put into looking busy, how my desk was always a mess of shredded *Interview* magazines I waxed into collages with the company waxer, or a puzzle of tarot cards deciphering Matt Dillon's destiny. Things were looking good for Matt. *How many times a day can you read your tarot cards, Michelle?* Julie chastised me. She was an older woman who looked like a rotund Sally Jessy Raphael. Those big round glasses. Oh, I'm Just Practicing, I said, embarrassed. I spent so much time alone and unoccupied in my cubicle that I would get real comfortable with my aloneness, and lapse into nose-picking. Or realize I'd been reading a book with a leg flung over the arm of my chair, my hand fiddling idly at my crotch. It was scary. I had to stay alert. Sometimes after lunch I'd be so drowsy with food and boredom I'd have to go into the handicapped stall in the ladies room and do jumping jacks. Someone would inevitably come inside and see my Doc Martens bouncing up and down beneath the door. I spent too much time with these people, forty hours a week, we were all doomed to know each other's weirdness.

Sara, who sat in the cubicle behind mine, was a forty-year-old obsessive-compulsive virgin who still lived at home. She was wan and bony with a thick black braid, forever in motion. I'd catch her embarrassing, repetitive gestures out of the corner of my eye as I passed her cubicle on the way to the break room. A speedy flutter, like a bird in a puddle. Sara hoarded everything—soda cans and gum wrappers and rubber bands, all stacked with a sickening order, crowding around her nervous perch at her light table. The fluorescence shone up at her face, a landscape of glaciers and caverns. Sara was the reason I bought a VCR.

I bought a VCR, she'd called out at me one afternoon as I passed by her box. Yeah? I paused politely. *Yeah, at BJ's, they're cheap.* It occurred to me that I could buy a VCR. I had this job, I could buy stuff. Real stuff, not records. Appliances. I guess that's the point of having a job. I already had a VCR, or rather, my parents did, but Clive didn't. Because his parents were hippies. His angry hippie dad had flung the family TV out the window many years ago, and Clive had only recently replaced it with his high school graduation money. I bought a VCR at BJ's, and installed it in Clive's bedroom. I'd never spent so much money on something.

When I'd summoned Madeline into my room for a meeting, I was solemn and scared. I was nervous. I'd told myself that talking about the creaks and my sister's long-ago suspicion of their cause did not mean I was saying it was true. Talking about it didn't mean I thought it was happening. It was just a discussion. It was just to make sure I was being a good big sister, making up for that moment in the past when I hadn't been, when I'd shooed her away so callously. But I was sick with bringing it up. It seemed like it could set something terrible in motion, something neither of us would be able to stop. I asked Madeline if she remembered when she'd come into my room years ago with her fears about Will. Of course she did. *It never stopped,* Madeline said, and her face looked hard. You Still Hear The Creaks? *Of course.* Did she still think it was Will? *Who else would it be?* She thought I was an imbecile. She'd written me off years ago, and had gone forward with taking care of herself in this house, nurturing a certain hardness, flicking up her middle finger when she heard the noises outside her room. I Do That Too! I didn't know how to move it all from suspicion and gossip to something more, hard proof. Madeline said she'd take care of it. The way she'd taken care of her graduation, becoming her class valedictorian, the way she'd taken care of a pile of flawless college applications, all delivered on time with sharp essays. The way she'd taken care of snagging a job, working the front desk at an investment bank downtown. Inside the bubble of our shared and denied secret Madeline had grown up, grown somehow capable, while I bobbed beneath her, stunted, scared and lost.

When the phone rang over in the telephone cubicle, it was for me. It was Madeline. *I found the holes.* What? I thought of goldfish. In the classic little bowl, glass and water. Little blobs of gleaming life, going in circles. I thought of glass and water. Something strange happened with my eyes, and everything seemed very far away or perhaps holographic. I reached out and touched the wooden shelves, the plastic binders. The black phone cord curled up at me. Where Did You Find Holes? I had to sit down. It was awkward to sit on the table, hunched beneath the shelf, but it seemed like pulling the chair out would be an exhausting effort. I couldn't deal with it. Part of my ass kept sliding off the table's curved edge. I thought about how horrible it was when this lady Mary collapsed in the hallway. She was one of the millions of people I worked with whose purpose in the company was a complete mystery. Actually, the entire company was a mystery. They published magazines, but I still have no idea which ones, or what they were even about. Mary was always cheerfully walking around with an armful of papers. Then one day she crumpled, and stayed there on the carpet that was the same hue of grey as the cubicle partitions, as the walls and the ceiling above us. *Help me . . . can somebody help me . . .* It was like her voice was streaming out of some scary portal, it was a ghost's voice, shimmering and weak. I was frozen at my light table, in the middle of reading Winona Ryder's tarot cards. I slid quietly from my stool and stood in the corner. Mary had fallen almost right outside my cubicle, it was all happening right there and I could not help. I tried to sink into the grey partition, my cheek pressed against a cool, glossy photo of Madonna. I couldn't bear to see the spectacle of Mary smeared on the floor, her big legs awkward in their pantyhose, her scuffed, flat shoes. I thought of fish in plastic, in the meat case at the supermarket. Anxious trills of shame tickled my insides. Mary was nice, I should help her. I huddled by the empty metal shelves in my box, and listened to the heaving of bodies and the voices that mumbled, *Okay? Okay? I can't walk.* That was Mary's voice. It was small and scared, tipping on hysteria. Somehow they got her away from the cubicles. She never came back. She had multiple sclerosis. *She's gonna die,* said Cherise, who worked in the cubicle beside mine, solemnly. If I fell off the table and onto the carpet of the telephone cubicle, I knew I would not get up, and I couldn't bear the people I worked with touching me. Madeline was speaking, her thin, disembodied voice streaming into my ear. *When you shut the bathroom door, there's a hole, there's a hole that looks right at the toilet.* I thought of the bowl, a porcelain scoop framed by the puffy ring of seat, blue. I liked the solid images my brain was shooting out to me. A nice, heavy toilet, all grounded in the linoleum. The flusher like a little comma, winking on the smooth white. *There's holes in my door, and there's holes in the back hall that look into your room.* Each of Madeline's words was a bulk of speeding metal that together formed a train, a brutal machine. Before we moved into this house, brittle with holes, when we had lived in the house that faced train tracks, I would sit on a patch of concrete, as close to the rails as I could be without dying. And the bells would start dinging and the striped boards would come down, and in the distance hovered a single ball of train-light, shining like the sun in the daytime sky. A faint rumble announced something terrible, but the circle of light seemed completely still, and slowly it came toward you, growing closer, and then suddenly with a roar it was upon you, like a jungle of animals leaping out at you. Its wind was thick and battering and your hair flew up like pigeons and the grinding wheels were right there, all crunching, crushing steel, alive and oblivious. It bore down on the rails and it was impossible to think that it would ever stop, it was a force, it blew by you and left trash bouncing in its wake, and your hair fell back down onto your head in tangles as the brutal wind was sucked away and the train's dark tail curved round the bend, gone, and you cried like something had just happened to you. *Michelle, are you there?* Yeah, I said. I tried to sound conversational. The company could fling up as many shabby partitions as they liked, but the truth was we were all sitting together in one big room, and I knew everybody was listening. There was nothing else to listen to. I could hear the tinny, monotonous whine of the Stone Roses coming from my cube. I hated them, but I hated all my tapes. I didn't know what to listen to anymore, and there was nothing new worth buying. Um, Are You Sure About This? I sounded chipper and mildly surprised—maybe someone was calling to tell me I'd won a prize. *Yeah . . . are you all right?* Madeline sounded small. She was small, she was a skinny, nervous, nineteen-year-old girl who worked too hard and would never go to an Ivy League school as she knew she deserved. I couldn't bear to think of what would happen to her, I knew she'd end up in a cube, too. I'm At Work, Madeline, I said tensely. Wanting to help her was like wanting to help lift Mary from the floor when her disease knocked her down, or comfort Will in his sobriety. It was like wanting to leap out of myself, or in front of a train.

After the men from the art department had carried Mary away, I'd told my sole company friend, Myra, how I had stayed inside my cubicle. Myra, I Just Stayed In My Cube, I said. My voice sounded scandalized, like I was gossiping about someone who wasn't there. *Why didn't you help her?* Myra sounded like she thought I was stupid, and my stupidity angered her. Myra belonged to Refuse and Resist and had political pins on her dark overcoat, she hated everyone in the department but me. I Don't Know, I Wanted To Help . . . I trailed. Myra hadn't answered just pressed the red nozzle on the bubbler and filled her teacup with steaming water.

Michelle, Madeline said anxiously. I'm Here, I said tensely. You'll Show Me When I Get Home. Was I mad at her? I felt brief punches of feeling, I punched them back and they were gone. I hung up. My vision was normal, the objects in the cubicle had resumed their normal positions. Everything was within arm's reach. I pushed my palm down on the staple gun and it spit a thin fold of metal onto the table. I did it again and again, a little pile of crumpled smiles. Julie Doule passed by. She glanced at the empty shelves where our work trickled in. *Waiting for a job?* she chirped fakely. Yup, I said, smiling an eager, new-to-the-workforce smile. I realized that now was my big chance to really have a breakdown. How luxurious, to have things finally get so bad that all you could reasonably do was flop on the floor like Mary and chew the carpet, howl and kick and cry and burn your cheek against the fibers until somebody more capable came to carry you off, one of the real bosses who didn't sit in partitioned boxes but had actual rooms with strong doors of buttery wood and windows full of sunlight and parking lot. Now was my time to really lose it, to drool and squawk and let somebody take over, and I couldn't. I sat at the table's edge, and when my ass slid off, my foot caught my weight and I stood, grabbed a pair of scissors, and walked from the department into the bathroom and gave myself a haircut. I pulled my bangs down into a black sheet, the split ends taut beneath my chin, and snipped a clean line above my eyebrows. Perfect. My mother used to sit me on the kitchen table and go back and forth with a tiny pair of shears, trying with each snip to even it out, my forehead growing larger as the mousy tufts piled up on the floor. I held the amputated locks in my hand. They looked cool, like dark little snakes. I thought how if I were an artist like Clive, I could use them for something, and threw them into the wastebasket. I walked into the handicapped stall and yanked up my skirt, tugged down my tights and dropped my ass onto the bowl. I stared at my boots. No matter how much I did in them, they still looked brand new and dorky. Crisp, shiny leather, red plaid laces weaving through the eyelets. I put my face in my palms and pressed until lacy patterns formed against my eyelids and slid around like lazy kaleidoscopes. Cry, I ordered myself, Cry. I felt crazy, kind of calm and floaty. Maybe nothing really mattered that much. I thought about Will staring at me naked, thought about it happening all the time. Who cared. I felt tired. It was after lunch, time for jumping jacks but I couldn't get off the bowl. This was my life. There was no reason to think it would ever be anything else. That's Not Right, I mumbled into my hands. My lip caught against the tight press of my palms and stayed there, I drooled. Pounded my face with my hands, slow and rhythmic, building in impact, *slap, slap*. No, No, I drooled and chanted into my hands, rocking on the toilet. I brought my hands down on my face, banging against my cheekbones. I heard the click of the door and the patter of pumps into the stall next to mine. Like the hive beyond it, the whole bathroom was grey. Working in that place could give you seasonal affective disorder, no matter what time of year it was. I stared at the pumps, beige like the pantyhose that rose from them. I stared forever. Was she waiting for me to leave? Fuck her. Fuck Her, I gurgled into my palms, and hoped it sounded like I was coughing. The pumps cleared her throat. Finally she let out some farts and tiny splashes of shit and a calming tinkle of pee. We both relaxed. I watched her pumps shuffle and heard the spin and crinkle of toilet paper, the scratch of it against her crotch. The rushing flush of the bowl. I thought about if toilets were like trains, how great it would be to sit tiny at the edge of it all and feel the giant suck and swirl of water beneath you, the fresh, clean water pouring down the porcelain curve like a violent waterfall. Crazy, I scolded aloud, a whisper. I couldn't cry. I left the stall and gazed at myself in the long mirror above the sinks. I'd forgotten I'd cut my hair. What was that about? The scissors were still there, by the metal spout that spit the horrid, institutional pink soap. I looked great. I should've looked awful, like anorexic, disturbed Sara, lit green by the office fluorescents. My bangs shone with glamour on my forehead. I headed back to the cubes. Radical Myra was moving down the hall with a Styrofoam cup of Ramen. *Look at your new hair!* she crowed, and turned into the hum of the typesetting room.

When I got home, Madeline was there, and no one else. Where were our parents? Maybe getting dinner, bringing it back to feed us like little birds. Pizza with extra cheese, big gobs of it to lodge in your teeth. A giant pizza we'd all snack on for days, cold, in front of the TV with lots of salt and a glass of Coke that clattered with ice. To eat the crust I had to crack it down the middle and dose the doughy center with a ton of salt. I'm Hungry, I told Maddy. *Come here,* she said. *See?* In the wood of the bathroom doorjamb was a crude, carved groove. It could have been any other nick in any other part of our banged-up wooden house, but it wasn't. Madeline grabbed the ratty doorknob and swung the door toward us, ran her finger in the corresponding gash. *You look,* she said, and shut the door. I bent down. The two grooves joined to form a little tunnel that delivered my eye to the bowl. *Look,* she said again, and slipped inside the bathroom. I brought my face down to the hole and saw a piece of my sister there on the bowl. A burst of feeling crackled in my chest, it rose to my brow like carbonation and made me dizzy. Was this hysteria? It made me need to move my body. I wanted to run. Madeline came out, and I moved into the bathroom and shut the door. It didn't look like anything, the hole. Just another messy nick. Below the knob that daily fell off the door was the old metal keyhole, stuffed with cotton. I looked at it, wedged into the crevice, fuzzy tufts of it poking out. I'd seen it a million times, and so had Ma, and so had Will. The keyhole stuffed with cotton. Everyone pissed and shit and wiped their ass and looked at the keyhole stuffed with cotton, and no one ever asked why. Madeline had put it there, to keep herself safe, a tiny, fluffy attempt. My eyes burned and I felt the saddest pulse of love for her. I remembered a dream I'd had, where Will had chopped off her head and left her neck a smooth, elegant curve, like a glass vase. Her neck just stopped, no head, but Madeline was alive. She was alive but couldn't speak or see or hear anymore, and it was my job to take care of her, lead her by her thin arm, try to discern what she needed and how she felt. In the dream I tucked her headless body into bed, her neck pressing into the pillow.

Outside the bathroom Madeline was calm. I followed her into the kitchen, past my bedroom door and the small pantry that held the fridge, into the narrow back hallway. A cracked stairway ran down to Ma's friend Lisa's, and the horrible children she was raising to be the next generation of racist white Chelsea. Already little Diana had hollered at a friend for raising a toy harmonica to her lips, because a black boy had been playing with it. *Don't, the black kid touched it!* she'd shrieked. Upstairs was Will's brother Ricky, and lazy Tracy, tormented by Will because of her big fat ass, and their wonderful son, who was so artistic and, I prayed, gay. I stood in the hallway and looked at the wall. My room was on the other side. A slab of fake wood paneling leaned against it. Madeline heaved it aside and exposed the giant hole, bigger than my fist, halfheartedly covered with a useless clump of duct tape. The tape had been peeled back from the hole so many times it had barely any glue, and stuck to the wall weak as dust. Madeline brushed it aside, it fell to the floor like a dead leaf. *Look,* she said. Like a science museum, when you peer into the darkness to find a magnified bug or a diorama. The Michelle's Bedroom Exhibit. Not exactly panoramic, but a good view. My bed with its jumbled mess of blankets and clothes, my aluminum wardrobe with the full-length mirror, the names of bands I liked or used to like scratched across the rough surface in colored chalk. I backed away from the punch of hole in that wall, and thought, They Could Have Been Stringing Electrical Wire. We were all stealing cable from each other, maybe that's where they pirated the wires. I was frightened by the combined degree of Madeline's and my paranoia. Bent like nervous crones in the back hallway, hysterical over a hole. Maddy, It's Maybe For Electrical Wire? My voice sounded like a little baby voice, a toddler. I had thought that if I saw the holes I would know, but the more proof I found, the more anxious and doubtful and uncertain I felt. My body felt like a wind-up toy, it clattered. I aimed it out of the gloomy hallway and into my bedroom. Madeline showed me the nicks in my wall. Little slits where the boards of paneling met, again each curve forming a perfect oval. So tiny, it was incredible that such a sliver provided such a sweeping view of my room. Awful, anxious rage bubbled. This is what it felt like to really need to hit something. How could you blame anyone for killing anyone, if this is what it felt like? Would I kill someone? I was losing my mind. What if this made me lose my mind, and do things I thought I would never do? What if all of this made me into a different person? Tears sprang, finally, but dried salty on my eyeballs, none of the soothing, hot release I craved. Everything just came apart inside me. I choked, and my face scrunched up like a sob—dry heaving, my tear ducts retching. My body was going through the motions, but I was dry. You try to be good, to be good and loving and nice and not hard, not tough, a sweet nice girl, not ugly, not full of ugliness, but people make it impossible. How could a girl be sweet in the face of this? A girl would die. I thought of Will, how he was a cabinetmaker, had learned it in the same vocational high school I had attended. Driving me there on mornings when I'd missed the yellow school bus, he'd proudly point at the sign at the head of the long driveway, Northeast Metropolitan Regional Vocational School. *I made that,* he'd brag. Back when it was known as the Yoke, before they tried to spiff up the school's working-class image by dubbing it Northeast Metro-Tech. Will, he was crafty, knew math, was an artist, knew how to work with materials, was clever.

I stormed into his room, and on his dresser found his knife lying amidst bottles of cologne, amidst cassette tapes and keys. I took his knife into my room, clamped my fingers on the blade's groove, and swung it out from the handle. I slid the point into the hole in my wall, it fit smoothly. More proof, and my will not to believe surged. No, my head thundered. I ran back into his bedroom and placed the knife on the dresser. In my own room I grabbed a bottle of black nail polish and globbed the stuff into the slit in my wall. It drooled down the paneling. I globbed more, blew air from my mouth to stiffen it. We Have To Catch Him, I told Madeline. We Have To Catch Him To Be Really Sure. I grabbed a copy of the *Phoenix* from my floor, brought it into the back hall and stuffed crumpled balls of newsprint through the hole, into that wall. Cotton in the keyhole. The dead duct tape on the floor snagged the heel of my boot, stuck there like an embarrassing bit of toilet paper. I pushed the slab of paneling back into place.

In my bed I could not sleep. I thought: Electrical Wiring. I thought: Paper. Balled-up newspaper, how Clive set his fireplace burning in his freezing house in Dorchester, how the crushed paper flared to ash so quickly. I was going to burn the house down. I had to get the newspaper out of the hole. I couldn't move in my bed. I thought of Will standing outside my room, and thinking about it brought him into my room, like a ghost, present and invisible. I burrowed like a child beneath my blankets. I'm Going Crazy, I thought again. Fear aged my bones into fossil. I couldn't move. I had to move, I'd burn the house down. I imagined flinging open the door and Will there in the dark, a monster. I imagined him wide-eyed and frothing, pouncing on me like a dog. He wouldn't do that. But if this was possible, anything was. Anyone could do anything to anyone. This was real. I flung myself out of my bed like pure light, heaved open my door. Layers of paint made it stick to the jamb, so bad that occasionally I'd been trapped, had to holler for someone to come rescue me with hipchucks and kicks. I pulled the door open into rich blackness. Nothing. I felt my way to the fridge in the pantry, and by its cold light located the lightswitch to the back hall. I moved the paneling and dunked my hand into the hole, yanked out the newspaper, eight crumpled balls of it. It was so late. I needed to sleep, to wake at dawn and begin the three-part commute to Newton, to sit in the grey and do nothing. I went back into my room and got a pen, and on the pale wall beside the violent hole I wrote, so tiny, "What are you doing? Please talk to me." I left Will a secret note. I would be his pen pal. I placed the board back over it. I went to sleep, slept badly.

The next night, I slept on my floor. I made a nest of bedding by my door, my ear to the creaking linoleum. I was a hunter, a ghost-buster. Dust lodged in my nostrils, I lamented my lack of cleanliness. In all the years we'd lived here, I'd never washed my floor. I could even count the times I'd swept it. When you sleep as lousy as that, consciousness bargains with dreaming and they work together to help you as best they can. All the long dark hours smooth into a calm hallucination. In old houses, the wood settles all night long. It shifts and creaks, and with every noise I shook awake, frozen, my ear to the door. Will was a big guy. He looked like Hulk Hogan, a big red guy with a wrestler's build and thinning blond hair. People told him he looked like the celebrity wrestler so often that he adopted his trademark mustache, the downy blond trimmed walrus-style around his mouth. *That's my maaaan*, he'd say when the Hulkster popped on TV in one of his Bullion commercials. I trusted that

Will's bulk would creak the floor loud enough to wake me, I would catch him and finally be free. I would know the truth and would not lose my mind. I would feel the linoleum sink beneath his weight, it would be unmistakable. All night long I twitched awake, rose frantic and yanked my door into darkness. Settled back onto the cold floor, the hardness bruising my hipbones despite the layers of blankets. I'm Going To Catch Him, I had promised Madeline. But after a few nights I gave up. Sleep deprivation makes you snap faster than anything. I was close to something terrible. I felt the distant rumble like the promise of a brutal train. I brought my blankets back to my bed and buried myself beneath them, slept.

INTRODUCING STEPH

Breaking up with Clive was easy, because we'd done it a few times before. Those previous cracks had lacked staying power—adrift in the ocean of free time suddenly available to us, we swam back to each other and clutched. But it was only a matter of time before I, like all of his girlfriends before me, left him to be with women. Poor Clive. He was just one of those kinds of boys, a last truck stop of heterosexuality where dykes fuel up before hitting the road. I think I broke up with Clive over the telephone, like discussing where we'd go for dinner or what movie we'd see. I Just Think I Like Girls, I said, and that was that. Clive was probably relieved. He needed a girl who actually liked his penis, not simply tolerated it the way you would a slobbering, needy pet, one your lover had acquired long before you entered the picture, one that it wasn't your place to ask him to get rid of.

Having sex with a girl seemed like the most romantic thing a girl could do. Freed from Clive, I drifted through my days like a character in a

Harlequin paperback, I flowed. Who would I fall in love with? There was Kembra. She was still holding on to her boyfriend too, and that worked for a little while, until I was too impatient for her to see the light and dump him. Linda was a shallow lezzie fag-hag, fun to go dancing with, but outside the club, we couldn't relate. I picked up Steph at a clinic defense action, the angriest girl, the loudest, hoarse from screaming murderous threats at Christians, and on the official shit-lists of all the professional feminists from NOW who were trying to look reasonable for the news cameras. There was Steph in her bra, strutting up to old, praying men and spitting, *I bet you want to fuck me, don't you? Or do you like little boys?* Steph oozed terrible, righteous danger, and I fell in love with her immediately. She was a rich girl from Connecticut who worked as an escort, and could never keep her story straight about where her loads of cash came from. She was catering—no, she was doing child care. With a swiftness particular to lesbians, I basically moved into her house, a brownstone in Back Bay, which she shared with her childhood friend, Dinah, another escort. I didn't really live there, but I slept there every night, rushed there on a series of buses and trains after brief stops in Chelsea to get fresh clothes and kiss my mother. We'd drink in bars, go back to her house to lick pussy, and stay up all night having hostile political discussions. Steph was against everything. It was mesmerizing. I'd never met anyone who took it all so far. I'd gotten used to being the most extreme thinker in any crowd, and here was Steph, making me feel like a moron, a coward. We fought about Madonna—was she empowering to girls? Of course she was. *No!* Steph blurted. Madonna was the same-old same-old. Drag queens—cool gender fuckers at the forefront of the war against homos? No! Exploiters and mockers of women, trapped in the heterosexist gender paradigm! Dildos were not fun sex toys for adventurous girls, they were pathetic props for unimaginative females. Ideas that would have seemed stale and dowdy coming from the humorless NOW feminists, who held similar views, seemed radical coming from Steph. Because she was wild and young, wore bras and go-go boots to art openings, sold pot and fucked men for money. Because she wanted to fuck shit up in a cataclysmic fashion, and sometimes she did. And when she did, it was incredible.

It was Steph's idea to terrorize the boy who assaulted Katy, another girl we'd befriended at the actions. Katy and Georgia were girlfriends, and worked for a communist youth organizing group. The focus was mainly labor and class, and they thought me and Steph were kind of dumb for being so worked up about sexism. *You know, I don't think it's the single most important problem,* Georgia confessed to me plainly one night drinking, and I was shocked. It wasn't? I was so filled with love for all these revved-up girls and their overanalytical minds. All of them were deep in the throes of their pain, the often serious pain the world had caused them. Katy's dad had kissed her once, a kiss with tongue like the boys of my youth, a wet mouth backing her into a wall. Georgia had had her ass kicked by cops, and Steph had been molested by a priest, and then raped on the street by a stranger. I didn't tell anyone about Will. I knew they'd make me do something about it, and I was terrified of what it would be. They were bloodthirsty, we all were, but Steph the most, Steph the craziest. I was afraid of what they'd do if they knew. When Georgia rang the telephone at Steph's house, we were drinking coffee, slowly waking up into the afternoon, watching daytime television as if for the first time, outraged at soap operas and talk shows. Calling Jerry Falwell's eight-hundred number and fighting with the Christians. If only Operation Rescue attacked clinics every day, we'd have left the house. Having no place to direct our fury, we could only spin out on coffee, television and crank phone calls. Then Georgia called, and told us about the party Katy'd been at the night before. A party thrown by an old straight friend who hung with a gruesome Bostonian crowd, lots of boys. And one boy just followed Katy around all night, finally into the bathroom where he shoved her up against the sink and shoved his hands down the back of her baggyjeans, stuffed his tongue into her mouth. Katy knew who the boy was, and where he lived—directly across the street from the party-house, where Katy was crashing until she found a house to move into. Katy said no, please, don't do anything, but it wasn't about Katy. It was about women. We recruited another girl with a simple phone call. Bonny Brooke Belligerence, a strikingly tall, pagan girl from the clinics. She and Georgia convened at the brownstone, Dinah was roused from her futon, and Steph master-minded the plan.

The boy's name was John. Everyone knew him, so collecting information about him was easy. All his wimpy friends told us everything we needed to know, between weak apologies for his behavior. John was an intern at the alternative radio station in Boston. The alternative radio station owned the alternative newspaper that Steph pretended to be a writer for. It was an election year, the first time I ever voted. Steph asked John if she could come and interview him, get his thoughts on the election and what the collegiate youth of America thought about today's hot issues. John was thrilled. Steph rang his bell, asked him to keep his door unlocked so her photographer could let herself in without disturbing their interview. Steph was professional, her little hand-held tape recorder angled up at the chiseled jaw of John, who jabbered pompously about the state of the nation. Out in his hallway were me, Georgia, Dinah and Bonny Brooke Belligerence. Katy was across the street with the blinds drawn, crying. We had bandannas tied beneath our flashing eyes, the cloth growing moist with our excited pants. I was so very excited. All of us had sadly agreed that the practice of non-violence was naive and idealistic. I felt a soaring permission—I was about to enter a home where any violence I wreaked was not only understandable, it was good. I trembled with it. Georgia was watching the minute hand twitch on her watch. A man walked down the stairs and started at the sight of us. Realizing we were girls, he relaxed and smiled. A costume party? *Let's go,* Georgia's voice was muffled, her bandanna fluttered with her breath. We pushed open the wood door. *John Thomas! John Thomas! John Thomas!* We were chanting, each on our own time, a chaotic round. Bonny Brooke, the largest of us, kicked open his bedroom door, and John Thomas looked up with a confused but delighted smile on his face. *What . . . ?* Steph bolted from her chair, tape recorder clutched in her hand. *You motherFUCKER!* She was a banshee, we were harpies. All of us screaming into his face at once. We hadn't rehearsed a script, no planned dialogue, it was each of us hollering all our hate and fury down at the boy who sat on a beanbag with a crumbling face. *What . . . ?* He started to rise, but we were looming above him, so close to the ground he was, on his squashed piece of furniture. *No, sit back down!* Bonny Brooke barked, and raised her hand in the threat of a smack. *Hey, listen—*John tried to assert himself, and I rushed up closer, beside Bonny Brooke. You Listen, You Bastard! I screamed. Somewhere beyond the bedroom door, which Georgia had kicked closed behind us, was a male roommate rustling sheepishly in the kitchen. He knew about our plan and, awash in male guilt, had agreed not to stop us. *You're a fucking rapist!* Steph was shouting. We yelled that we would kill him. Do You Know That? I demanded. Do You Know That We'll Fucking Kill You? He nodded, paling. Eventually he would cry, thrilling us. *When a woman says no, what does she mean?* Steph grabbed his head. *No,* he mouthed. *She means NO!* Steph affirmed, and we all started chanting, *No, No, No, No,* bringing our fingers down at him like a legion of scolding teachers, a move we'd learned from ACT-UP radicals, who would surround their targets and chant "Shame!" in a similar fashion. A flock of witches fussing over an evil cauldron. The friction of our voices, our energies, spiraled into a thick cloud above our heads. The air was charged, and I felt that we could hurt him, we could really hurt him, and it would be okay. I couldn't be the first to strike, but I could jump in. I felt a shift in my body, like the beginnings of a drug crash, as I realized that this probably wouldn't happen. We'd taken it so far, but none of us would go all the way, give him the punch in the jaw that the arrogant set of his face begged for. The moment was dissipating. There wasn't much more to holler without getting repetitive, and we couldn't let our outburst sag. Like a single mind, we turned to leave. I gave him a swift kick in the leg, and Bonny Brooke kicked his bed and flicked her hands above it. *I cursed his bed,* she told us later, satisfied. *He'll never be able to get it up in that bed again.* We filed triumphantly out the door, and saw the roommate like a scared cat at the end of the hall, poking his head around the corner. We slammed the door behind us and ran down the stairs. Infused with energy once again, we shrieked, scorching our throats as we ran through the doors and out into

Allston. From a bag I'd brought I whipped out a can of black spray paint, and tagged JOHN THOMAS IS A RAPIST in thick, dusky letters, cramping my trigger-finger, getting my skin inked up with the sooty, sticky paint. We ran back to Steph's car, and drove back to her house.

We were gloating when Katy called us. Katy, who we'd all but forgotten about, though the assault was of course in her honor. We were rewinding the tape in the tiny, hand-held recorder, listening to the event again and again. How you could hear us coming down the hall like a ghostly parade, our voices growing louder. When we all roared NO, I got chills. It was too perfect, it sounded staged. You could hear the quiver in John's voice as he began to cry, and the clunk of Bonny Brooke's combat boot as it struck the frame of his bed. Katy called us, freaking out. John Thomas had simply walked across the street, across my libelous mural, and banged on the windows of the first-floor apartment where she was, alone, banged until the glass shook, rattled at the doorknob, shouted in the street for her to come out, or let him in—why did she send a bunch of fucking dykes into his home to threaten to kill him? *That bastard!* Steph shrieked. He hadn't believed us, hadn't taken us seriously after all. We had told him, it he went near another girl, if we heard of him bothering another female, we'd slice off his cock with a knife. We had to go back. I could hear Katy wailing through the phone, pleading. *She doesn't want us to.* Georgia translated, torn. But there was no time for waffling, one glance from Steph and you were ashamed that you even thought of maybe not responding. She had those weird blue eyes that burn like a gas flame, pale and spooky. We dashed back to Allston, speeding in Steph's car. When a girl took her time crossing the street, Steph

honked, and Dinah yelled, *Move it, bitch!* out the window. *Hey,*
Bonny Brooke Belligerence said, confused. *Don't call her a bitch.*
Oh . . . yeah, Dinah conceded, distracted.

In front of John's door, which was locked, I braced myself
against the banister and the wall, lifted my body up by my arms
and battered the wood with my boots. Thud, thud, thud, my feet
shot out, black Doc Martens laced with red plaid laces, I tried to
kick the door in. *You motherfucker!* Bonny Brooke screamed. *Did*
you think we were JOKING? With every two-footed kick, the door
sagged and buckled on its hinges. A splinter ran up the middle
like a crack in an ice floe, the wood there raw beneath the var-
nish. *I'm calling the police!* John Thomas yelled from inside his
house. His voice lowered as he addressed the cop on the other
end of the line. The five of us clustered around his door and
pounded the wood with ten fists. *Yeah, call another white man to*
come protect you! Steph shrieked. Coward! I hollered. Come Out
Of Your House! Inside I was doing the math. How many seconds
till a call went out, till the squad car turned in our direction, till
a stocky Irish cop began his laborious climb to John's fourth-
floor apartment. Come On, I said, and the girls followed me. We
dashed down the stairs and back into the street again, pausing at
a pay phone to call in a final threat. We wouldn't be scared off by
cops. It was the cop who answered the phone. *What is going on*
here? he asked, in his talking-to-a-crazy-bitch tone. Like he was
bored, tired of shenanigans like these. He Sexually Assaulted My
Friend! I hollered. *Then your friend should come into the station*
and file a report, the cop recited. Oh, Fuck You, I spat and hung
up. Was the call being traced? We were mere blocks from John's
house. We sped home.

John Thomas didn't have to end, me and Steph decided. John Thomas could be just the beginning. Since none of us hung out with boys—except Katy, who didn't want to relinquish her old, stupid, straight friends—it was a bit hard for us to come up with our next target. Madeline knew lots of horrible boys whose legs should be broken with baseball bats, but I was afraid to offer her up as a potential source of assholes. What if it came back on her, like it had on Katy? Inside I knew I was a coward, I had that private knowledge, and it shamed me. I longed to be as fearless as Steph—I acted like I was, but my heart was a safe house that kept my family and all their crimes protected. We thought maybe we could put the word out on the street, let all the straight girls know that an underground band of dykes was ready to take out their last rotten date. A nonviolent version of this already existed, in a disorganized way. Women writing the names of their attackers in ladies' bathrooms across Boston. I saw it all the time, in bars, in the public library. *Names of Rapists*, one pen scrawled, and beneath it, in different pens and pencils and markers, in different handwriting, a list of names. If we could only let those girls know we were out there. I read Andrea Dworkin's *Mercy*, and the inspiration rattled inside me.

Steph decided to stop eating meat, and I followed. We weaned ourselves, from the bloodiest on down to fish, one week at a time. Then we stopped buying anything but organic. Soon we would no longer be able to eat out at restaurants. We needed full control over what we ate—who knew what cooks used, what awful, poisonous foods they served us? Steph talked about moving to Tucson, where it was easier to live natural and not harm the earth or other people, and I knew I would follow her there when she went. She made it sound like heaven, warm and beautiful with tiny cheap houses and cacti. But before she left she wanted to do things. She thought blowing up a movie theater showing a violent, male-oriented action film would get rid of a whole bunch of pricks in one fell swoop. We argued. I thought, Madeline Goes To Those Movies. With her awful boyfriends, who do deserve to die, it's true, but what about their girlfriends? *That's what you get,* was Steph's answer to that. *They shouldn't be in there. They shouldn't be supporting that culture.* Steph thought about going, dressed up like a dumb slut, to one of the millions of frat parties that raged through Boston on the weekends. Sitting like bait in a short skirt, and the rest of us could be waiting nearby, bandannas wrapped around our faces. Almost every day Steph had a different plan, brainstorming next to the telephone as she waited for her agency to send her out on a call. Her tricks would be too hard, she'd reasoned, because the agency had all her information, would trace the crime to her so easily. Every day the things that men did and got away with piled up in the world, growing like trash, like trash on a barge with no place to dock. In bed next to Steph, night thickening around us, I racked my brain anxiously, trying to shake out a plan of retribution, but nothing came.

HAPPY BIRTHDAY CONNECTICUT

Steph knew about a little bed and breakfast in some little town in Connecticut. Connecticut was close to Massachusetts, but I had never been there. Maybe driving through, not stopping. It was a boring place, like Rhode Island. Nothing of interest had occurred in Connecticut, historically. It took a second to cover it in Social Studies back in fifth grade. Connecticut was scenery blurring by on a car trip with my grandparents, a whole state of that, monotonous trees with the occasional New England home peeking through, a white triangle of roof, a backyard with a clothesline strung and flapping—you wondered who lived there, but only for a minute. Steph grew up there. Lots of rich people do. Not millionaires, but rich compared to me. Which was Steph. A very privileged person who believed that by becoming a dyke she negated all that, the sex we had canceling out her well-cared-for teeth and that way that moneyed girls carry themselves, uptight and comfortable at once, radiant like health personified, wealth sitting on their skin like a good tan. Steph clung to her dykeness like a fatal disease, so that she could be alive but dying too. Finally her blond hair didn't matter so much, and she could relax into being an outlaw, or a victim. She took me to Connecticut, this neighboring country she hailed from.

There were a few reasons for the weekend trip. The first and most practical was a really great store that sold camping equipment wholesale, and since me and Steph had decided to spend the rest of our lives living in the wilderness, living off the land, living the way humans are supposed to live in this world, we would need a lot of gear. Also, Steph had a score to settle with the state of Connecticut. Things had happened to her there, a grade school teacher had sexually harassed her, stuff like that, and she had to go and look that landscape in the face the way *The Courage to Heal* tells you to confront your abuser. Lastly, as it happened, Steph's best friend Brad had a nephew who was having his second birthday, and there was some big party at his mom's house, and we would drop him off there. So the entire trip had little if anything to do with me, and that was fine. Right then I was very into being pulled along by the tides of other people's destinies. It was about all I could do—being an observer, offering advice when asked, taking a stand when it was really necessary. My own life being too overwhelming, it was nice to vacation in the lives of these blond, white-toothed kids who came from Connecticut. Like watching TV. Sure, I'll Come With You, I said to Steph. A supportive girlfriend. Not that she even wanted me there. She dumped my ass in a state park, and said she'd be back for me in a few hours. She was going to go look at her old grade school. I thought it was great that she was investigating her life, like a girl in a book.

I sat among the trees. I was trying really hard to like nature, I figured I would have to since we were planning to live in the middle of it for the rest of our lives. I understood it to be the natural world, the place that was true before humans ruined everything. I knew it was the righteous place to be, and more than anything I have always wanted to be righteous, so I wanted to like nature. I walked into the middle of the park, my boots on the dusty path, trees and tangles of green the margins of this page I moved into. But what do you do in nature once you are there? I wanted it to be more than it was. I wanted to be awed, or at least have a revelation of calm, but I was only myself—restless as always, and not a person in sight. I sat down in a small clearing, with some jutting rock I could climb on. There were ants. I worried about them getting into my stuff. I had a bag with some snacks, I had a book about shamanism, which is, of course, about the glory of nature. I had hoped it would prompt something but it didn't. Mostly I thought about being raped. There was nobody around, anything could happen. What good was a tree if you were being raped. I ate an apple, and flung the core into the mess of green that just kept coming up from the earth with no one to stop it. I took off my boots and walked with my toes in the ants and the dirt. I lay back on the rocks and masturbated and thought about being raped in the woods. Where was my girlfriend? I wanted out of this creepy place. I picked up some heavy sticks and played drums on a rock. It felt good hitting the stone, I pounded hard and the branches chipped and splintered then split and broke, and I grabbed more sticks and kept playing. I sang out loud, I sang Ani DiFranco songs, playing drums on a rock. I felt I captured it for a moment, the elusive nature of the natural world that supposedly we are all innately connected to.

I hated it. Imagine if you really had to live out there. All the time, like it was your life. Maybe there would be one second in the morning, right when you were waking up, when you would hear a nice sound, a pretty gurgle from the beak of a bird, and the air would smell good and fill up your lungs, and you would slowly begin to feel the stiff creaking of your body, which had slept on natural hardness all night, a rock or stick poking into your side, and you'd lift yourself into a day of physical labor and boring monotony, like carrying water or tending a fire, tedious shit. When that's done, what do you do? You look at trees. I hated it. It seemed impossible that this would be my new home, a tiny sloping tent for a bedroom. I had agreed to it only because I could not imagine it ever happening. Maybe if there were twenty other girls, and they were all insane and drank all night and smeared mud on their chests and told stories and howled, maybe something like that would be okay. But the idea of me and Steph alone forever in these still trees felt like incarceration.

I had to get out of it. I hiked back down to the road, where there were a couple of houses, and a fenced-in pen of reindeer—incredible, branches of antlers with a thin fuzz like moss, like nature come alive, which I guess *is* what they were. A manmade pond thick with green algae. Cars drove by, the sound of their tires on the smooth pavement soothed me. I read a newsletter I picked up at a health food store, about how corporations were using nuclear waste to irradiate food so it would sit longer on the shelves in the stores. I thought about fat red strawberries, gigantic and crimson but white inside, dry with no juice. And those tomatoes that looked like something big and bubbly you'd inflate with a pump. Radiation. A guy in Brazil who worked in a junkyard found a container filled with dazzling glitter and he brought it home and sprinkled it all over his daughter's bedroom. She loved it. She died. He killed her, it was radiation. He died, too. I put the newsletter down. I opened the shamanism book. I wanted something to erupt from my brain and save me. A really excited dog kept diving into the lake and emerging coated in that thick green sludge. He'd run over to me and shake it off and it would land in my mouth like spit. Go Away, I motioned with my hands. I said the same thing to the bees. The dog kept doing it, hopping into the pond and running right to me like I was his friend. I was his friend, but I didn't want that shit on me. Finally Steph came, and I got in the car. *How was your day?* she asked in this breathy voice that meant she'd been smoking pot. Oh . . . It Was Really Nice, I said. It Was Really Peaceful. Grounding. She smiled. What Did You Do? *I was standing in the schoolyard of my old school*, she said, *and I found this*. She lifted a black feather. *It's from a raven*, she said, her voice heavy with significance. Wow, I said. She nodded and put it on the dashboard.

Steph rented a room at the little bed and breakfast. It was pretty great. We walked into this lobby that was classic rustic New England glory, real wood dark enough to cancel out the sunlight streaming in through lace-curtained windows, polished to gleaming. Someone calm and sensible took our money and gave us a key and we climbed the solemn staircase with carpet that quieted our feet, a banister too large to fit your hand around, shining dark wood. The bedroom was an explosion of sunlight. White walls, a bed with a white chenille covering that looked soft and welcoming. Wood headboard, old lamps, white bathroom. A single pathetic fan in that heat. It was so hot. Hot like a New England summer, the weather an overbearing relative who's been away for so long she wraps you in all her musty stinks and you cannot twist away. Why would you want to? It was delicious. We took off our clothes and spread our skin on the bumpy bedspread. The fan blew our smells around the room, the windows let some flies in. It was beautiful and perfect the way my time with the trees was not. This is what had been missing, the small porcelain sink hung on the bathroom wall, the light fixture on the ceiling dangling its switch. I loved Steph's body. It meant I was a dyke, the tanned length of it sinking into the bedcover. The external symbol of everything inside me, her wide hips, breasts much larger than mine, not firm but soft, the skin like crinkly tissue paper. Something lush I could lose myself in. Only, Steph was a bitch. Really mean. But lying quiet in this setting, I could make her what I wanted her to be. We kissed a little, she always seemed bored. I think she was just waiting for me to pounce on her, rough her up like her boyfriends had, but since I was waiting for the same thing, we only lay there, doing this half-assed kissing until we fell asleep. I had a yeast infection. My pussy felt itchy like the rest of me in that heat, like it had never seen soap and water. The pillows were hard. All night the fan whirred in the dark.

Why did we go to the birthday party at Brad's mom's house? We weren't wanted there. They were Mormons. It was fascinating, I had read about their sacred underwear, long Johns marked with mystical Mormon symbols that they had to wear all the time, even in the shower, dangled off an arm, held away from the spray so it wouldn't get wet. Brad promised he'd try to steal me a pair from his mother's drawer so I could wear them out to clubs. Brad was Steph's best friend from high school. He was the cute boy who'd worked at Burger King, so as a joke Steph and Dinah had gotten jobs there too, took pictures of themselves posing sexy in the ugly uniforms with the stripes at the shoulders. It was performance art. They didn't need to work. Brad was difficult to be around. He was just like Steph, and if Steph were a guy I would've hated her. These arrogant kids from Connecticut, always laughing at everything. Their families had so much money, and now as adults they were forever bitter about having to actually work, hold jobs, make their own money when they were so aware of that wealth of parental cash, all locked away. These parents knew that their children were spoiled brats. Steph and Brad had to fight and threaten for a dime. In Boston Steph and Dinah got work as prostitutes, and Brad hooked up with boys who had money, and lived off them. Eventually he was a prostitute, too. Then he found out he had HIV. I was at my mother's house when Steph called. *Brad is positive. You can come over if you want.* I had keys to Steph's apartment, I let myself in the front door, climbed the stairs to their flat at the top, music growing louder and louder until I opened the door and the sound fell onto me like steam from a shower when you walk into the bathroom—the Beatles, "Happiness Is a Warm Gun." It was blaring, the room was dim, they were all stoned on the couch. Wine bottles, some empty, some full.

Want to see my report card? Brad asked. *I got H-I-V-plus.* Nobody knew what to say. I didn't. I sat in the dusky room and drank the wine and sunk into the stereo. It was such a depressing time. We were all funding Brad's life, especially his new rich boyfriend, Jim, who worked at the stock exchange. Not his rich Mormon family, they wouldn't help at all. They thought he deserved it. He was gay—what had he expected? So we all went down to

Connecticut, and showed up at the Mormon occasion. It was absurd. I looked real shabby, and they all knew I was Steph's lesbian girlfriend. The mom was pretty nice, a big woman, apologetic like she'd been apologizing for everything for so long it had become her manner, rushing around, filling up paper cups with caffeine-free soda. She wasn't the family problem as much as the dad was, your classic abusive asshole dad. The mom was forever in the process of divorcing him, but I guess that's kind of difficult if you're a Mormon and want to stay a Mormon. Brad's little brother, who used to be a skinhead but supposedly was better now, was freaking out because he'd lost his pet iguana. It was a big animal, and he was in the backyard, rummaging through the bushes, calling to it like it was a dog. There was a kiddy pool filled with water, which we sat in. There were a couple of Mormon "elders," those young boys in the suits who walk around your neighborhood with their spiritual imperialism, missionaries. They had their suits on, with the little plastic nametags like they were working, and I'm sure they were wearing the special underwear. Me and Steph plopped down beside them on the couch in the living room, all of us with our little cups of caffeine-free soda. *So,* Steph began, *how does it feel to not think for yourself? Does it bother you? We think for ourselves,* one answered. *Did you know,* she continued, *that America dropped nuclear bombs on Nevada throughout the fifties, only when the wind was blowing toward Utah? They observed the effects of the radiation on the Mormon communities there, they did nuclear testing on you guys. Do you like your government?* The elders got up with their sodas and left. Brad's mom glared nervously at us. Then the dad showed up, and Steph ran out onto the lawn to intercept him. I was right behind her. Actually Brad got to him first. It was a long time coming. Brad was crying, shaking red—*I have AIDS.* The whole Mormon family clustered inside behind the screen door, listening hard but not coming out. The dad was awful. *You didn't have to do those things. Anal sex,* he spat. It's almost not worth telling, it's so cliché, but he said these things to his son. *It's your own fault.* Me and Steph stood there on the manicured Connecticut lawn. He Is Your Son! You Are Evil! Brad just cried. His face was like a sunburn. *You get out of here,* the dad said to us, *or I'm calling the cops.* Call The Cops, White Guy, I hissed at him, Go Call The Fucking Cops, Have Them Arrest Your Son For Having AIDS. Steph loved that I said that. What was I doing in Connecticut? The dad stormed into the house and the mom tearfully asked Brad to come inside. *Just Brad, please,* she added.

One by one, the party guests left the house. *Thanks a lot,* the mother of the birthday child hurled at us as she climbed into her car and left. Me and Steph sat on the front lawn in our hippie dresses. I had an *Utne Reader,* with a big article about a feminist who liked pornography. I put it down, I couldn't read it. Tiny pale green bugs hopped on it and hopped away. Brad's brother came out and started up this perfectly bizarre conversation about how Brad's dad would beat Brad as a teenager, because sometimes he just spontaneously shat his pants, and maybe it was because he was gay and having sex with his ass and couldn't hold his poop in anymore? We just stared at him. *What?* Steph asked. Maybe You Should Go Find Your Iguana, I suggested. He was about sixteen. When the dad left, me and Steph were allowed back in the house. The mom was on the couch, beside an end table decorated with glass swan figurines. She collected them. *I love Brad,* she said. It seemed a struggle to get the words out. She was trying not to cry anymore. I Know You Do, I said. I felt awful. We took Brad back to our bed and breakfast. He slept with us on the wide, white bed, the covers kicked into piles at our feet.

On the drive back we went to that camping store. I was so bored. It was like shopping at Lerner's with my mom when I was a kid. I didn't care about any of it, the aisles of different tents popped up on the linoleum, racks of sleeping bags hung like cocoons. I just gave Steph money. She bought us a tent. I got a really expensive synthetic grey sleeping bag that I never used in the wilderness. In the car on the drive back I spooned white globs of yogurt into my pussy and lay across the back seat with my feet raised against the window, letting the microscopic bacteria annihilate each other.

MASKING TAPE

Every day I waited until the house was empty, Will and Ma at work or visiting the neighbors, Madeline at work in Boston, or out on a date with a new boyfriend. In the dusty back hallway I would slide the slab of paneling away from the wall, and peer down at the tiny message I had graffitied on the wall. My mousy plea for communication. Each day I lamented its static progress, and worried. It seemed the longer it sat there, unanswered by Will, the more likely that someone other than Will would discover it. What if Ma's occasional cleaning frenzies suddenly extended to the musty back hallway? What if our cable fritzed out, and Ricky upstairs needed to dig into our walls? What if Lisa downstairs wanted to use that extra bit of paneling for her children's rooms? The small mark of my handwriting on the wall made me anxious, and I grew more certain about our sisterly false hysteria. Will hadn't been back there, would never see my minuscule SOS. I stopped checking daily and moved to weekly. And then one week, it was gone. What Are You Doing?

Please Talk To Me. I whispered my message aloud in the cobwebby quiet. That's what it had said. It had been written in pen. I thought of those weird, nubby pen erasers, white, that sat on the tips of the most ancient pens, useless. How do you get rid of pen? I imagined Will licking the tips of his fingers and smearing it off the wall. I studied the space closely, moving my head in till my bangs brushed plaster, till my eyes blurred. Nothing but the bumpy topography of paint and plaster. And the hole itself, the crumbling gape. It was taped up now, meticulously. Row after row of masking tape, narrow beige layers resting atop each other like shingles on the side of a house. Stripes stretched across the void with a neurotic, anal precision. This was not a single slab of duct tape, easy to slap on and tug off. There was no way to casually peel this masking-tape creation away without destroying its deliberate arrangement. The hole had been sealed.

This new quilt of masking tape was my proof, proof that Will had been out in the back hallway, and recently. That he had pushed the paneling aside, and noticed that pathetic bit of duct tape gone. Had he known he was busted? I imagined him squinting beneath the dim bulb to read my childlike scribble. This new masking tape was a quiet, secret apology. He had bound his temptation up in gluey strips. It was a message that communicated itself, doubtless as any string of words. It made me feel creepy to be communicating with Will in this hidden, dusty way. Notes left in back hallways straight out of a haunted-house movie. Replete with gauzy spiderwebs and the scattering brown bodies of the arachnids that wove them. I grabbed a pen from my room, left my note on the masking tape this time, the ink sinking into the texture, bleeding like lipstick. *What is going on? What are you doing?* I moved the paneling back over it, switched off the light and pulled the back door closed behind me. I would wait for his reply.

SWEET EMOTION

Ever since he entered our family, Will had wanted one of those big-ass luxury cars, the kind that only broke people who can't afford nice cars dream of. Just a bit too large, too showy. A Lincoln Town Car. He finally got it. It was long and black. It had a T-top, like a sunroof but shaped to shine only on your balding scalp and the scalp of your passenger, a T-shaped pane of glass that held blue sky. Will did well in nice weather. When the sun finally roared out and filled your eyes with glare, heated up the world with a slight electrical smell, Will just expanded. It was like a big, public party, and he was the host. He loved giving rides in his car on those summer days, blaring a little Led Zeppelin, a little of the hometown boys, Aerosmith. Steven Tyler's screeches, like an angry cockatiel. *This song always makes me think of you,* Will smiled, and cranked "Sweet Emotion." Will was cool, Will knew that I had told whopping lies to Ma all through high school, lies that allowed me to stay out until sunrise, drinking and joy-riding with kids unhampered by curfews. I went to *Rocky Horror* every weekend, the Saturday and Sunday shows. Once, I accompanied Vinnie and Greg on an overnight drive to Pennsylvania, when Ma thought I was at Carla's. I *was* a real good liar. The backstage door part of the song, being obsessed with rock 'n' roll, with goth, with punk or whatever—I would wait for hours, on the verge of tears, for bands to emerge from their hotel, their tour bus, the infamous backstage door. Though making out with that guitarist from the tiny eighties glammy rock band from Britain was as close as I ever got to setting any celebrity pants aflame. I liked that Will thought I was that cool, as cool as a girl in an Aerosmith song. It wasn't until later that it struck me as creepy, how the song's all about the search for the slutty girl who would actually fuck you, would fuck Steven Tyler back when he was a high school dweeb, and now, as a rock star, about looking for that slut-girl at the backstage door. Maybe a weird song to remind you of your daughter. Unless your daughter's not your daughter, but your rock 'n' roll peepshow, your MTV.

Riding in the car with Will, on a day so sunny the shine formed blisters of light on the cars, on the windows of shops we cruised by in his Lincoln Town Car. Sometimes he'd have the trees hanging from the rearview, duking it out with the larger, yellowy smell of nicotine that swirled through the car, sinking deeply into the seats. Sometimes he'd have a little spray bottle of cherry-scented stuff to just squirt into the air or onto the upholstery. The windows whirred down with the press of a switch in the door; above our heads the sun bore into our skulls like a magnifying glass held over an ant colony. Air from outside whipped my face, and the radio blared WBCN, maybe the Doors were on, something like that. Something from Will's time that I liked too, something we could share.

Once, I had been obsessed with a thirty-year-old gothic French tarot reader named Bertrand. He was tall and willowy, and had seen Bauhaus live. His hair was long and black and wavy, and his voice dripped with other places. In the tarot reading he told me that I had been a flapper in a past life, a party girl in a fringed dress, a feather bobbing from my sequined headband. I'd smoked my cigarettes from long, thin holders, and I'd drunk my liquor straight from the bottle, defiantly. My hair danced around the nape of my neck and my eyes were wide with liner. I fell in love with Bertrand. He told me I often dreamt I was flying because I was part fairy, and in those dreams I *was* flying—flying in another dimension. I smiled and blushed and did not tell Bertrand that I never, not once, had one of these flying dreams I'd read about in dream books. I didn't tell him that I often dreamt I was swimming, swimming in pools of contaminated water that my skin absorbed the way the seats of Will's car absorbed nicotine. The water would kill me slowly, from the inside, and there was nothing I could do, it was too late. Like asbestos, it only took the tiniest bit, a splash on your skin to doom you, and there I was, immersed in it. I didn't tell this to Bertrand, because I didn't want to make him feel bad about his shoddy psychic ability. I didn't tell him, because I liked that he saw me as a girl who dreamt of flying through skies, and not as a girl trapped in poison. I didn't tell him, because I was swiftly becoming so infatuated with him, and I wanted to be associated with flirtatious flattery, not corrections. I was eighteen years old then, barely. I had just realized I could actually go out with a thirty-year-old man. I was legal. Not jailbait. I could play bingo, and make out with adults. I'd learned something from that run-in with the obscure British rock star, and I vowed—if cute, rocker guys viewed me as a bona fide adult, I would act like one. At home I told my family about Bertrand the French tarot reader. He had given me his card, and I intended to call him. My mother was tense. It's Legal! I crowed. I'm Eighteen! There was something ill about the way I shared so much with my family. I just wanted it to be okay, and not uncomfortable, but that was like wanting a different family altogether. My mother of course was concerned about what kind of man would want to spend time with a child like me. He's Goth, I explained patiently. Our common subculture made age difference irrelevant. We were above such things, the petty moralities of the mainstream. He's Seen *Bauhaus*, I gushed. They've Been Broken Up *Forever.* Will started grumbling about not being able to trust a guy who lives in the past, holding on to the music of his youth. I looked at him, my black-lipsticked mouth hung open in shock. What Do *You* Listen To? I accused. The Who, Black Sabbath, Ozzy but old Ozzy, not the new MTV incarnation. Ozzy when he still had Randy. Will was not so deep into his thirties, the same age as Bertrand, more or less. The conversation ended, and forever, since Bertrand had more sense than to involve himself with one of his eighteen-year-old tarot customers, making himself available for more useless, incorrect psychic consultations, but resisting my timid invitations to have coffee with me and talk about France, about Bauhaus, what Peter Murphy looked like twisting on the stage, a scrawny funnel cloud, storming.

In the hot and breezy Lincoln Town Car I leaned into the deep grape upholstery and breathed through my cigarette. Inhale, exhale. Will breathed through his, occasionally flicking the tip out the window and sending a squall of ash back into the car, flying hot and brittle into my eyes and mouth. I sputtered and my eyes teared. *Sorry there, hon.* I flicked my own out the window with the utmost carefulness. My biggest fear was chucking the whole spent butt out the window, only to have the wind knock it back inside, into the back seat, to smolder, ignite and kill us. It never happened. I was rigid and shaking with the question I was about to ask Will, right after I finished my cigarette. I finished it, and realized that I would want something to fidget with, something to distract me from his face and voice, something to occupy myself with, I lit a new one off the car lighter, puffing ugly as the dry tobacco tip began to spark, the glowing orange ring cooling. Dad, Why Are There Holes In The Back Hallway Walls? Behind My Room? The long pause didn't mean anything. I mean, you couldn't really read into it, because Will was so slow. Sometimes he just wasn't there, had to be reeled in slowly with your voice. Maybe it was because he smoked pot, but he didn't anymore. Now he was sober. Meetings made him nervous, such a *culture,* but he was off the sauce and the smoke. Like many living the sober life, he'd become a huge consumer of coffee, and perhaps his cigarette smoking had increased. *Well, ah, there's been electrical work back there, threadin' wires, stuff like that.* They're From Electrical Work? *Yeah.* I angled my cigarette out the corner of my open window and let wind shave the ashes off. We were pulling into Wellington Station, the orange line, where I would catch a train into Boston. Faster than the bus. I Wrote You A Note, Did You Get It? *A note?* He looked alarmed, and his face seemed to grow, to widen, as it cast its focus on me. Yeah, A Note, I stammered. I pretended to be such a hardass, but inside I was nothing more than paper lace, a doily for a heart. I should have turned on Will like John Wayne, drawn what I knew from my gut's holster, aimed and popped him.

I should have let all my scary crazies out right there in the front seat, to drool and convulse and shriek gurgled shrieks, so he could have seen what he had done to my mind. Yeah, A Note, I said again, blasé. *No, I didn't get any note,* he said. Yeah, he seemed nervous. I gulped. I Should Push it, I thought, Push It. I hesitated. *All right then sweetie, I gotta get to work.* He leaned the block of his head over, gave me a dry kiss on the cheek, the sound of his whiskers against my skin like a dry leaf blown into the gutter.

PHASE ONE

The next time Madeline called me I was working a new job as a receptionist at an off-Newbury Street hair salon. The hair salons that were actually on Newbury were famous, exquisite. Someone brought you a glass of bubbling champagne while you waited, flipping through avant-garde hair magazines. My salon was a discounty place, like Supercuts, staffed with hairdressers—called "designers"—who, for one reason or another, could not hack the competitive glamour of the couture cutteries around the corner. I got the receptionist job despite everyone's concern that my own hair might scare away potential clients. I was hired because of Kingsley Carter, my old fag friend from high school—his fag-hag sister, Andi, owned the place. Andi liked me, she'd once lent me her wedding dress for a lip-synch performance. She was divorced so the dress meant nothing to her, and she hadn't even cared that I'd drooled fake blood from my mouth onto the dress's pearled lacy collar, gargling and frothing as I mouthed the words to

Madonna's "Like a Virgin," as performed by the Lords of the New Church. This was in the auditorium of the school me and Kingsley had survived. I'd thought I was spectacular, and truly in the running for the one-hundred-dollar prize, but it went to a group of basketball cheerleaders who'd worn trash bags and white gloves and mouthed the words to "I Heard It Through the Grapevine."

Andi was currently in love with one of the designers—Jessie, a big queen who pretended he was bisexual in order to keep Andi interested. She would load him up with money—he'd ceased having to even ask to borrow cash, she'd just slip him cash from her tip jar as he dashed in and out of the salon on his customized, erratic work schedule. Sometimes weeks would pass without Jessie showing up to work. He'd be on a gigantic bender, booze and coke, and wind up in the clink for hustling, or possession. Jessie was both effeminate and butch, and his own hair was a disaster, a calico mullet of failed frosting attempts. He wore those awful tank tops guys wear, the kind that scoop way down low, offering you an eyeful of man-tittie.

Ralphie was another terrible designer, a dyke with a tattoo of her cat on the skin of her fleshy upper arm. Once, I let her cut my hair, and it was so bad that Andi let me have a half-day off, paid, while other designers worked to fix it. Andi gave me an apologetic handful of free styling products, and sent me home early. Ralphie used to work at one of the fancy shops on Newbury Street, styling the hair of celebrities like Grace Jones, but the salon was a competitive whirl of cocaine and all-night drinking at chi-chi Boston bars, and her life had fallen apart. Ralphie was sober now, and happy to have work at this humble shop, out of the limelight. There was once a span of time, about two weeks in length, when she could not stop nicking the customers' ears with her scissors. It was terrible to look up and see blood trickling out the slash in a dainty, whorled ear, staining the towels crimson, the client screaming, Ralphie dashing around for a first-aid kit. Andi gave her a week off.

Armando was a black queen with long black braids and intense blue contact lenses. He was my favorite, he would cellophane my hair for me when the shop was dead, leaving my locks shot through with deep, unnatural reds and purples. At night Armando would take me to various hipster bars in Back Bay, where he knew all the bartenders, and we'd drink for free—Alabama Slammers, big fruit-punch drinks. They really fucked you up, some of the more collegiate bars in Boston refused to sell them, because students would occasionally get severe alcohol poisoning and die. It would be on the news for a week or so, a string of outraged exposes about binge drinking among college kids, like everyone was just figuring it out. Like Jessie, Armando also took obscenely long lunch breaks, swishing back into the salon hours late, drunk, his long, leather coat floating behind him like a cape. *Hi, honeys!* he'd crow. Andi was such a fag-hag, she'd let him slide. When the end of the day rolled around he'd hoot, *I feel like I didn't work at all today! YOU DIDN'T!* Andi shouted. Also like Jessie, Armando was on a lot of cocaine. Sometimes they'd go on little benders together, though they didn't really like each other at all. Jessie would tell Armando about all his exploits in bathrooms with other men—turning tricks, doing it for fun, and Armando would cluck his tongue and say, *You're a mess, child.* I was shocked to learn that Armando cut hair so high and frenzied on the white powder. *I learned to cut hair on cocaine, girl! I'd fuck up if I was sober!* He laughed. Later I would see Armando as Amanda, his drag name, looking just like a girl, hustling out front of Playland, the absolute sleaziest Combat Zone gay bar. So skanky not even Vinnie and Greg, connoisseurs of skank, would go inside, afraid that sinister old trolls lurked there, waiting for young boys to drug and sodomize. Outside Playland, Armando/Amanda was fighting with another hooker, who was screaming, *At least mine's real!* and slapping at her spandex crotch. *They don't want your skanky snatch, bitch, they want dick!* Last I heard, Armando was in prison, Walpole State.

When Madeline called the salon, I was behind the counter where the appointment book was splayed open, scratched up with pencil and torn with eraser from cancellations. There was a little wicker basket of fragrant Spritz Forte samples. The place smelled so clean, like gallons of shampoo, and the air was misted with fruity gusts of hair product. Every so often I would get up and sweep the hardwood floor, collecting spooled nests of different colored hair: wiry and straight, kinky, permed, fried, healthy. Andrew was there, the only straight-guy hair dresser, older and sort of rock n' roll, with long hair and craggy bad skin. On slow days he would shampoo my hair, because he liked to give scalp massages. It was sort of creepy, but irresistible, because his strong fingers sliding across my head made me sleepy and chilled, it felt marvelous. *Your hair will grow faster if it's massaged,* he'd ooze. Afterward I'd feel as if we'd been sexual together, and would have to ignore him for a few hours until the sensation faded. The big white queen was there, too, ancient, who was so loud and racist. It made me nuts to hear him yell the N word so proudly, and refuse to cut black people's hair, and no one—not Andi, not even Armando—no one but me would tell him to shut up. *That's just George,* they'd wave their hand at him like he was some pesky sitcom character.

I sat at my little station, flipping through an old hair-styling magazine that had survived the eighties. I looked at a picture of a huge ratted coif that a stylist had titled "The Tarantula." My own hair, though a toxic red in color, was flattened with product in a poor imitation of a bob. My wiry locks gathered into clumps and began to frizz, to curl upward in rebellion. I was trying out these new, chic styles, but my angry hair wanted to be a Tarantula. I slapped the dated magazing shut and threw it in the trash. Behind me on the wall, where the credit card machine hung, was a list of every state in the nation and their different credit card codes. Every day I'd do eeny-meeny-miny-mo to see where I would move. Alaska, Montana, Pennsylvania. It was the vacant portion of my day, when no customers filled the chairs, and the floor was swept, and the raggy little shampoo towels were washed and dried and folded in the cupboards—those lulls were filled with my daydreams about my future, my next life. That day was Tennessee. Maybe Nashville? It was warm there, and it sounded kind of campy. I'd thought of my friends saying, *Michelle ran off to Nashville.* I'd wear skirts and cowboy boots. Any place, I thought, could be a romantic place to run away to, simply because running away was such an act of romance. The phone behind the desk rang. Phase One, I chirped. It was amazing how many hair salons called themselves Phase One. I knew of four in Massachusetts alone. Andi was always hurt when I brought her news of another sighting. She'd thought it was such an original name. It was Madeline on the other end of the phone. She told me she'd talked to Will. She'd bluffed. She'd told him we *knew*, we knew *everything*, and it would be best for him just to admit it, own up to it all, because he was busted. Madeline was unwavering. I trembled behind the counter, awed at my little sister. Her frail-looking body of slender bones, her Snow White, anemic complexion, all of it housing a reserve of power, of determination, of righteousness so tough it made my head buzz. Will, of course, had denied everything. He had acted outraged, concerned that we had such a terrible misconception of him. He had shaken his big, meaty head, as if it were so absurd—he denied and denied. I would have cracked. I mean, my face would have cracked like a vase and leaked water down my chin, I'd have cried and blubbered and felt a geyser of deep shame spurt its steam. I would have rushed to Will with my arms wide to wrap around him. I would have apologized and begged for him to forgive me for thinking such terrible things about him when he had been so good to us, when he had loved us so deeply. From our first Christmas with him, when he gifted us with Sony Walkmans, until now, with his constant bowls of chili and rice, money for concert tickets, the way he intervened in my fights with Ma—dumb fights about my hair or my clothes. *Ah, who cares, let her dress the way she wants.* I would have been struck with a panoramic view of my life with Will, the kind people claim to see as they die, a reel of all his kindness. I would have cried, apologized and that would have been the end, forever. But steely Madeline had pushed. *We won't tell Ma, we won't tell anyone,* she promised. *It's okay, we'll get you therapy, we know.* It was the "we know" that wore him down. Will burst into tears like a little boy, caught. He apologized. It was only while he was drinking, he claimed, and he'd stopped so long ago. This did not synch up with the creaks and weirdnesses that had continued to happen long after Will put down the bottle, but Madeline let the specifics slide, because now *we knew.*

I thought maybe I'd leave the salon, go home early, go freak out, but then I didn't want to go home, really—not ever again. Steph was out of town, and I didn't know where else to go. I had been staying at her house so much that it felt like home, but her sudden trip to Connecticut had locked me out of this place I'd deluded myself into thinking was mine. There was only one place for me to go, only one true *home*, rotting in Chelsea on its old, chinked beams.

When my shift ended at five, I walked down Newbury Street to Back Bay Station, took the orange line to Haymarket, and climbed upstairs, back out into the world, to wait for the Woodlawn 111 bus to Chelsea. I stood in a violent clump of people, each one hell-bent on being first on the bus, for the luxury of picking their very favorite seat, and I, too, was all elbows—jostling up the steps, dumping my quarters in the little collection machine that ticked and hummed, and then dashing down the aisle to one of the few single-seats that lined the left side of the bus. The best seats, just you and the window, all of Boston streaming by beside you—the edges of the North End and their curving, Italian streets; the border of Charlestown with its hills and projects, and that one monument like a huge sewing needle pricking the sky. Then the bridge and the harbor. Then Chelsea. Then my house, which was empty of everyone but Will, who sat alone in the kitchen, his chair faced out from the table, facing the wall, just staring at the wall. The house was so still, like the horrible moment of his confession had preserved everything as Vesuvius had done to Pompei. None of the lights were on, and the house was dim with the onset of dusk. I was sure that Will had been sitting in that chair for hours. His *Hello* was weak; probably he was unsure if I knew. A normal, cheery Hello would be sick if I did, but a moping, scared Hello would seem odd if I were oblivious. And my eyes seared his for a moment, and in that second he knew that I knew, he knew as I dashed into my room like a cat and knocked shut my door.

Will was at my door. *Michelle, can I*—there was a rattle of doorknob and I screamed. Do Not Come In Here! *Michelle, I*— Shut The Fuck Up Go Away Fuck You Fuck You I Hate You I Hate You Go Away! Then I was throwing things. The feelings coursing through me, down my arms, a physical feeling. I had a statue of the Virgin Mary that Clive had painted. He'd brushed a black skeleton face over her benevolent gaze, very Day of the Dead. It smashed into chunks on my floor, paint chips from my door fluttering around them. *Now, stop it*—Fuck You Go Away Go Away! I hurled fistfuls of clothing that landed unsatisfyingly, nailpolish bottles that whirred like bullets, pens that clattered—it was like that scene from *Poltergeist,* when the family, frightened, opens the door to Carolann's room and finds a terrifying kaleidoscope of children's toys, clothing and furniture spinning through the air, a circus of destruction. I flung a heavy wooden crucifix, and as if Will were Satan, this last threatening thud silenced him. I waited to hear the famous *creak,* the sound of him moving away, back to his post in the kitchen. It was silent. I Will Kill You! I screeched like an aging rock star whose vocal cords have been scorched by drugs. A gurgled, dry scream. My throat felt harsh. Will moved away from my door. I could hear him crying, had heard the strain of it in his voice as he chanted, *I'm sorry, I'm sorry, I'm so sorry,* and I screamed back, Shut Up Shut Up Shut Up! trying to smother his voice with my own. The pathetic timbre of his fear and apology made me want to run out of my room and comfort him, hug him, tell him it was okay, please don't be sad, please don't be sad. I wanted to take care of him, which then made me want to kill. I slammed myself onto my bed. Was it okay? What if I walked into the kitchen, and sat with him there at the table? It's Okay. My plastic blue phone sat on my lumpy mattress. I called Vinnie at his mother's house in East Boston, where he was visiting. Vinnie, You Have To Get Me. You Have To Come For Me Vinnie, Please. I told him what had happened. He had been my best friend for years now, and never had I told him about this, about this possibility. Vinnie would come. I sat on my bed and trembled. Will approached my door. *Please don't tell*—Fuck You, I Mean It, I Will Kill You! I Swear I Will! I grabbed my backpack with a book to read and cigarettes, and I left the house. Will's sobs were at my back. Out front the streetlights were on, and night had started. By the yellowy light I opened my book and read from it. I'd go pages and realize I hadn't really been reading, flip back and try again. I lit a cigarette. A car pulled up, and it wasn't Vinnie. It was Ma. One of her nurse friends from work, dropping her off at the curb. *Okay, see you tomorrow!* she hollered with a smile as she shut the car door behind her.

Ma said, *What are you doing out here?* with a smile, because she was happy to see me. She bent her cheek to me and I kissed it. I'm Waiting For Vinnie. *Oh, you two doing something? You want to go to bingo?* No, We're Going Out. *You're going to hurt your eyes, reading out here in the dark.* She'd said this to me since I was eight, maybe younger. I felt sick with wanting to tell her. I shook with it on the dark, hard stairs, the air chilling around me, cramping my fingers. It was selfish, my desire to break down to her. I craved her comfort and her love, but I'd have to ruin her life to get it. And I knew that I would, just not then, not with her sore feet still cushioned in her soft nursing shoes, her crisp white uniform scratching at her knees.

Not with Vinnie on the way in his mother's borrowed Hyundai, not with me, speechless and numb. My mother stood there in the streetlight above me, smiling. I knew it was one of the last happy moments she'd have, and this knowledge made my insides cave in, a sinkhole. I wanted to sit there on the steps with her forever, waiting for Vinnie, who would never come, and Will would never come down the stairs, and Ma and me could just sit out front and smoke together, watching the streetlights fade beneath the encroaching sun, watching them turn on again as the days rolled over.

Kaliuah Hawaiian was the Chinese food restaurant closest to Vinnie's house in East Boston. Not a single Chinese person worked there, it was all trashy Italian, and the food somehow was great— fried lumps dunked in sweet sauces thick as puréed apples. Duck Sauce. We started going there in high school because the waitresses never carded. They would bring us gigantic ceramic mugs with mottled tiki faces, paper umbrellas stabbing fruit that dangled over the lip of the glass. Patricia was our favorite, long blond feathered hair, fake blond, from the bottle. The shrillest accent, always happy—happy to bring us our Blue Hawaiians, our Scorpion Bowls with the long, thin straws. Greg did her hair for her, had actually gone to her house and saw where she lived, bleaching and coloring her locks in the bathroom. Patricia was biting her lip because she was in trouble. She was pregnant, and her husband had had a vasectomy, so she couldn't even pretend it was his. Shit, we sympathized. *I know,* she bit her bottom lip, chewing off the pink. It looked like she was biting her smile away, like she was going to giggle, a little girl caught stealing candy and not a knocked-up, cheating hussy.

Whattaya kids havin'? We ordered cocktails and egg rolls, saucy chicken wings. I told Vinnie everything. He was stunned. He didn't know if I should tell my mother, he didn't know what I should do. I smoked cigarettes, and Patricia returned to take more drink orders, to ask about Greg—her roots were coming in. I wondered if I could live at Vinnie's house. Maybe down in his basement, on the couch. Letting myself in and out through the bulkhead. No, his mother—retired from the phone company and always on alert for intruders—would hear me moving around and call the cops, or worse, come downstairs and pummel me herself. Vinnie's mother was an hysterical, older Italian lady who, when upset, would yell through her teeth while gnawing on one of her knuckles. We all started biting our knuckles, too, as Vinnie's angry mother grew into a sort of cult figure. Partly we were making fun of her, but we also loved her, the way we loved Joan Crawford, or any female who radiated strength and insanity. She had only wanted Vinnie to be normal. Most of our parents had experienced this tragedy. I Don't Know, What Am I Going To Do? I asked Vinnie. Two drinks now, and my head felt lighter, my body relaxed, a dull ache in my shoulders as the muscles there finally unclenched. We talked about other things— messy gay people, crazy Greg, Patricia's embryo. Eventually Vinnie would take me home like any other night, pausing at the curb as I dug for my keys, zooming away as I stepped inside and locked the door behind me.

I always thought insanity was a white room, and now the room was mine. So white it crackled. It was like time had slowed enough for my eyes to catch each flicker of the fluorescent lights that normally strobed just beyond my perception. It fucked up my head, the shrill light. At my bedroom door Madeline cried and spoke, her voice vibrating with the strain of keeping her sobs contained inside her tiny rib cage, a nest. Her face bubbled with it, like something boiling. She was begging me not to leave. Like when we were little and slept all night in bunk beds, me on top, her in the cavern beneath. I remember nighttime weeping, Madeline begging me not to run away. We were so small. Where was I going to go? I thought perhaps the park some blocks away, where jagged, rocky hills rose above a baseball diamond. I could hide in the crag of it and never be found, live off grass like an animal. I would drape my head in a scarf and be sad. Maybe I would simply live out front, on the steps, like a neighbor. Huddle beneath the awning in the rain. Panic rolled out from Madeline's eyes. It annoyed me that she cared so much. If no one cared about me, I could be truly free. I had to promise Madeline I would not run away. Soon she would believe me, or become so tired that her salty eyes collapsed into sleep, and I'd climb the rungs up to my bunk and dig myself beneath the covers. Sometimes I'd snake my arm down the skinny place between the wall and the bed, and Madeline would reach up and grab my hand and we would clutch each other's fingers and drift away, palms in each other's hands, two girls sleeping.

Madeline's long-ago fear of my leaving had smashed out of the past, and into our real life, now. Into a new, foreign house that Ma had found for us. Just around the corner from the old place, the home with the holes. She had needed to move after a falling-out with Lisa, the landlord, her best friend since they were both twelve years old. You can't keep living upstairs from a break that strong. They drove each other crazy. Lisa was bitter, she was mean-spirited and cranky. She could work a friendly gossip session into a shit-talking jag that left you feeling bad, like you wanted to take back half of what you just said, apologize, but there was no one to take it to. Most gossip, I had learned, was just sport, it was like writing—what metaphor could you dredge up to describe that woman's hairdo, what slicing comeback had you spat when that bitch at work cut you down. It was storytelling, often other people's stories, but it was kind of innocent. My mother was just as likely to cluck her tongue in sympathy at any of the poor bastards she ragged on, it was just talk. But Lisa was really feeling it. The breakup of their friend-ship was sad, there was such history between them.

Lisa was who I'd been dumped with the day my mother went off to the hospital to have Madeline. I'd sat on Lisa's carpet before the television blaring soap opera histrionics, watching her dog trot around. A small pet dog with a small Kotex pad belted between her back legs because, unlike Ma, the dog was not pregnant. One of those short, white-haired dogs that start looking mangy real quick, the fur matted and wet by her runny red eyes. The pad looked like a diaper, which made me think of babies, like the one my mother would bring home. A baby that looked like a clown, Madeline. *What d'ya do all day?* Ma asked me over the telephone. *Lisa let you watch soap operas? Do you miss me?* I didn't. I was playing, watching grown-up TV and observing the weirdly decorated dog. Ma was having a terrible time in the hospital as her hormones dipped and surged and the doctors shot her up with drugs and took her new baby away because Ma had a cold or something: they wouldn't let her cuddle Madeline. Ma spent her birthday alone in the hospital, and Madeline spent hers a few rooms away, also alone, and I was with Lisa. Lisa was married to Pete, a garbage man, a grody job for sure, but you make lots of money hauling trash. Later she popped out Pete Jr., born with a testicle that wouldn't drop and legs that required metal braces, his feet stuffed in clunky old-man shoes, but he was just a small, small boy. Then she had Diana, C-section. They sliced open her stomach like a watermelon, and plucked the baby from her gut. Diana was a preemie and lived a while inside a little tank, and whenever my mother talked about it I thought of the giant egg-shaped hatchery at the Museum of Science, where, round-the-clock, chicks broke themselves from their eggs. When Lisa's kids got older, I would baby-sit them, ten bucks to corral them into bed at an hour generously past their bedtime. I'd spend the rest of the night sampling everything in the cabinets and fridge, eventually passing out on the couch. Pete would drive me home, baby sitter and dad alone in the dark station wagon. He never did anything weird, but I was always on guard. It was a power dynamic I knew about from countless teen novels and made-for-TV movies.

But Lisa. She was just so naturally bitter, life rushed to deliver her reasons to back it up. Initially it'd been great that we'd moved into her house—she was family, and I always wanted everyone I knew clustered around me, walking in and out of rooms, just tons of people, a dormitory. But Lisa would fog the air above our kitchen table with her extra-long cigarettes, talking a mile a minute about the horrors she had to endure at her job at the free clinic. She was the first person you talked to when you got there, all frenzied with medical trauma. This bitchy white woman. She'd bring the stories home. Puerto Rican moms bringing in babies that had roaches trapped in their ears. She was disgusted. It was too much to hear her talk about it. As if it were all hardest on her, having to take these people's paperwork. Having to be that close to a cockroach, one wiggling inside a screaming baby's ear. Their friendship buckled beneath the weight of so much bitterness, Ma couldn't deal with the relentless diatribes after a point, and so she found us a new place to live. And all the proof, the hard physical evidence of what Will had done, was gone, just like that. The new house was just around the corner from Chelsea, but now we were in Everett, a better place. And I was leaving. Madeline was crumbling. Every stupid thing that belonged to me was taped up inside the jumble of cardboard boxes that sat in my new room. They would go to the dump that way, undisturbed. If I unpacked, it would mean that I lived there. I thought maybe I would never live anywhere ever again, maybe this family had only been a holding tank. Madeline in the doorway looked like she was at the end, like she was ready to slam her head against the jamb, crack that egg and let the bird fly out. I told her she could come with me. I would go to Steph's, and she could come—Steph wouldn't turn away a girl escaping an abusive father. I wasn't abandoning Madeline, not the way she thought I would when we were small and slept stacked on top of each other like Tupperware. It was weird how when she was so little this fear, so big, would keep her up at night. Maybe because we were children, and still powdered in the psychic dust that clings to kids. Maybe Madeline could feel it, that eventually I would leave, that she would be left without me, crying.

Looking around my new bedroom scared me. If this wasn't my life, what was? The enormous plaster angel on the floor, propped against the metallic radiator. I'd dared a boy to bring her to me, to wrench it from a giant manger that had been set up in a nursing home's front yard. Somewhere in Cambridge, the night so cold it froze us like chunks of meat. There were a few of us, drunk, moving through the city with our booze in paper bags, disguised as juice. I liked when it seemed necessary to drink. It was so bitterly cold, the whiskey was a warm medicine for our bodies, making us rosy and numb. The manger on the nursing home lawn was big as a backyard tool shed. Splintery wood, and though Christmas was still weeks away, little Jesus was already affixed to his rickety crib. That's Not Right! I pointed at the setup, offended. I was an authority on few things, but I knew about Jesus. He's Not Born Yet! I raged. You Don't Put Jesus Out Till Christmas Eve! That's the way we did it in my house. Jesus lived in the junk drawer with the loose nails and nubby Crayolas and electrical tape, gestating there until the twenty-fourth, when you plucked him from the clutter and brought him to the tiny manger beneath the fake evergreen, where his painted fam-

ily had been waiting amidst the molded plastic donkeys and camels and sheep, the Wise Men hovering at the edge like hopeful groupies. You plopped Jesus in the middle, and then you stuck a skinny candle in a Hostess Cupcake and sang "Happy Birthday." The nuns had suggested this snack as a way of reminding the children that Christmas was about the stunning birth of our savior and not, you know, toys. So we had a chocolate cupcake with a white frosting ribbon, we sacrificed it along with some sugar cookies for Santa and a carrot for Rudolph. Went to bed and twitched like speed freaks all night, waiting on morning, and presents, and the incredibly vanished snacks. I was indignant that this nursing home had put Jesus out early, like a Caesarean preemie.

John was the name of the boy I dared to jump the fence and pry the angel from her bolted perch atop the small barn. John had a crush on me, so he did it. I was impressed at his daring, but already knew John to be a thief and chameleon, and I didn't like him. But I loved the blond angel, with her robe and grand wings and the length of frozen cloth she stretched between her hands like she was about to swoop down and swaddle the Christ child like a little burrito. I had managed the fantastic thing all the way home, drunk, and then Uncle Markie had dropped it in the move, and half a wing had crumbled away, revealing the wiry skeletal system of angels. She looked cooler that way, broken. I resisted the urge to take her with me. The familiar push of want, I aimed to master it. What did I really need, anyway? A change of clothes was the most I came up with. Libraries had books, and the government had food stamps, and if I had to I could steal, could find girls to love me, and fuck me, and grant me a night in their bed. I could even sleep outside and pretend I was camping out for concert tickets—first in line, excellent seats. When Boston got really cold, all the people with no place to go slept on the wide heating vents behind the library. They laid themselves across the grates like burgers on a hibachi, and the surplus air flew up and warmed them. I'd be fine. I hardly needed anything at all.

Madeline's pajamas were dusky pink and spotted with roses, frosted with modest lace at the collar. Her hair was long and naturally dark, thin clumps of it stuck to her wet face, naturally pale. I realized with an anguished plunge that Madeline was not ready for this, the disintegration of our family. The only way to ride it was to train yourself to want nothing at all, something Madeline was almost pathologically incapable of achieving. She wanted so many impossible things, and wanted them so desperately. It wracked her thin frame like illness, something grand and old-fashioned, consumption or tuberculosis. She stood there watching me walk toward my closet. Oh Madeline, don't try to stop me because maybe I would push you. Oh god, don't bring me toward pushing you because what if it became hitting, what if I hit Madeline and the hitting never stopped? Some awful horse reared up inside me, big eyes rolling, wanting to trample. Madeline had always wanted so very much from our gasping, reeling family, while I had weaned myself off the very basics as if they were breast milk or drugs, things to grow out of, things dangerous to become dependent on. I had done this until I was actually looking forward to sleeping on the fumy grates behind the BPL, all the smashed and interesting people I would meet there, a new family. Madeline had dumped all her hopeful eggs into the wrong basket, and now she was trapped in everything she thought she needed—love, food, clothes, private school and safety. Trapped in her sweet pajamas, coming apart at my door. I'm Leaving.

In my closet were some clothes my mother had unpacked and hung on hangers for me. The plasticky plaid backpack I'd gotten from the Gap when I had thought that maybe I needed schooling, too, and in the grand New England tradition would attend college, wearing a backpack studded with political pins. I zipped open the bag and dumped some clothes in, nothing frivolous. Took a swing at the urge to grab the vinyl miniskirt, or the crushed velvet dress the same color as my broken angel's robe. I decided I didn't really need underwear, no one did, it was another of capitalism's conspiracies. I thought that anything I loved was in my heart anyway, so leave it. If you loved anything it would live there in your body. Leave it. I had my body, and to the best of my knowledge it wasn't dying, so I'd be okay. *You promised*, Madeline accused, her face like a windshield in the rain, and I the drunk driver. *You promised you wouldn't go.* I thought about Ma, asleep—how could anyone be sleeping right now, in this house? I Will Go In There And Wake Them Both Up, I threatened my sister. My voice was some kind of sewer grunt, the voice of something mean. *I promised him we wouldn't tell Ma*, Madeline cried. *I told him we'd get him help.* I zipped up my bag. It was light. I Didn't Promise Him Fucking Anything. Madeline sobbing. Come With Me, I pleaded. I didn't want her in that dark house, like a carnival ride with the power cut off, trapped in her little car, wobbling on the track. I Have To Go, I said. I couldn't cry. I felt thin, sucked out, a mirage. Madeline would wake in the morning after dreaming that she'd had a sister. *What will you tell Ma?* I Don't Know, I shifted. I'll Make Something Up. *Michelle,* she whispered, she was a little sack of a girl. All wet with crying. The digital clock on my floor snaked out from the wall—the face flickered the late hour. The last bus had left Everett. Boston shut down early, trapping everyone in all their desperate holes. I looked at Madeline. She needed too much to be okay, why hadn't she taught herself not to want? It was the only freedom. I wanted to blaze the house with lights and fill it with scream, freak out on the cold floor, fetal and gone. But you had to really believe that someone would help you, to let yourself do something like that. I dropped my backpack. I was so tired. The buses started rolling again in the morning, before the miserable sun could even be prodded into the sky. Come Sleep With Me, I said. I would try again then, try to leave the house and stay gone. Me and my sister fell into my bed and slept.

PRECIOUS

Madeline refused to be there when I told my mother about what Will had done. Partly because of the promise of secrecy she'd sworn to Will—part of the grounds of his confession. But I'd promised him nothing. Madeline was also unconvinced that our mother should ever know about what had happened, a notion that just corroded me. How could Ma not know? What if I needed her comfort? How would I explain the sudden hatred of Will? If we kept Ma in the dark, I would have to keep sitting in rooms with Will, smiling, brushing his cheek with my lips, bringing him a glass of Coke, like nothing had happened. The images sickened me. The thought of Ma's face sinking with my news sickened me, also. I thought if I were a mom, would I want to know if my husband had watched my naked daughters? I thought about all those books on sexual abuse and how confrontation was key— why should you protect your abuser? Why should I? Why should I make Will's life comfortable, now that he'd ruined my own?

I brought Steph with me. She took her place at Ma's kitchen table, still cluttered with glassware wrapped in newsprint, from the move. There was Tracy our old neighbor, then Ma, and then me and my lesbian girlfriend, Steph. How could Steph have been a comfort to my mother? I had thought, idiotically: a female, a supportive female. But Steph was only a rich lesbian from Connecticut, sitting in my mom's kitchen with her cold, weird eyes. As a young girl I had read many paperbacks about girls with eyes like that. In the books they were all murderous witches. Steph's eyes were the color of sky viewed through the thick glass of an icicle. The big ones that stabbed down from winter roofs, their sharp tips slowly dripping onto the slushy ground. Ma had always warned us to keep back from the icicles, crystalized, shimmering ornaments, when they began to drip and melt. The sun was loosening their frozen grip on the buildings, soon they would dislodge completely and sail down sharply, as if flung from the fist of a knife thrower. Those gigantic icicles could kill you. If you were in the wrong place at the wrong time, which is all death is anyway, I guess. Lingering just a minute too long beneath the wet and glittering spectacle, transfixed by the frozen ripples, the way it held the sunlight solid at its core. A *crack* and a *whoosh* and you were impaled. Steph's eyes were like that. Entire violent cycles of desire looped in each glance. I brought her with me. I brought her with me so that she could witness me being strong. I brought her with me because I was terrified, my stomach was sinking like a bombed-out ship, and I wanted her thigh near mine, for me to press my fingers into. I brought her with me because when she was out of my sight she talked shit about me, so I liked to keep her close. For me, I brought Steph, and for Ma, Tracy. I knew Ma's first impulse would be to shut herself away in shame, telling nobody, as if it'd been *her* eyes sneaking peeps at the doorjamb. Ma would stew in her hurt and eat it for comfort, she would waste away with it. I thought that if Tracy was present when it all went down, then she'd be someone Ma could always go to for help. Tracy was disturbed about what had happened, but not too bad. She heard it with the ears of someone accustomed to hearing about the mundane horrors of men. Vaguely sympathetic, not alarmed. She sat beside Ma at the kitchen table as the words left my mouth. Each word leaned a bit heavier on the detonator, slid it down the shaft until the family exploded. I wasn't crying. I was racing inside. I rushed out of myself like carbonation, fizzing into the kitchen air. Ma's face numbed tightly, blank, then it rippled with twitches, then crumpled. Her face was a flutter of eyelid and tears. She looked scared, small, and I thought, There's No One To Take Care Of Her. Who Will Take Care Of Ma? Maybe we could all take care of each other, I dreamed. I felt sick, watching the information strike Ma. Everyone was silent. She said, *I trusted him with my most precious things.* Her voice was dry with bitter tea and the heat of cigarettes. *I trusted him with my most precious things.* Her first impulse was her love for us, her precious things. That was her heart's first pulse, before everything else roared in like a sour tide—her fear, her complacency and her awful, beautiful, perfect love for Will. That love that women's hearts churn and churn, produced inside their bodies as steady and irrational as hormones, that clinging, desperate, triumphant love. Could this maybe be a love story, after all? Perhaps it is. But before the horrible loyalty to her husband crashed in, there was that first, still moment when we were her precious things, me and Madeline. Soon we would argue the specifics of Will's behavior, as if the import or extent of what he'd done could be negotiated like a court settlement. Soon she would rage New Age about my toxic anger, my monstrous lack of forgiveness, soon she would let Madeline leave her home rather than clear Will out, she would be his spokesperson in every conversation, she would want to die and all of it, somehow, would be left to me. But forever there are her first words. Soft, a comfort easily blown away. *I trusted him with my most precious things.* I thought of treasure, a treasure chest sunk deep, wedged in wet sand, spilling gold and strands of jewels, me and Madeline.

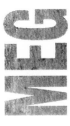

Ma told Meg, our former next-door neighbor, about what had happened. Our new house in Everett sat on the edge of our old neighborhood in Chelsea, making it easy for Ma to maintain her friendships. Meg was a big woman who was just fantastic-looking: robust, gold curls on her head fat as a baby's fist, twirling and bobbing like toys. Meg looked simply healthy in her body, despite the fact that she was, by neighborhood standards, fat. Bigger than my mother, who had taken to attending the twelve-step meetings at Overeaters Anonymous, adopting an OA-prescribed diet of chicken cutlet with raspberry vinaigrette dressing that was so exotic in its simplicity, infinitely preferable to the greasy meat combinations prepared separately for the rest of the family. A regular box and can dinner for me and Will and Madeline, the kids, and then this clean-looking, pink-drizzled delicacy for herself. It sat on her plate like a food photo from a women's magazine, elegant and sparse. Occasionally I would nibble at her sweet and tangy meat. *Get away,* she'd swarm in like a mama animal protecting sustenance. *This is MY food.* Sometimes Ma would rear up against the ritual of sharing that motherhood had forced her into. Nothing my mother possessed was hers alone. I'd rummage through her dresser for sweaters, for underwear in desperate times. I'd swipe her fantasies from the dirty books she hid, and steal cigarettes from her pack when she locked herself in the bathroom to pee—I took everything. Sometimes she'd rebel, like with her sweaters. She hated having to charge into my room and pull through the lumps of clothes and junk on the floor, looking for what was hers. *This is MINE,* she'd lay a thick boundary of words in the home, a tiny verbal fence that would keep us, for a moment, out of her bedroom, away from the refreshing new clothing options stuffed in her drawers. It was like the tits we never got to nurse in the hospital became all she owned—everything she had was ours, and she didn't have much, but occasionally I would want it. Like the citrusy chicken that tasted so good. She ate it proudly as we wiped grease from our chins with our wrists. Us, her three-headed offspring with the many grasping hands. She had so few opportunities to separate herself from our need, to not be a mom, and her entire non-mom identity became symbolically encapsulated in that one sweater I was not allowed to wear. The heavy knit one with colors that faded so gently from the collarbone's pink, to darling blue, to the hem's arresting purple. The perfect sweater. Or the chicken, trim and graceful in its gelatinous raspberry pool. It was for Ma and her body, which we had imposed upon for so long, our basic economic drag propelling her to supermarket aisles stocked with boxes of Hamburger Helper, the cheapest ground beef, tiny nodules of fat glistening out from the moist red squiggles.

Meg next door didn't do diets or cults, she was so supernaturally confident, with her inground swimming pool, and the legion of ceramic gnomes that leered out from the tangle of shrubs that wound around its border. Meg didn't have to work, her husband did that. Meg took care of their kid and made hundreds of ceramics, knitted afghans. We'd get something every holiday. Halloween was a glazed ghost with a pom-pom spider on its head, and if you bopped the spider with the palm of your hand it would trill a cheap electronic spooky noise. Christmas was a new afghan to replace the mangy one that hung over the couch all year, the one you drowsily tugged over your shoulders when you fell asleep watching television. If she hadn't been so generous with her pool, everyone probably would have hated Meg for having it so easy, a house all her own. She lived in all of it, didn't have to split up the floors and rent them out for extra money. Summer nights the whole street was over at Meg's pool. All worn out with the day's sun, sitting in lounge chairs around the umbrella table, drinking iced tea and beer and talking shit while the kids splashed in the dark water till the air finally began to chill, and parents said, *Your lips are turning blue, get out of there.* And it was true that our chins trembled and drooled with the cold chlorinated water, but we loved how weightless and elegant we felt inside it, how our feet streamed behind us like a mermaid's fin when we dove beneath it to touch the bottom. I loved tumbling in the water, gathering my body into a curl like an insect, a beetle on its back, flipping in a perfect circle, a pulse inside the warmth of the pool. Backward flips seemed obscene, the way your crotch would stick above the water for a moment, knees bent and open and the nylon flash of your swimsuit curving over your privates, hung there for a moment like a flag until your body's motion pulled you into the water like a wheel.

So much happened at Meg's. The one table, umbrellaed and round, where the adults would sit, sagging into the weave of lounge chairs. The ceramic gnomes and rabbits poking out from the bushes. The yard was all pool. We would beg our parents for one, we had begged Lisa, our former landlord, to get the useless dirt and grass out of our yard and please put a pool in it, fill it with water. You could see the thought of it flicker chemical blue across their eyes for a moment. But pools like that cost money. You could get a pool like the one the neighbors on the other side of Meg's house had, one of those cheap jobs that sat, round, atop the ground, plopped there. You climbed up a ladder to get in, not down like in Meg's. You could hear that neighbor and her kids, little girls, splashing around on a hot night while we were luxuriously floating the length of Meg's, and there was a dim sense of pity for them, for their poverty. Their pool was a glorified Mr. Turtle. Better not to flaunt our own poverty with the installation of such a shabby pool, better to keep treating Meg's like the local country club that it was. Meg was so generous. Even if my parents weren't hanging out over there, I could sheepishly ring her bell and ask if me and a friend could hop in. *Can she swim?* she always asked. Oh, Yeah. One time she couldn't. She wasn't my friend, she was a friend of Marisol's who seemed slow, kind of stupid. One of those friends you had from an earlier time, before you had really located your true personality and linked up with your new soulmate-friends. We were thirteen, and the social realm seemed split between new friends who matched your burgeoning teen reality and old friends you'd been sort of set up with by parents or school or location, and you still had to hang out with them, and it was awkward and made everyone feel weird. This girl couldn't swim, but who cared? You just stay in the shallow end, or you cling to the edges, tiptoeing around the top of the slope that spilled down to the eight-foot bottom of Meg's pool. And the girl slipped—like a sled, she just slid down the tiny aqua hill and began to flounder, a mess of water smashing crystal all around her hands that beat the surface wildly, groping at wet nothing, punching blind waves into the pool. Wet animal cries from her mouth sucked in air and water, choking and crying. Our dead-end street was still, pure summer, a weekday. No charred Saturday cookout smell in the air, no voices or cars. Me and Marisol looked at each other, alarmed. It was weird to think that someone could drown in Meg's pool, this playground where kids splashed constantly. It wasn't like it was the ocean or anything. We waited a second for the girl, Joan, to gain composure, kick back to the ledge and breathe again, but she didn't. I lurched over to her and grabbed the meat of her arm, and she beat me off like the water that flooded her face. She was really drowning. I felt a terrific surge of panic. People really drowned. Life was just a series of things I'd read about coming true. Things in the paper, in books or on TV. The gasping, drowning girl. It's not like it was hard to haul her over to the side of the pool, it wasn't. I gripped the side of the pool with one hand, scratching my fingernails on the concrete, and the other tugged Joan through the water. You feel so weightless in water, but it's worse than gravity. I reeled her in through the heavy liquid, and when she hit the wall, her personal panic subsided and she stopped fighting, hung on, coughed and spit and breathed. Meg was at the top of the back stairs, pulled from her inside world of soaps and snacks, the pearly glaze of ceramic figurines. *Is she okay?* The pool owner's horror, a dead kid belly-up in the blue. They could get sued, it'd be their fault. By law the fence around the thing had to be a certain height.

Joan sputtered, red-faced. She's Fine, I called. I sounded like I'd almost drowned too, breathless. Marisol was just wide-eyed. *I'm fine,* Joan croaked. Meg went away, and we all left the pool.

There was this thing about Meg's husband, Jim. He wasn't her first. The first, I'd heard, was a bastard. It's what you heard about the guys who weren't around anymore. It was kind of hopeful, actually: the bastards leave. You heard about them, but they weren't there anymore. Our bastard, Dennis, had left. Meg had had her bastard and they had had a daughter, Rachel, around nine or ten and really nice, ordinary and nice, just a girl, tanned poolside skin, and sandy hair the same shade. Very blue eyes that shot up the monotony of color that was her hair and skin. Jim was Rachel's stepfather, and he treated Rachel like shit. Everyone talked about it—at dinner, inside our own homes, not by the pool. How he whistled for her when it was time to come home, two fingers between his lips. *Like a dog,* my mother said. It was because Rachel was the bastard's daughter, not his own. He had had his own daughter with Meg, tiny Rosie, the plump princess, around five or so, so how bad could she be? But, word went around: *She's a little bitch.* A little five-year-old bitch. Starting trouble and blaming Rachel. Kids are manipulative, dumb and cunning. Her tiny, plump brain, grey baby fat, understood that Rachel was always the bad one, and she went with it. Tongues clacked. It wasn't right. But what do you do? You don't get in people's business. Especially people who have a pool. The way Jim talked to his stepdaughter, the word "stupid" just dripped from his chin like chlorine. You could smell it. Fuck that, you could see it. Just sit by the pool.

Another thing about Jim was that his younger cousin, a woman, had called him on the telephone and confronted him about molesting her a long time ago. When he was like eighteen, and she was maybe twelve. It was a very whispery thing. I had to tug it like taffy from my mother, who acquired the information during different telephone converations during which I would be kicked out of the kitchen. Into the living room with the TV down low. I had to strain to hear, but I heard only tone, not words. A low tone, serious and gentle. Jim, of course, had done nothing. He'd only been jerking off in his bed like a normal eighteen-year-old guy, and his twelve-year-old cousin had just burst into his room and flung herself onto his exposed boner. Twenty years later she was in therapy and making phone calls. *You don't know,* my mother said noncommittally, but we all knew. And we all thought about Rachel, privately, inside our brains. How he hated her, how guys like Jim always fuck girls they hate because they hate so many, really. I mean, nobody said this. But Jim was a creep. Loud and macho, round and balding, just a big tanned globe sliding skinny cigarettes in and out of the hole in his face.

Maybe, just to be nice, I'll say that Jim never touched Rachel, never touched her with a sickening sweetness after a night of being mean out at the pool. Maybe when he was eighteen he had some kind of horrible lapse into badness, like a puppy's nose at your panties. I know that a twelve-year-old girl is not a puppy. Maybe Jim figured that out too, and never did anything bad to a girl ever again. He was just eighteen, he fucked up. What I'm trying to do is hear the inner maneuvers of a woman I haven't seen in eighteen years, Meg. What must it be like for straight women to have to live with the fuckups of their teenage husbands. Just knowing they did that, even once.

Ruining one girl's life to come to the grand realization that they shouldn't ruin the lives of any others. The ways that guys fuck up. A slip of the dick and maybe you get a phone call twenty years later, but probably you don't. Just make up a little story if you do, play it down. The wife blows it off, everyone forgets about it. How about the way girls fuck up, since we're talking here about youthful fuck-ups. A slip of the heart and you're pregnant, you're dead, whatever. Maybe in twenty years you make a phone call, reach out, finally cry or maybe just kill yourself. Jim stayed there in his home, his castle, the courts gathered nightly by his moat and many Budweisers were cracked. And that was it.

I was glad that Ma told Meg about what happened, about Will. What I was afraid of was Ma telling no one, staying in it all alone, no help, no community, lots of nothing, lots of quiet, lots of shame. Meg was furious. At us, me and Madeline. We think we were sexually abused? I imagine her golden face, her white eyes widening, a vehement head shake that turns her head into an avalanche of hair, shaking curls. *They think THEY were sexually abused?* Meg had been molested, as a girl. *Really* molested, with hands, her stepfather's. *They don't know what it's like to have someone's hands on you.* Would she have rathered we did? Meg fumed, *They don't know what sexual abuse is.* My mother told me what Meg said. Every statistic, quote or anecdote about sexual abuse that I pulled from a book, she countered with this. Her friends thought me and Madeline were crazy, even her HMO therapist, the one I had begged her to see: Get Therapy Ma, Please. She did, and her therapist said, *Why do they want to tell everyone? They want to tell your father? That would kill him*. She didn't know Papa. World War II didn't kill him, a French beach that exploded with wet limbs and ocean. I wanted to tell Papa about it because the cloak of shame and secrecy was claustrophobic. I wanted someone to hug me and tell me that what Will had done was awful, someone who wasn't a man-hating young feminist. Someone from my family, an adult with comfort power. Ma's therapist claimed that sharing the news with Papa would be the death of him. The therapist tried to put Ma on Prozac. Ma! I protested passionately. *What do you want me to do?* she cried. *Become a lesbian?* Is that what it came down to? Because all men were like this, all men were the same? A couple of naked teens in the house, girls, duh. A twelve-year-old girl in the house and what is the boy, the eternally teenage grown-up boy, supposed to do? Me and Madeline didn't know what sexual abuse was. He hadn't touched us.

I remember a summer night and me in my Garfield nightshirt. Will was drunk and it was late. Something had happened earlier, a celebration worth getting tanked for. My graduation, eighth grade. Earlier I had been in my room and Uncle Markie had been at the table with Will, beers and cigarettes, Budweiser and Kools, and I was awake well into the night. It would be like this forever, I never wanted to sleep. I liked being on my bed with the cool of sheets against the back of my legs, my window open to the warm night, my record player spinning music, Bon Jovi, Prince. *Around the World in a Day*. A book in my hands, a paperback, something about a girl in trouble. Drugs or boys, maybe a baby, maybe cancer. Maybe she was psychic, that had its own hardships. Maybe a mass market horror story already fattened and pulpy from Will's hands, voodoo or serial killers. Maybe a magazine, *Seventeen*. I knew it was dumb to want to be like the girls inside it, and I didn't, but I wanted the stuff they had. I would allow myself one Want from one ad. Randomly, I would eeny-meeny-miny-mo my way through the thin color pages and land on my destined advertisement. Maybe it would be easy, Bonne Bell Watermelon Lip Gloss, no problem. Two bucks, I could do that. That mascara in the pink and green tube. But maybe it would land on a pair of Candie's. Fuck. Where do you even get Candie's? Not in Chelsea. Probably in Boston. Or a Gunne Sax gown. Get real. Maybe if I were in high school, maybe if I had a prom. I slapped the magazine shut and yanked the sticky door to my room open with a sucking wrench. The men at the table, in the kitchen. Uncle Markie with his very fucked-up face, the watery bloodshot eyes blearily fixed on me. *Well hel-lo, Mee-shell.* Hi, I waved, and plodded into the bathroom. Uncle Markie, I heard him. *She sure is turning into a little woman, did you see that?* I slammed the bathroom door, the paint of the jamb locking it in a moist little lock. I knew he was talking about my tits, and I felt a weird swirl of anger and pride. I was glad someone had noticed, but Uncle Markie? I felt creepy. I stayed on the bowl forever, reading the *TV Guide* that we always left on the wicker hamper. We called the bathroom "the library'" in my house. People went in there for a half-hour at a time, reading magazines. *Cheers and Jeers* was my favorite. Finally I emerged. Uncle Markie was gone. I was sitting at the table with Will, a landfill of cans and butts. Ma was sleeping, Madeline was sleeping. Will, a red man normally, was extra red. I loved the damp, stale stink of a million cigarettes smoked. It's a terrible smell, and it's terrible that I enjoyed it. The curse of a child of smokers. It smelled like Christmas morning, the minute before

I woke up Ma, when I sat by the glistening tree with its miracle of gifts beneath, luxuriating in all that beauty and promise and stillness, and the ashtrays overflowing from the party the night before. That stink permeated the excitement and became a memory. That and the artificial tree smell that you sprayed from a can.

I sat at the table with Will, and he promised to take me shopping in the morning. Into Boston, real shopping, real city. I had graduation money. I knew all the things I wanted, jewelry from the carts that lined Downtown Crossing, fairy earrings, makeup from Woolworth's, rock posters and fingerless gloves from Stairway to Heaven. Records from Strawberries. Then Will started talking to me about sex. Just telling me I could always come to him. Assuring me. Okay, I said. Boys my age didn't know what they were doing with girls, he told me. They didn't know like older guys knew, what to do. He knew. Okay, I said dumbly. I really thought he was just being cool. The cool dad. The cool dad I'd wished I'd had, on the level, just talking to me. It made me uncomfortable. Don't be a baby, Michelle. Sex was cool, Will was cool, I was cool. Nothing happened. It was mostly a monologue, Will drunk and rambling. I was stupid, listening. You know when you really believe in someone, you think if they sound weird or dumb it must mean you are. You just don't get it. He just went on about the sexual ineptitude of teenage boys and how older guys knew how to do it. *Don't believe boys who say they love you cause they just want to fuck you.* Okay, I nodded. He said, *Don't tell anyone we talked about this. They get the wrong idea and I could get in trouble.* Okay.

I wish he had just grabbed my tits. I wish he'd asked me to do something. I've thought about that night so often and I wish the tension between what was said and what was not had taken the form of

Meg

353

a bad hand in a soft place because then I'd have been abused. Years of an eye on a body pale next to the indisputable trespass of a hand. Ma would have been mad at him, not me. I would have been sexually abused. Now I'm this other thing. I think about that night and I think about Meg and I think about Ma saying, *He never touched you.* If he had, I could have plucked it off and screamed. I was a loud girl, ornery and full-grown when Will got me. I'll never know if he would have touched me if I'd been younger, shyer, more scared by the world. I'll never even know if it would have even mattered. If Ma might have said, *He was drunk, it was just once, he won't do it again.* None of us, we don't know anything but what happened, and what happened wasn't enough. Will was so hungover the next morning, he just slept and slept, no shopping in Boston. I creaked open the door to his room, and hated the sight of his legs sprawled beneath blankets, the lack of light, the old beer breath. I shut the door and sat in the parlor for a while, waited. Went outside.

CLASS

My mother really liked that movie *Stella*, an eighties remake of an old Barbara Stanwyck movie, with Bette Midler in the starring role. Ma had a dramatic fear that she herself was a Stella figure, and that the tragedies of class betrayal would be sprung upon her by us, her daughters. We would marry into wealth; ashamed of our white-trash, Chelseaen upbringing we would disown her, Louisa, our mother. She would give us up in a final grand gesture of maternal self-sacrifice and self-loathing, she would peek through the church window as we moved without her into a life of riches. We would be in big white gowns, Cartier tiaras twinkling on twists of hair. Something like this would happen. Of course, my recent lesbianism threw a bit of a wrench into this ruinous fantasy, but Steph was loaded, and it showed. My mother didn't want to discuss her, though it was clear that a lot of questions rolled through her mind. Occasionally, one would tumble out: *Where is she from? Oh, Connecticut. What do her parents do?* Stuff like that. It was apparent to me that Ma was put off less by Steph's baseball hat with the word "Dyke" stitched onto the brim than she was by Steph's wealthy background. When I'd brought her to the confessional table, Steph had sat in her wooden chair with a steely, detached look on her face, unspeaking. I read her visible arrogance as that of a Sapphic warrior forced to face another brutal example of how men ruin lives; to Ma it was the face of a rich girl sitting in a ramshackle kitchen, taking in the grease-stained curtains, the torn corners of linoleum tiles—a voyeur to the shameful struggles of a dysfunctional working-class family.

It was days before Thanksgiving, and me and Ma were meeting in Boston, to have a Thanksgiving moment together, since I wouldn't be coming home for dinner. We met in a little café in Back Bay, seated at a round table. Outside was slushy grey November. I had promised to stop trying to get Ma to leave Will, and she had promised to stop trying to get me to speak to him. As these were the only things we wanted to talk about, we simply chain-smoked and commented on our coffees. Somehow it had become my fault—and also Madeline's—that our family was ruined. That there would be no Thanksgiving this year. Because we were so angry and demanding, so unforgiving, my sister and I. A two-headed monster bent on oppressing this poor sorry man who was just so *sorry*, he was *sorry*, and we would not forgive him. Any mention of Steph was also sure to start an argument, so I kept quiet about her as well. It was uncomfortable, processing sexual abuse and coming out at the same time, because of course Ma just thought I was damaged. Damaged and vulnerable to the man-hating rhetoric of a girl like

Steph, who also played a key role in the destruction of my mother's family. It was Steph who made me hate men, and I in turn converted my sister, so really it was Steph's fault that there would be no Thanksgiving. And Steph was rich, and I was going to spend my Thanksgiving with her this year, in Connecticut. A rich place, where rich people lived in giant houses, and my mother was Stella Dallas, slipping me twenty dollars as I hugged her to me in Boston, and descended into the subway. I hated taking the limp green bill.

Steph had gotten me a job as a prostitute with her agency. Every night the phone rang for me and a cab pulled up at my door. Dressed in Steph's clothes and clutching a purse loaded with condoms, I ran a series of odd errands throughout the greater Boston area. The cab dropped me off at a variety of men's homes, I dashed inside, fucked them, left with money, and was delivered to another man. It was a whirlwind, a blur. A landscape of heaving chests, scribbled with hair and hung with belly, corrugated with ribs. Each man astounded me, again and again, with his complete obliviousness to my hate and my absence. I was not there, except when a spool of rage would suddenly unfurl itself and shake me. The men had rented the space between my legs for one hour, and that is what they occupied themselves with, nothing more. It's True, I thought. Everything You Hear About Men. All Your Worst Fears, All Of It, It's True. I lay back in a random bed and felt strangely vindicated. I thought about Ma, about all of the good women out there with their men, how their closeness to them sheltered them somehow from reality. How only the ruined girls knew, the whores and the dykes and the crazy women, only they knew what this world was really like. I was slobbered on, my tits slick and spitty. I was sore. Late at night, when the men had stopped calling, I washed myself gently, petting my pubic hair like a scared animal that might react. I cooed to it, I did not want it to feel unloved. I thought we were in it together, me and my pussy, and I hoped she understood. Otherwise, I was afraid I'd get cancer down there, believing, as I did, in the mind-body connection, the ability of the body to manifest disease in its least-loved pockets.

I had tons of money stuffed in a box at home, an untaxed cash stash that grew nightly. Ma couldn't know this, so I was forced to accept her twenty-dollar bill. Her weak but true attempt to care for me a little, to do something. I crumpled it into the little square pocket of my leather jacket, snapped it shut, kissed her wrinkling cheek goodbye. It was awful to watch her turn into the crowds of Boston, this city that frightened her, was so much bigger than her, it gulped her up and she was gone. My heart rang out toward her, I felt the quick panic of a lost child, Where Is My Mother? I smelled like her cigarettes, tasted them in my mouth with the bitter coffee. Vantages, with little tunnels in the filters that turned deeply yellow as you smoked them.

I was conflicted about Steph being rich. Sometimes it made me feel grumpy and resentful, but I kept it to myself. Me and Steph bickered enough without me having issues about her wealth. Sometimes where she came from seemed irrelevant, meaningless, occasionally I thought it was interesting, like having a friend from Europe. In high school I'd hung out briefly with Tanya, who was from France, and I thought that was really exciting. I would introduce her to people, saying, This Is Tanya, She's From France! I didn't understand why she wanted me to stop. I never introduced Steph by saying, This Is

Steph, She's Rich! but I would refer to myself as "white trash," and Steph and her friends were bothered. *I don't like to hear you putting yourself down,* Brad said. But I hadn't been. It was like being Polish, or a dyke. How could I have thought that a white-trash party would be fun? I had thrown one. At my mother's house, while she was out of town with Will, back when me and Steph had first started going out. I put deviled ham on Saltines, with little bits of olive. I cooked Tuna Helper on a pot on the stove. I put on my mother's clothes: stirrup pants and flat-heeled shoes, a thin gold chain with its clump of twinkling charms—"#1 Mom," an Italian horn even though we were Irish, a teddy bear. The guests were Steph and Dinah, Brad and his new boyfriend. They didn't get it, they were rich kids. I brought a plastic bowl of bright orange macaroni and cheese into the parlor, where everyone was watching the vice-presidential debate on TV. They were laughing at Perot's running mate, that senile old guy. None of us could get over him. This was slightly before our group plunge into vegetarianism, but Steph, Dinah and Brad wouldn't eat the food I brought out. They were laughing at everything. Laughing with, laughing at—I understood the difference, and it was unexpected. My mother's worn shoes were tight at my toenails, her weighted necklace swung out when I bent to place the food on the table. I was a monkey shelling peanuts. I was my mother, I was Stella Dallas. Brad's new boyfriend was from Idaho, he had just come out of the closet and was all big-eyed, blue-eyed and blond. Like all of Brad's boyfriends, he looked just like Brad. He was eagerly eating the Tuna Helper, and they were making faces and laughing at him. *You're not supposed to eat it! He doesn't get it!* He was like Perot's running mate.

I sat on the floor and ate some deviled ham off a cracker. If you could forget about how the stuff looked when you first opened the can, the translucent gel clumped to the sides of the can, if you could forget about that first part and stir it all in, then deviled ham could be quite tasty. Salty on the crackers with the pickled bit of olive. *Eeeew,* said Steph as she scrunched up her face, laughed. They all left shortly, to go dancing. I stayed behind in my mother's empty house, Steph wanted a night out with *her friends.* I was alone in the kitchen that stank of warm tuna. If Ma had seen me, there in her pumps, making a joke of her to my new friends. I walked into the bedroom that smelled of her smell, unclasped the necklace and placed it gingerly on her dark bureau. Before Brad left he had taken a bunch of pictures hanging in the hallway and turned them all upside down on the wall. Then he'd stolen one of my mother's figurines. She had tons of them—Precious Moments, ducks, bunnies. Sweet children, with bonnets and puppies. Brad put one in his pocket and left. He gave it back to me later. He just thought it'd be funny to steal one for a while.

We went to Thanksgiving at Dinah's parents' house in Connecticut. The joke was that Dinah's parents were nouveau riche, they had acquired their money later in life and, not being born into it, had terrible taste. Steph told me all about it. *It's like if all of a sudden YOUR parents got money,* she said. Supposedly they had two original Salvador Dali lithographs. They didn't know anything about him, they just bought them because they went with the dining room. They were hung on a side wall, almost out of view. Elongated figures in pale pink and blue. They weren't anything spectacular, no magnificent Christs or rose-headed ladies or melting clocks.

Dinah's parents' house was huge, and it was a big uncomfortable deal that we were there. Dinah's gay friends. Where would everyone sleep? Dinah approached her mother in the kitchen. *I wanted to talk to you about the sleeping arrangements,* she said, and her mother asked, *What would you like?* There was an awful formality between Dinah and her parents that scared me. I'd almost rather they hit her or something, their coldness was so creepy. *Well,* Dinah started hesitantly, *Steph and Michelle would like to sleep together . . .* pause *. . . and I would like to sleep with Brad. WHAT?* Her mother popped like a cork. She was too uptight to really explode. She was horrified—there would be no boys and girls sharing beds in her nouveau-riche castle. Even though she knew that Brad was gay, and she knew that me and Steph were girlfriends. *Is Michelle the partner?* she had asked Dinah, well read in *Newsweek* lesbian chic. Everyone was very informed about us right then. So me and Steph could sleep together. Because we were so cuddly, with no penises. We got this really nice bedroom with a four-poster bed, and Dinah and Brad got separate rooms. Cats prowled the halls all night. One looked like Morris the Cat, it was orange and friendly but if you petted it, it began to drool uncontrollably. The other cat was so ugly, it was like a small dying cow. Its eyes were milky and blind, its belly hung like flabby udders and it had the markings of a dairy cow.

In the morning Dinah and Brad hopped into bed with us, and Dinah's mother came up to say good morning and she would not enter the room. She stood in the hallway and sent her disembodied voice in to us, and we all cracked up. We had this whole conversation with her hovering just beyond the doorway. She had set up a great breakfast for us downstairs. Meaty red grapefruit in cut crystal bowls, with jagged spoons to eat them. It was such an array, I was impressed. Countryish baskets with cloth and warm scones. Steph's cruel analysis had been pretty right on—Dinah's parents were into the same "country" aesthetic my mother liked, but they had the money to really do it right. Tons of geese and bunnies, blue and white embroidery. What I couldn't get over were the grapefruit accessories. Those little spoons, evil and cute with their sharp teeth. Dinah let me keep one. They were amused by my enchantment with the mundane ornaments of their culture. I was a monkey again. When it was time to set the table, I couldn't help. I didn't know how. They had these little bundles of silverware wrapped in pocketed flannel envelopes, an excessive amount of silverware, multiple everything, special spoons, special forks, and they all went in this particular arrangement around the plates. It was such a ritual. Steph was real showy about it, sliding a spoon from the cloth sheath and with a grand gesture placing it in its special area on the table. I was useless.

Lots of people came for dinner—cousins, brothers, girlfriends. They were pretty boring. *Watch Dinah's mother,* Steph whispered. *She sits in the chair closest to the kitchen so she can serve everyone. She is so oppressed!* The mother was perched on her seat, poised to leap the minute a bowl emptied. The father sat at the other end, by the Salvador Dalis. I guess it was pretty uneventful. The mashed potatoes were good, and they had real, homemade scalloped potatoes, which I loved so much and had only ever eaten from a box. There was a special bowl of stuffing for us that had no sausage. At one point, Steph and Brad smoked pot in the bathroom and Dinah's mom smelled it. That was a problem. At night we went to some awful sports bar to laugh at all the kids they'd gone to school with, kids who still lived there. We came home drunk, and took more wine out of the fridge and brought it into the Jacuzzi on the back porch. I remember Steph talking about how foot massage really turned her on, and floating her wrinkly feet at me. We went downstairs to the rec room and watched MTV and crank-called the kids from the sports bar. In the morning there was grapefruit again. We sprinkled it with sugar and scooped it with the spoons and sat on the couch watching TV. I had my period, and left a big red stain on the cushion, so we had to flip it over.

PASTA

My mother's new kitchen had nothing to do with me. Ma and Will had moved again, and there wasn't a place for me in the entire new house, paid for with Ma's tossed, cracked back, vertebrae snapping out of place like Legos. The house didn't have a bedroom for me, or Madeline, but that was fine. We wouldn't be sleeping there. It felt strange to have no connection to the place my mother lived. It made me feel tiny to have nowhere to go now. There was no empty room waiting for me to inhabit it. The world held no room for me, yet every night I slept. Steph's room wasn't mine, but it worked. I felt a bitter, ascetic pride in my years and years of doing without, years of preparing for the absolute nothing I had suspected life had to offer. The teenage years of making do and making no requests. I knew it would pay off, and it did. Probably I would leave Steph's bed, at some point. I knew that I would, only because I knew that everybody leaves. My mother's devotion to Will through this horrible time only confirmed this: if you didn't leave, it was only because you were too weak to do it. I'd leave. Again and again. I didn't know where I would go, and in the midst of this dull misery it was a fabulous jolt. What is that Janis Joplin song? I would go out into the world.

To get to my mother's brand-new house, the one she had just bought with the snapped nerves of her back, broken at work trying to hoist a bedridden old vet, I had to take the orange line out of Boston. To Malden, a city I hadn't been to since being born in the hospital there twenty-one years before. I followed her awkward directions, past bakeries and second-hand stores and Chinese take-outs. The new house sat across from a big green park, one of those parks that are just green, no clanging swing sets or plastic jumbles to climb and slip and crack your head on. It was a white house with a fortress of boxy hedges squaring it off from the street. A sedate street, a nice neighborhood, Malden. I got to the house on my own time. I almost didn't get there at all. Maybe I didn't want to see Ma. *I'll make you dinner,* she had offered on the phone, a shy and unsure voice. So small it filled me with a rotten love, so lousy I wanted to squash it. Push it down like choking the neck of a kitten, this is how good people go bad, I thought. This is growing up, having to stomp out love, this is how people turn terrible. I snatched the little sprigs of tears from my eyeballs. You Don't Know How To Cook For Me, I said coldly. The whole world had been reduced to poison. In particular the realms that claim to comfort, including the realm of food. *No, pasta and broccoli and garlic, you eat that, right?* She knew I'd been laying off the meat, one beast at a time. Cows first, the hardest, sure, but the bloodiest.

I'd worked up to it for a bit, grossing myself out every time I ate a steak or a burger. That's Blood That's Blood That's Blood, I meditated as the juice, no, *blood*, squirted against my teeth. I thought about it being a dog, or another person. I'd seen a chopped cross section of a human thigh in one of Ma's medical books, and it looked just like steak, a T-bone. I read *The Sexual Politics of Meat* and *The Dreaded Comparison*, and stopped eating pigs, rereading *Charlotte's Web* for staying power. I stopped eating chicken. Next was eggs, then milk. It's For Baby Cows, I snapped caustically to anyone who cared. All those cows, girl cows, trussed up on their rape racks. To keep them pregnant and squirting milk, their babies sold off to the slaughtershacks. Just like life, the women keep living and the men are sent off to be killed. The women keep living with all their particular female agonies, the pain of pregnancy and tits endlessly feeding everyone. I didn't want that milk. And the chickens with red lights shone in their eyes all night so they don't sleep, not ever, they just keep dropping eggs. Do you know what I'm like when I don't sleep? I'm crazy. I mean it. Everyone's out to get me and the whole world is sadness. You think I want to eat the eggs of psychotic chickens? I tell you, this is the only sane way to be in this world. Saying No, again and again. The problem is, it keeps going. Food in cans, what's that about? Where did the food come from? Someplace bad. I didn't want to eat it. Poison sprayed all over it, people paid shit to pick it—whole social movements have sprung up around the evil of produce. I didn't want to assist anyone's misery. I was perhaps dying and nobody seemed to care, and the least I could do was not participate in the hurt of a people, a person, a cow. If I ever wanted anyone to help me—and I needed help—then I had to help others. I had to care about the badness, all of it. Charity is selfish, and maybe that's okay. Maybe that's community. But it is very hard not to hurt anyone in America.

I told my mother I would come to her home and eat the pasta and broccoli and garlic if she could please use margarine and not butter, which was no big deal bacause she used margarine anyway. It was as if caring about the world was some sort of destructive addiction, I couldn't do it socially, like normal people. It was a huge obsession taking over my life, every injustice leading logically to a related and worse injustice until I was standing in the center of a pulsating ring of pain and torture and oppression and the only real solution was to just kill yourself. Just get off the fucking fucked-up planet. I couldn't do that, but I could whittle away at my existence until I was simply immobile on the couch, eating raw organic produce and doing bong hits.

I told my mother that I'd come for dinner in that way you say yes to something you're not totally committed to, and for some reason you think the other person understands this, even though you've just agreed to hang out. I told her I'd be there at four, but wasn't it a theoretical four? Like, maybe I'd be there at four, maybe a little later, maybe I'd hop a Greyhound and never speak to her again, that kind of four. I arrived at seven o'clock to my mother's tight face, and the endless gasping barks of her new dog, a Corgi. The dog made me crazy. It was an emblem of everything I felt was wrong with my mother. Her deluded attachment to an earlier time, when she was simply the provider for something helpless that didn't hold opinions, that never questioned or accused or got angry. The dog was like a new baby, but one that would never grow and destroy the family. It had been bred by humans to have legs that were little more than flippers. It could barely propel itself up the stairs, a mutant dog. I hated the humans who had created it. The same terrible pulse that inspired people to shine those lights at the chickens. I was perhaps experiencing schizophrenia lite. Everything was connected, and all of it was terrible. The dinner, the family dog. The mother's love, now useless on her daughters, was to be showered on a canine.

My mother said, *I thought you'd be here at four.* She said it in a lonely way that made me feel murderous. Did I? I asked. I Meant, You Know, Whenever. Her tense and breaking face, catching itself again and again, something behind the muscle was falling. I could not give her anything. It would be too much, and then she'd need more, and then where would I be? I spaced out, staring at a Sears portrait hung on the wall, me and her and Will and Madeline—normal, happy. It was from only a year ago, but it seemed like another life. My lips were glossed a thick red, the skin of my face dusky with powder from a compact. I cringed at how recently I wore such foolishness, how close I was to this feminine idiot. I'd grown so much, made intense progress, and it wasn't fair that such a document existed, mocking me. In the picture, my cheeks glow red beneath the muddy cosmetics, lit up with food, ruddy with beef and plumped with cheese. Nothing like my present countenance, cheekbones crashing like broken rock, my mouth grotesquely large, the hole it made in my face big as a meteor crater.

I made you food but it's all cold now, Ma said. I plucked the shining lid from a pot on the stove and gazed down at a congealed brick of spaghetti. Some limp branches of frozen broccoli collapsed into sickly green heaps, crunchy nuggets of dehydrated garlic like a spray of gravel. We never had real garlic in my house, it was a foreign food. My stomach, already shrunken to the size of a pea from all I wasn't feeding it, shriveled a bit tighter. This wasn't organic, it was barely food. I thought: This is the food I was raised on. How am I even alive? Why doesn't anyone know how to take care of me? My eyes felt scratchy. The little shaker of garlic sat on the stove. Ma, You Know You Can Buy Garlic Fresh And Just Chop It Up. I loved chopping garlic. Great stinky piles of it to be baked into bread. The way the smell rubbed into your fingers and clung there for days, like girl-stink. Soap can't wash it off. You Can Buy Fresh Broccoli, Too, I continued, as if she were a moron. And You Can Buy Organic, No Pesticides. Imagine If Someone Just, Like, Sprayed Raid On This Stuff? You Wouldn't Eat It. Would You? Ma shrank away like my stomach. I didn't need food, anyway. I was running on something else. I didn't understand it, but I could feel it rushing in my body like drugs. A certain hysteria. I was different in a good way, I didn't need food or mother or any family at all. Something else inside me rocked my heart, kept it beating. *Have you eaten today? No.* It was hard to eat when food was so bad for you, bad for you and hurt so many things on the way to your plate.

Ma fired the blue gas flame beneath the pot. She could cook the best spaghetti sauce, the red sauce my Italian friends called gravy, though in my house gravy was brown, and went over meat. Ma's red spaghetti sauce held chunks of pork that just fell apart in your mouth after soaking in the warm tomato juices for hours. I told my mother that there was another way to eat, and she could learn how. Her face was crumpled like an old potholder. My hard and empty stomach had felt stuffed with a nauseous fist the whole train ride over, because I did not fully trust my mother. I hadn't trusted that Will would not be at the table when I got there, smoking a Newport with a cup of Dunkin' Donuts regular. But Will was at work, taking care of guys with severe head injuries. That was his job. He liked it because he could relate to them, they were all old street punks, it could've been him. Just luck had kept his own skull from getting dented with a pipe in a street fight or something. The men Will cared for were all bad news to start with, worse once they got their brains smashed in. Most of them were pure rage. Will got his nose broken more than once at that job. He was there dodging fists while Ma worked at the pasta block, breaking it up with a wooden spoon. *It was hot at four,* she said. What had I been doing at four? Fucking around, watching TV, reading gay newspapers and getting angry. Wondering if I should go to my mother's.

I pushed an Ani DiFranco tape into my mother's stereo and pushed play. I really thought I could save my mother. Words were saving me, why not her? I read and I listened and it all came together: the world a web of badness, each bad thing feeding the other. I saw it so clearly it nearly killed me, it was supernatural, a flash. *I know so many white people, I mean where do I start? The trouble with white people is you just can't tell them apart,* Ani trilled. *Is she white?* my mother asked tensely. She Is, I said proudly. I'd found back-up.

When I was little, I would start the morning by asking Ma if we could cuddle that night. After supper, on the couch, in the TV's glow. Curled into a shrimpy wad on her body, her hand on my head like Jesus' halo. It was my favorite thing to do. I was as loved as a cat. Sometimes, in the afternoon, she'd ask, *Do you want to cuddle tonight?* She liked it too. To cuddle me now would snap my mother's bones. I'd have to kill her if she tried. How could I even let her touch me? She lived inside this new house, with only one bedroom, her and Will's. I had no more bedroom. I felt a spurt of panic. What had happened to my bed, my pillows?

I cracked the kitchen window, to let out some of the cigarette smoke. I thought about having no bed. No bed and no bedroom and no family. I had a plate of pasta. I stabbed a wilted, olive-colored stalk of broccoli with my fork, and mushed it with my tongue. I wondered how little I could get by with. How much I could do without. I felt a rush of whatever was keeping me alive without food or love—whatever it was, it was great. It flared inside me like something that paid visits to saints, and then it slunk back out, and I grabbed a pack of cigarettes from the table. Vantage, my mother's. Ma cringed as I rattled one loose. *Oh no, you're smokin' again, am I upsetting you?* No, No, I'm Fine. I lit up and breathed. It was like an inhaler, something that helped. It hit my lungs with a shock, and dizzied my head. I thought about getting a drug habit, something bigger than pot, but how did you even get drugs like that? It was like, if I could do something just really supremely fucked up, my mother would understand that something huge and serious had happened. If I tried to kill myself, or filled my body with heroin. But I wanted to live. That lousy desire inside me, wanting to live ruined everything.

Ma, How Can You Stay With Him? My ash fell into the pasta, the cigarette was making my hands shake. Ma, He Was Looking At My Cunt, Right At My Cunt! My voice rose like heat. *Don't say that word, I hate that word.* Disgust on her face, like I was gross. Like I was the dirty one, my dirty cunt peeking out the keyhole at my stepfather. Cunt cunt cunt cunt cunt. You Looked Through That Hole In The Bathroom Door And All You Could See Is Cunt, I said, the shrillest slicing voice, crying. How Madeline had sat on the bowl for me, shut the door and latched it. How I had lowered my eyes to the tunnel in the wood, carefully worn into the frame, a half-circle that perfectly matched the half-circle in the door, a periscope. That's what Will saw, a little circle of body. Was it better that it was only that, crotch, cunt, like a torn bit of paper? No face, no me, just a kaleidoscope hole of skin and hair, a hunk of meat.

How do you know that? My mother challenged darkly. I Looked! I screamed. I Could Show You . . . I looked at her new bathroom door—clean, new house, no girls lived here. No holes anywhere. Everything erased. A girl could go crazy just trying to stick to her own story when everything around her conspired to knock the past away. I Looked Through The Holes, I said, and shook another cigarette from her pack. Is not wanting to believe someone the same as calling them a liar? Was Ma calling me a liar? Wasn't that the very worst thing a mother could do, short of shooting her kids in the head to a Duran Duran song because her boyfriend didn't like them? What about the kid whose dad set him on fire with gasoline? That was worse. Was this worse than being hit? Ma never hit me. One time I was being a little bitch and she gave my cheek a swat, and I rubbed and rubbed the skin till it was raw, so everyone would know. It had made me feel so bad that she'd hit me. It hadn't hurt, but it stung my feelings so bad, it seemed that it should show. If someone hurts you, it should show. Shouldn't everyone know about it.

I never saw any holes, Ma said. Even though Will himself had admitted it, she still talked like that. *He is sorry,* she said strongly. Her voice was rearing up like an animal. *He is so sorry, you do not know what this is doing to him. He wants to kill himself.* I Want To Kill Myself! I screamed. *Well how about I kill MYself,* my mother stubbed out her cigarette, tears making her face all wet. This is how it went in this family, this is always how it went. It made me crazy. You couldn't ever get sick, or threaten to kill yourself, because someone else would beat you to it, beat you to it or crowd you out. I cried. I did want to kill myself, but I knew it was for the wrong reasons. You shouldn't kill yourself unless you truly want to die, and I didn't. I just wanted my mother to understand that I *wanted* to die. *He wants to die,* she repeated. *He is so sorry.* He Got Caught, I shot back. Everyone's sorry in jail, sorry and finding God and getting law degrees. The thought stopped me. I Could Put Him In Jail, I said. We sat with that for a moment.

The hub of the controversy was when, exactly, did Will stop looking at us through these holes? He claimed that it had stopped when his sobriety started, and Ma believed him. But I had continued to hear the creaks as he climbed the twelve steps, as he got a therapist, as he stopped filling the fridge with cans of beer. How convenient for it to have been part of his alcoholism, which we all understood was a disease, no one's fault, and we must have enormous compassion for such sick and brave people. It would be years until my own alcoholism would bloom into an identifiable blossom, until I could go: So? I get drunk too, am a drunk, do I do that? Terrible things? No. Just get sloppy and cry. Try to make my lovers pay for the pain of my past. That's bad, sure, but that's all. It was like Alcohol had looked at us, not Will. He wasn't there, it was a can of Miller aiming its sloshy eye into the keyhole. *Creak, creak.* No one could prove anything.

My mother cried. I hated her for being such a jerk that I could not hug her, because I wanted to, I wanted to hug her. I wanted to cuddle her, her sad wet face on my shrunken belly. I wanted to pat her thin blond hair. Fuck her for making it impossible for me to love her. Love. It spat itself from my throat like a bit of bad food. I chewed it back down, this stupid love, I'm not a kid. Only kids love like that, blind and hopeful. I ground it with my molars and kicked it back down, wherever beaten love goes. I made my way back to the subway, through Malden, leaving town before Will got home from work. I was someone else. I didn't know who, not in this strange suburb. Some girl, some new girl, an orphan.

ACKNOWLEDGMENTS

Many thanks to Rona Jaffe and her generous Foundation for the incredible assistance they lent to the completion of this book. Thanks to Cari Campbell for being the on-call computer genius and also for being my friend. To Kathleen Tomasik for being such a noble and superb sister. To David West for feeding me well and slipping me vitamins and believing in me, and to Peter Plate, also for his friendship and encouragement. Thanks to Leslie Miller and Jennie Goode for their patience and focus and vision, and to Christina Henry and everyone at Seal and Avalon for their help along the way. To Ali Liebegott, Sara Seinberg, Ida Acton, Tara Jepsen, Anastasia Kayiatos, Ricky Lee, Lynn Breedlove, Bucky Sinister, Clint Catalyst and Chelsea Starr for pure inspiration. To Sini Anderson for adventures, to Merry Williams for letting me live in her house so that I could remember New England. Thanks to Crissa Cummings and Rachel Pepper for keeping me around. To Jessica Lanyadoo for her super superpowers and friendship. To

Sash Sunday for her incomparable Sash-ness. To Peter Pizzi for long-term greatness. To Ted Robitaille for the grim missives from Chelsea, and for making me read Bukowski. To Petunia for sitting on my lap while I edited. And to Rocco Rinaldi Kayiatos for letting me read him stories at four o'clock in the morning, for making me feel sane and pretty when I'm a psycho mess, for making my life so magical and completely interesting, and for loving me with such a gorgeous, dirty, enormous love—I love you the same.

© LYDIA DANILLER

Michelle Tea is the author of several books, including the Lambda-winning *Valencia* and the illustrated *Rent Girl*. Her novel, *Rose of No Man's Land,* was declared "impossible to put down" by *People* magazine. Her writing has been published in *The Believer, The Best American Erotica, The Best American Nonrequired Reading,* and *The Outlaw Bible of American Literature.* She was voted Best Local Writer of 2006 by the *San Francisco Bay Guardian.* Tea is the founder of the all-girl performance happening Sister Spit, and artistic director of Radar Productions, a nonprofit that stages underground, queercentric literary events in the Bay Area and beyond.

Selected Titles from Seal Press

For more than thirty years, Seal Press has published groundbreaking books. By women. For women. Visit our website at www.sealpress.com.

Without a Net: The Female Experience of Growing Up Working Class edited by Michelle Tea. $14.95, 1-58005-103-0. A collection of essays "so raw, so fresh, and so riveting, that I read them compulsively, with one hand alternately covering my mouth, my heart, and my stomach, while the other hand turned the page. Without a Net is an important book for any woman who's grown up-or is growing up-in America." -Vendela Vida, And Now You Can Go

Intimate Politics: How I Grew Up Red, Fought for Free Speech, and Became a Feminist Rebel by Bettina F. Aptheker. $16.95, 1-58005-160-X. A courageous and uncompromising account of one woman's personal and political transformation, and a fascinating portrayal of a key chapter in our nation's history.

Valencia by Michelle Tea. $14.95, 1-58005-238-X. A fast-paced account of one girl's search for love and high times in the dyke world of San Francisco. By turns poetic and frantic, Valencia is a visceral ride through the queer girl underground of the Mission.

Nobody Passes: Rejecting the Rules of Gender and Conformity edited by Mattilda a.k.a Matt Bernstein Sycamore. $15.95, 1-58005-184-7. A timely and thought-provoking collection of essays confronts and challenges the notion of belonging by examining the perilous intersections of identity, categorization, and community.

The Testosterone Files: My Hormonal and Social Transformation from Female to Male by Max Wolf Valerio. $15.95, 1-58005-173-1. A gripping transsexual memoir that focuses on testosterone's role in the author's emotional, perceptual, and physical transformation.

It's So You: 35 Women Write About Personal Expression Through Fashion and Style edited by Michelle Tea. $15.95, 1-58005-215-0. From the haute couture houses of the ruling class to DIY girls who make restorative clothing and create their own hodgepodge style, this is the first book to explore women's ambivalence toward, suspicion of, indulgence in, and love of fashion on every level.